CONTENTS

ACKNOWLEDGEMENTS

Thanks to those who read and commented on parts of the book: Jonathan White and Jeremy Howe; to Ken Plummer for his vast knowledge of musicals; to Felicity Baker for interesting discussions on some of the subject-matter of the text; to Francesca Franchi from the archive department of the Royal Opera House for help and Professor Jay Boyer from Arizona State University, who kindly answered a point. Sussex University provided some needed money in order to see some films I needed to watch, and John Banks at Manchester University Press gave the whole project some pushing which was important, and Pauline, whose book this is, gave the most stimulus of all.

INTRODUCTION

Opera and film. Though these two cultural forms are not often thought of together, they have actually existed in an interesting symbiosis, influencing each other in the time they have been in co-existence, equally: film has wanted to be like opera, and opera has not been above learning from film. In Britain the growth of the opera industry has been marked since 1946 when the Arts council began to subsidise productions (as a product of the nascent Welfare State and 1944 Education act thinking— and this State support has been part of a 'culturism'—'the belief that a wider distribution of culture through society is desirable and that it is to be secured by public expenditure').[1] It has ensured that opera has now become not so much of a fashion, nor so much as a tying-up of bonuses for the privileged—as it was in the days of Beecham in the 1930s, and was (is?) at Glyndebourne. Covent Garden gives 'only' 140 of its seats away on an annual basis to companies and banks and so on,[2] and so operagoing has become a badge of middle-classness. And the result has been that films have started to work on operas: those I discuss in the second part, for instance, are all post-1970. And there are other opera films I have not written about. For this book is not in any way a complete treatment of the subject of opera and film: there are large omissions in it, as will be seen by looking at any summarising treatment.[3] In particular, I have not dealt with the Russian *Boris Godunov* (1954) directed by Vera Stroyeva, who also was responsible for *Khovanshchina*, Shosta-kovitch's edition of Mussorgsky's work. Nor the Tikhomirov versions of *Eugene Onegin* (1958) and the *Queen of spades* (1961). Such films, using the Bolshoi theatre, and with a strong feeling for the chorus—not making them faceless, but important, as embodying the nation's history—and distinguished for the use of locations, have been seen too few times in the West, and I could say nothing about them. Another time, another place. Nor do I write about some films which might be claimed for opera, or for musicals, or for films with musical accompaniment:

Clair's *Sous les toits de Paris* (1930), where the title song is chanted by various Parisians, while the camera moves from person to person, house to house, gaining a view of a whole community, or Demy's *Les parapluies de Cherbourg* (1963). This last, with no dance or chorus, but with three principals who sing in a melodious recitative, written by Michel Legrand, could not be classed as the first opera to be written for film (Menotti is earlier), though it is early enough, but it is eccentric for my purposes. That is to say in its whimsicality and gentleness, it is out of the circle of the issues that I would like to deal with, which have more to do with operas that are defined as such since they belong to the repertoire of the opera house. Because these belong to the culture that is summarised in that word 'opera', and the symbiotic relationship that this culture may have with film is my subject. It is a relationship that has often been by no means hostile, as when Strauss said apropos of *Der Rosenkavalier*, which was to be filmed in 1926, that he would write a film for his music, 'allowing the spirit of the music to suggest appropriate action for the screen', and wrote out his ideas for the director, timing the action with a metronome.

Some friends of mine when they heard I was working on this book wanted to know why I was writing about film, and some wanted to know why I was bothering with opera. Not a lot wanted to hold the two together, to think them in the same thought, and few in the second category had been interested to see the opera films that had been made: they suspected them to be traps: operatic material new style, but the newness merely cosmetic, and as establishment-based as any other aspect of what is defined as high art in Britain, with the addition that they display the effects of 'culturism': holding up that 'art' and 'excellence' within the field of opera in a way that 'naturalises' it, and makes it seem not the reactionary toy for the rich end of an elitist culture, but something of universal significance: which gives it a certain accessibility that can only work to ensure the continuance of opera houses, with the class and conservatism, both political and intellectual, that they provide a projection of. (The letters that come in to the relatively amiable monthly *Opera* protesting indignantly about any new production that tries to be new—for instance the 1985 Pertilie production of *Rigoletto* for Welsh National Opera—are well worth looking at for their sense that there are some things that are hard to forgive.) In the opera house, at least, tradition is something we all understand and salute. Covent Garden provides the illustration. It keeps about forty 'central' operas in its repertoire which it shows every three years or so, then runs also occasional minor works of distinguished composers—all these, so far, set firmly in the past—and then only hopes to commission a new work (and then it would be one by a known modern composer) every two years.[4] Like the past, the opera house is another country: they do things differently there. There would, of course, be no public for the new opera: this seems the point of contrast with the theatre—though no one is going to say that, for example, the National Theatre does much better than Covent Garden in commissioning new work, and the National Theatre is often less adventurous, with its neatly-laundered productions of the classics, than is Covent Garden, when it puts on a fresh revival. But when opera remains so inbred, is it not, functionally, a good thing that film should extend its appeal, allowing people to see what they have missed? The cultural corpus is aired: its limits delineated; its representatives defined; its interpreters made plain.

Yet Walter Benjamin's essay 'The work of art in the age of mechanical reproduction' offers the possibility of thinking the two together: of asking what happens to the cultic value of opera in the opera house when it can be 'democratised', as Liebermann wished to do by making *Don Giovanni* as a film. These things do not work univocally: singing operas in English is enough of a cultural shock to many operagoers: an insult to the 'original' sense of the work: that the English National Opera, with its policy of translation, moved into the West End in 1968 becomes a reminder of the other subversions of that dangerous date. Opera screened—and what do you call the result? Filmed opera? Opera on film? Opera film?—its ontological status is denied by the deprivation of a satisfactory name—looks a radicalism of a different sort. There is the threat imposed by it to remove the ritual, the class associations, the sense of elitism and exclusiveness that masks itself under the guise of a self-confirming appeal to the best. (The best defined by the best.) Pierre Boulez, in radical and no doubt teasing temper, suggested in *Opera* that opera houses should be blown up: some readers' letters responded by wishing him to be blown up instead.[5]

Not that the films have all necessarily been motivated by the radical desire to remove the aura from the work of art, and to reaccentuate its possibilities. 'Culturism' has worked: the elitist values have been internalised and naturalised and opera *is* increasing in popularity in Britain: Welsh National Opera, Kent Opera, Opera North, Scottish Opera are all companies that have grown since the 1960s; touring companies have been set up, and transmissions of stage productions are common on British television. As for the United States, Bertolucci in an interview at the time of *La luna* affirmed that there were eight hundred opera companies in America. There has been a considerable cross-over between popular and classical musical tastes, where Bernstein and Sondheim are seen to be in the middle, accessible to both, and singers continue to be marketed like film stars, as they were from the very beginning of the star system in the cinema. It is evidenced in the careers of, for example, Te Kanawa (royal weddings, advertising, singing popular music), Domingo (the indispensable tenor in opera film, it seems, as well as a popular singer), Raimondi (who acts in Resnais' film *Ma vie est un roman*), Ricciarelli (by her recent marriage to Pippo Baudo, the Italian TV personality). And like the Labour Party, opera is a broad church. It is seen as belonging to a gay culture[6] —the diva in *La luna* says that she is 'always a big hit with faggots'—as if to suggest that one marginal and irrational activity (hitting top notes) has a fit with another. At the same time, it belongs to the indispensably top social class. The *Observer* runs weekly profiles in the main newspaper part, not the social chat sections, dealing with the great and the good, and the last two I saw before writing this, of 16 March 1986 and 23 March 1986, on Lord King and Jacques Chirac, both found it necessary to refer to their subjects in relation to their nights at the opera: neither figure is to be instantly identified with operatic music in the public mind, of course, but they do go. So liking opera (not necessarily going to it regularly) is like voting for the Conservative Party: it demonstrates to yourself that you are able to buy into that way of life, that you wouldn't want to think of yourself as beyond it. Of course, most people who go to opera do so because they like the music. But musical taste is not produced in a void: the economics of the market dictates endless Strauss and Puccini, and the Italian tradition, and that it is Mozart and Verdi and Bizet that have been filmed is no coincidence. And musical taste proves oddly confirming of class position and of the kind of education received.

So it is not surprising that opera films have begun to appear: that Gaumont, (*Giovanni, Carmen*), Accent films and RAI (*Traviata*) and Cannon (*Otello*) should have produced films that over a longish period of time should do well, financially. And the work of art is mechanically reproduced: is changed thereby, loses its status as ritual and exclusiveness.[7] It is true, as Fredric Jameson says, that Benjamin's optimism about the mechanical functions as a state of mind simplistically in attributing change simply to technical alterations: it thus leaves out vital historical determinants: the theory 'offers a feeling of concreteness comparable to economic subject matter, at the same time that it dispenses with any consideration of the human factors of classes and of the social organisation of production'.[8] But what is affected is a mode of thinking: discourse—the whole fashion of thinking, and acting, in ways created ideologically, and therefore not really subject to conscious inspection—can be altered. A text—operatic, filmic, literary—is multi-accented, polyphonic, as Mikhail Bakhtin, the Russian literary critic, insists, and the possibility of reaccentuation of what functions as a sign in society is always there. Through film, operatic texts are opened up for a new kind of examination that cannot assume the simple hierarchical structure of the opera house, which imposes a way of seeing on the audience, and also a way of hearing: 'the spectator-auditor in opera is not to be led to focus on narrative—which is a form of referring to external reality in an objectivist mode—or description, but to experience a number of scenes in a mode of presentation and reception which suspends any engagement in the natural structures of the objective world'.[9] Opera in the opera house gets little opportunity for character development; presents, instead, a psychological state in a frozen form. I am not sure about the use of the word 'natural' in that quotation: a structure is not that; but artifical, created, as the conditions of the reality in which people find themselves are. But that said, it seems important that the heavily generalised and imprecise values that are presented in opera should be articulated more precisely in film, with its narrative stress, its ability to handle detail and ability to make something of objective reality. At least in the cinema, opera becomes the art that speaks its name.

And in that way, it can make the musical-dramatic text show itself as it cannot in the opera house, make it apparent what is being articulated there. It can show what ideologies underlie the works, which, because of their strong attachment to tradition—and to a single consideration as 'the opera'; as though the precise work, with its differences, did not matter— are too little questioned, only described. The differences of opera from film are crucial, yet the switching of codes involved in moving from one to the other, may prove enabling. Opera is usually thought of as being slow and static, hence unfilmic: though it would be truer to say that its pace represents not inherent slowness but an entirely deliberate desire to accentuate actions in different modes: at the end of *Trovatore* note the lingering pace of the singing with Manrico and Azucena, and the very fast speed of the end, with the deaths: this is part of a controlled signifying practice, and suggests a dramatic sense that could well be given a cinematic equivalent: is not, that is, simply a problem that opera is slow, and film is fast. Close-ups of singers (perhaps indifferent actors) performing coloratura may look unpleasing. The Russian films, such as *The Queen of spades* experimented with having 'singing in the mind' with an unmoving mouth, in moments of soliloquy, and this has been used since in the West in films derived from stage productions; this film also used (as did Syberberg) actors to mime to singers who were pre-recorded. Edith Clever's Kundry in *Parsifal* is very strong as a result. These solutions are only two that have been devised: inherently there seems no reason why opera film should not free itself from the static nature of the stage, as the Hollywood musical made so much of a virtue of the moving camera.

In this book I look at the two phenomena of opera and film from different angles. I begin with an examination of the dependence of film on the opera—such is the power of opera-house tradition and mythology—even when the opera itself is actually absent: *Carmen* provides a useful illustration of this, and it demonstrates how little there is of an 'original' work: to try to get back to what the composer meant, as the readers of *Opera* advocate, is illusory: there is no original text, and ways of seeing belong to different discourses that change historically: to understand at all is to understand within history, not in some absolute sense. I continue by examining how cinema has wanted to use operatic excerpts, techniques, ideological stand-points and ways of signifying. In the third chapter, the subject is turned round: how has opera used film, and what part has mechanical reproduction had in the construction of twentieth-century opera and contributing to its modernism, its ability to question its ways of signifying?

Here it turns out that composers have responded to film. I have instanced Schoenberg, Berg and Hindemith and Britten, most traditional, yet inventive of opera composers, but could have mentioned others. There is Martinů, with his Paris opera of 1929, *The three wishes*, to a libretto by the Dadaist and Surrealist Georges Ribemont-Dessaignes, which has its first two acts set in a studio where a film is being made of a middle-aged married couple's unhappy use of the three wishes (for wealth, youth and love). In the third act, the film is shown as a silent short, while in the epilogue, the dream-world of the film-factory and the dream-world of the characters are ironised by being played out mockingly in a New York bar called 'The three wishes'. 'The audience is left to question whether life is like a piece of celluloid action or if the film recreated a life of dreams or a dream-life'.[10] And there is Milhaud, who set the drama of Claudel, *Le livre de Christophe Colomb* (1928). This reads as a series of historical tableaux, beginning with Columbus in old age, and as an opera, first performed in Berlin in 1930, it works on the epic scale: with forty five vocal soloists, an off-stage orchestra, and with film insets. 'When Columbus is reading Marco Polo's travels, blurred images of tropical landscapes flit across the screen as in a dream: in the scene where Columbus takes leave of his family, the same actions enact the episode in a different way, thus duplicating and hence reinforcing the effect; when Columbus questions a sailor concerning a piece of wreckage found near the Azores, the same scene, immensely magnified, is thrown on the screen in a way that seems to prolong its mystery, with an inner universe opening out from our own.'[11] Claudel's play, with its punning on Columbus's name as that of the colombe, dove of peace and Holy Spirit, sent out indeed only as the imperialist, is reactionary. The opera, which Milhaud revised, and which was performed again at Graz in 1969 (making topicality out of the film insets: the Statue of Liberty greeting Columbus), has hardly survived, none the less, the interest is in the wish to connect three dimensions: the immediately visual, language and sound. These works are relevant, and add to my argument as to how twentieth-century developments have incorporated a film at the opera.

In the fourth chapter opera's claims are put alongside the musical, and especially the musical film, which may well provide a neat contrast, existing as a specifically American music, and form of opera. Bernstein's *On the town, American town* and *Candide*, as well as *West side story* look operatic: the contra-puntal setting of 'Jet song' against 'Tonight' belongs in that tradition, but however much there is of middle ground in musical terms, the labels are sharply differentiated, to opera's loss, since it becomes the more rarefied and separated from a common life in being insulated. The second part of the book applies some of the theoretical considerations to the six examples of operas that have been filmed and which I discuss: one the Britten commission, *Owen Wingrave*, and then two Mozart operas, *Don Giovanni* and *The magic flute* that show how differently Mozart can be accentuated according to what is wanted; and two others that represent twin aspects of Western filmmaking: the very faithful and modernist treatment of *Moses und Aron*, and the glossy-looking Zeffirelli *Traviata*, which with all its chocolate box manner—yet there was something else there too—was significantly praised by David Cairns in the *Sunday Times* (13 March 1983)—'it leaves every other opera film I have seen nowhere'. Verdi, then, continues to be the draw. The last film to be looked at is the Syberberg *Parsifal*, deliberately oppositional to Bayreuth and to the quasi-religious ritualised status that this opera holds there, and dwelling, perhaps to the point of cliché, on the politically reactionary tendencies of Wagner. Like the Losey *Giovanni*, it is the film that determines to be independent of the original material it works from. None the less, while working on the Bayreuth myths, Syberberg is victim to his own, and there is a quasi-mysticism at work in the film.

Film might act as a challenging contrast to opera: the work of art be relativised by mechanical reproduction: but it becomes more evident that these cultural changes do not exist in isolation: they are determined by the interests and ideology of a society, and it is evident, at present, that the government, for example, will have opera stay as it is. That needs substantiation: in 1983–4 the average cost per seat for opera amongst all the subsidised companies was just under £10, and each seat was subsidised by £20. Of the 0.3 per cent of public expenditure spent on the arts that year (£92 million), £10 million went on opera and ballet at Covent Garden, and about half that went to English National Opera, leaving the 'regional' opera houses with a very small slice of cake. In 'culturist' terms, there is nothing here for the government to be proud of, of course; quite the reverse, and there is no reason to doubt that even with the inflated fees for 'top' artists, (which are, of course, passed on in increased seat prices for the nonce), that these subsidies are too small, and could not be dispensed with. In comparison, *Opera* in 1985 could quote figures of £26 million going to Paris Opera, £12 million to Frankfurt, £17 million to West Berlin, £16 million to Cologne, and £15 million to Hamburg. The Arts Council demands more and more that companies look to private sponsorship, thus ensuring that the reign of the well-known and safe is perpetuated, that the links between culture and the capitalist State are affirmed by making the cultural products overtly advertise the interests of the State, and that only the establishment companies get the sponsorship, since few companies will advertise themselves via unknown or marginal groups. None the less, when over a tenth of the Arts Council pittance goes on the three Royal Opera House companies with the opera company unlikely to say or do anything subversive, or even relevant to anything contemporary and political (and if it did, as some productions do, use a topical slant—Greenham women in *A midsummer marriage* at English National Opera, for instance—it would seem pretty marginal); and which has as those members of its audience who are strapped for cash to get in (on Moser's testimony) 'young lecturers, or young civil servants or young solicitors'[12] —a *jeunesse doré* indeed—then there is leave to wonder what interests are being served by opera as an institution, as part of the dominant discourse of British society. It accounts for some people's puzzlement when I said that I was working on the subject of opera, for it is not clear that the form as presently constituted can say anything useful at all, because of its imbrication in that discourse. Cultural activities are of course, political: as 'culturism' is in its naturalising of ruling-class values and making them into the whole middle-class consensus. Perhaps, however, the sense that there are differences within operas, that they were not all produced in one way and with one aim, whatever homogenising appropriation they have received, and that even the property of that culture might be freed from its present placing, and be seen to be capable of reaccentuation, makes the extension of opera to film possible and even necessary.

NOTES

The place of publication is London, unless otherwise stated.
1. The phrase is Alan Sinfield's, from 'Royal Shakespeare', an essay on the productions of one of the other companies (National Theatre, Royal Shakespeare, Royal Opera House, English National Opera) the Arts Council seems committed to upholding, in *Political Shakespeare* ed. Jonathan Dollimore and Alan Sinfield (Manchester, 1985), p. 164.

2. See Sir Claus Moser, 'The appeal and cost of opera', *Universities quarterly, culture education and society* 37 (summer 1983), p. 190.

3. See the entry 'Film opera' in *The concise Oxford dictionary of opera*, ed. Harold Rosenthal and John Warrack (Oxford, 1979), p. 169.

4. Moser, *op. cit.,* pp. 194–5.

5. Pierre Boulez, 'Opera houses? Blow them up', *Opera* (June 1986), pp. 440–50.

6. Michael Bronski, 'Opera: male queens and other divas' in *Culture-clash: the making of gay sensibility* (Boston, 1984), pp. 134–43. Susan Sontag, in 'Notes on camp', *A Susan Sontag reader* (Harmondsworth, 1983), pp. 105–19, finds Bellini, Strauss and *Trovatore* to be examples of camp; which she links to homosexual taste. Both these views, however, seem to be finding something ahistorical and essentialist about 'gay sensibility'.

7. See John Berger, *Ways of seeing* (Harmondsworth, 1972), chapter 1 for a discussion of Benjamin applied to the visual arts.

8. Fredric Jameson, *Marxism and form* (Princeton, 1971), p. 74.

9. Fabio Daschra, Anthony Blasi, David Dees, *The sociology of music* (Bloomington, 1984), p. 28.

10. Brian Large, *Martinů* (1975), p. 47. His discussion of Martinů in Paris in the 1920s is all relevant: see him, too, on Martinů's American television operas, *What men live by* and *The marriage* (1952), pp. 102–4. See too the review of *The three wishes* in *Opera* (1971), pp. 790–2.

11. Darius Milhaud, *Notes without music* (New York, 1970), p. 213.

12. Moser, *op. cit.,* p. 191.

Ideology in the cinema: rewriting *Carmen*

Though opera has been cast in the mould of one of the oldest art-forms in its combination of music and drama, it may well be seen as one of the youngest, and to have changed shape so often in its short history that an attempt to homogenise operas under the one genre-heading of 'opera' may be deceptive. Certainly the palatial and plush opera houses that most spring to mind as centres for the live performances of opera belong to the last third of the nineteenth century often enough, (Bayreuth is the obvious example, 1876); and to the sense that a Western industrial society, with its bourgeois controls, needs the invention of tradition, this being so aptly provided for by the ritualising of opera in the quasi-aristocratic, stylised world of the opera house. Many opera houses are older, naturally, but changes towards ritualisation (e.g. in the dimming of the house lights for performances, greater textual reverence by such conductors as Mahler and Toscanini), are everywhere present, and do much for the idea that opera becomes a mode of cultural production that aims at the elite, and which suggests that they are preserved within an established tradition. The movement towards having operas in repertory, rather than having a constant flow of new ones, is significant here, and is well documented as regards Italy by John Rosselli.[1] When operas become established for regular revival, more than the work becomes fixed; so does taste and so do standards. It seems a pity that Eric Hobsbawm and Terence Ranger did not include a discussion of the upward movement of opera in class terms and the ritualising of operatic discourse in their *The invention of tradition* (Cambridge, 1983): it would have provided an apt illustration to go with such things as the development of ritual attending on nineteenth-century monarchies. The innate conservatism of so many opera productions, the fêting of the star singer over the music, the little rituals that attend on each performance, the whole hierarchical organisation of singers and conductor, the existence of productions some twenty years old in an opera house's repertoire (imagine the same thing being done with a production of Shakespeare)—all these work towards the continued establishment of opera as, not the most youthful art-form, but the oldest, the most fixed, and the most serving the interests of conservatism. (Even the heavily naturalistic sets, most familiar in works in the Italian repertoire are relevant here, serving to fix the myth of a Europe unchanging, known, and mediated as a form of knowledge through great art. Those interiors of Sant' Andrea della Valle or, indeed, exteriors of Nuremberg have played their part in the creation of myth.)

With access to opera houses so restricted, it seems, too, difficult to believe that opera could easily serve the interests of any but the establishment; certainly its reactionary character seems apparent in contemporary Britain. Filmed performances of opera productions, such as the Chéreau *Ring*, have done much to break down the inaccessibility, and their impact is not being minimised because I do not discuss them in this book. But they remain stagey none the less: the camera is restricted by the limited nature of the set, and close-ups of singers often appear embarrassing as then the singer's art cannot conceal the techniques of singing. The static quality of opera, its absence of acting opportunities other than those of the most straightforward, the facial fixity required of the camera's gaze, and the length of operas, characteristically, work against the successful filming or televising of the medium. Further, the filmed stage version is inscribed within the tradition of the opera house, the physical surroundings being often foregrounded by camera-work: the faces of the privileged are played over as they wait for the performance to start, and the television or film director works to ensure that the aura of the opera house

Carmen. Placido Domingo (Don José) and Julia Migenes-Johnson (Carmen).
Courtesy Gaumont.

is preserved. 'Aura' may be defined in Walter Benjamin's terms as that which is eliminated when a work of art is reproduced: its vaunted uniqueness, its sense of having a mysterious whole-ness. Benjamin goes on to say that 'the technique of repro-duction detaches the reproduced object from the domain of tradition',[2] it being, of course, no coincidence that the growth of opera as a highly specialised, unique phenomenon, with the invention of tradition attending on it, should have occurred just at the time when 'mechanical reproduction' makes possible the breaking of this aura, and so the democratisation of art. The use that the establishment has put opera to preserves something of the myth of art as hallowed, as separate: it belongs to the *l'art pour l'art* ideology, with which it is historically synchronous; aestheticising art.

Filmed performances of opera, though of course they are 'mechanical reproduction', often work to return the auratic dimension to the opera house, thus excluding, by implication, many who watch the film or televised performance from the rite going on in the theatre ('It is significant', says Benjamin in the essay quoted from (p. 225), 'that the existence of the work of art with reference to its aura is never entirely separated from its ritual function'). Who is not familiar, too, with filming of overtures where the camera plays on individual performers in the orchestra, fading in and fading out on strings or woodwind, or conductor, thus effectively adding to the sense of mystique, of the arcane and wonderful—again, trying to put back the aura, and silently separating the audience for the film from the activity? The starting point of this book is that opera filmed in the theatre is unlikely to offer a radical experience, one that can be used by its audiences in a way that frees them from tradition and ritual, but that film itself might well offer a new approach to opera. Here, reproduction, in Benjamin's terms, 'reactivates the object reproduced', and in that the 'most powerful agent is the film', that most democratic and, again, young, art form, which may often offer ritual, but does so in a way that is its own parody, and which may create its own auras, as with the star-system, but which has shown the capacity to allow the cinema-goer to create a reading of the film. There is an active role for the reader–viewer: I assume here the impact of such books as Fiske and Hartley's *Reading Television* (1978) and James Monaco's *How to Read a Film* (Oxford, 1981). Modernism and post-modernism have had their effect on the cinema, not so much the opera house, despite the impact of such modernist texts as *Wozzeck* and *Lulu.*

This is not to free the cinema from the charge of having sought to capitalise on the auratic aspects of the opera house: that the recent Rosi film of *Carmen* should have used Domingo as its José seems to indicate that passivity before the idea of the opera remains embedded in the film-maker's consciousness: the star system is not obviated, despite Domingo's obvious miscasting in terms of age and looks. It is a miscasting, indeed, more tolerable in the theatre, where distance may lend something, if not enchantment; in film close-up it is misjudged and artistically suspect. That opera stars have constantly been wooed by Hollywood, from Geraldine Farrar onwards, adds to the sense of a myth being involved here: Pavarotti recently made a film, *Yes Giorgio* (1982), directed by Franklin Schaffner, to continue the tradition. Nor has the cinema taken great advantage of the idea of filming opera: the examples of operatic films have been few, though there have obviously been many more than I have elected to discuss.[3] In the next chapter I intend to discuss some of the less obvious ways in which the cinema has used opera, in which it has made operatic material into part of its own discourse, and used operatic glamour to sanction its own ideologies, or has managed to question that glamour. At the moment, it will suffice to stay with renditions of opera in filmic terms, where the opera has been conceived anew cinematically, not in terms of the opera house.

The comparative fewness of these films may be explained in commercial terms, and in terms of the elite nature of the operatic form. The artistic difficulties above with reference to filming stage performances are relevant often when it comes to recasting the whole idea of the opera as a film: there are restricted opportunities for acting (even if opera singers were less the notorious poor actors they have been historically), and close-ups of singers rarely please or flatter. Furthermore, the mix of genres has worried many: only a consideration of the possibility of affecting a reaccentuation of opera through this most startlingly different medium could free the director from worry on this count. For one of the most interesting aspects of opera as film is the way that it has the power to call in question the authority of the text. The deliberate conservatism of the operatic establishment is relevant here, and though there is no homogeneity with regard to taste amongst 'serious' musicians, that conservatism about the text is a feature too of music criticism. Thus Losey's film of *Don Giovanni* could be dismissed by Julian Rushton as an 'elegant imbecility',[4] presumably because of the way that in his eyes it lurched into irrelevance by its disdaining to accept the whole original text as authoritative for the way the opera should be performed in 1979. The idea of the weight to be placed on the author's intention and the sacrosanct nature of the text as given lies heavily upon all kinds of writing and consideration of the arts. It will be noticed that most of the films I give an account of have radicalised the operatic text in some way, and this is no coincidence, or a simple matter of my choice, but has to do with the way that opera has recently exerted its appeal upon cinematic directors. The parabolic nature of Werner Herzog's *Fitzcarraldo* (1982) is significant: the desire to build an opera house in the middle of the jungle is paradigmatic of the desire for an opera and for an art generally to be situated outside the commercial pressures that have previously constituted the arts the way they have been. Fitzcarraldo will enter the system—claiming territorial ownership in the rubber barons' community by producing a given amount of rubber in a stipulated time—in order to fulfil the objective. The system is used, equally, by Losey and by some of the others described: the attempt is to renew the power of opera, not by remaining servile to the voice with which it has traditionally spoken—that tradition not being an innocent thing, in any case, but ideologically created—but by making opera speak to the present.

The issue perhaps turns on the question as to what is a text, and whether there can be said to be any authority in it. Customarily a text is referred back to its writer, so that it becomes a matter of biography, and of course the equation between 'author' and 'authority' is easily made. 'The *explanation* of a work is always sought in the man or woman who produced it, as if it were always in the end, through the more or less transparent allegory of the fiction, the voice of a single person, the *author* "confiding" in us.'[5] That is Roland Barthes's point of departure in 'The death of the author', an essay first published in 1968: against that may be put the idea that explanation in this sense puts its own critical closure upon the work, resists its possibilities of continuing signification. Then, too, that the assumption of the individual artist (Barthes's discussion, in 'Musica practica', of Beethoven as the paradigmatic 'individual genius' of bourgeois criticism, is relevant here) as a 'single person' invests too much in the originating nature of the mind. It displaces the importance of the way the author is the creation of language, is, as it were, a text written upon before he begins to write: works of 'art' are products of ways of writing themselves. That is not to imply mere continuity, that the artist can only go on in the old modes; continuity in history (or 'development', or 'tradition') is itself a metaphysical idea; it might be better to argue for discontinuities, for breaks, for fissures as characterising history and equally the way in which one text moves out from another. The work of Derrida since the middle 1960s has to do with the way that one text moves out from another: there is no directing 'presence' or being in the text that would impose one way of reading or another upon the person who receives the text; rather, how that text will be accented and nuanced will depend on questions of power, on the controls that are placed upon the production of meaning at any moment. Knowledge, on this basis, (it is the argument of Althusser, most clearly) is not free from the constraints that are placed upon other kinds of production. There is no merely objective knowledge that rises out of a text. That knowledge has to be produced. What is in question are the uses to which Mozart, Verdi, Wagner are put. We have the illusion that art is inherently humane. It is nothing inherently: it is waiting to be used, as a series of signs, a series of rhetorical strategies that is ready to be taken up and used at any point, not only in the production of types of knowledge, but also in the formation of power-relations. What are the implications when Rushton can assume that he knows what *Don Giovanni* is, and what representations of it should be like? What follows from the assumption that Mozart presents life-enhancing values? What but the creation of an elite who are in contact with those values, who alone can appreciate them? And what in terms of power flows from the creation of that elite, whose guarantee of rightness is the self-justifying one that they have access to this art and can appreciate it?[6]

Derrida's work is useful in its refusal of the idea of the truth of representation: the text, in his terms, can never offer an approximation to reality: representations fail to do what they say they do, since they are caught up in a particular epistemology, are bound to a current metaphysic. The 'representation' is ideological. The point perhaps may be acceptable in terms of literature, but it may seem harder to take as regards music—that non-representational art, as Schopenhauer argued it to be; non-representational even when billed as programme music, or sung. But even to agree with that philosophical position would not take from the idea that music has its *uses* in a society, and that those uses have characteristically, involved arguing for the 'naturalness' of tonality and for the sense that a language of music may be derived from seeing the way that musical phrases and combinations of notes move towards or recede from this naturalness.[7] It is not hard to derive from this a sense of the centrality of nineteenth-century music, with opera as one of its main manifestations. There are created by this such assumptions that recognisably 'human', non-historically positioned, but rather central, feelings and experiences are registered in the music that is characteristically in the operatic repertoire, as also in the concert. (The conservatism of that repertoire will be confirmed by a glance at any opera house's list: the canon of works to be put into the repertory was what was being fixed, to a certain extent, towards the end of the last century, thus adding to the idea of 'tradition'.) Though the way in which music has been taken to be referential, and to deal with—and exalt—certain states of emotion remains elusive, it does nevertheless seem that one of the uses to which romantic music has been put (as also, partly, the music of the sonata period), is the privileging of certain states of mind, certain heightened forms of awareness as natural. Thomas Mann plays ironically upon this theme when he deals, in *The Magic Mountain*, with Hans Castorp's 'favourite records' (Chapter VII, 'Fullness of harmony')—these turn out to be the final duet from *Aida*, the Debussy setting of 'L'après-midi d'un faun', the duet from Act II of *Carmen* for José and Carmen herself, where love and duty clash, the prayer from Gounod's *Faust*, and Schubert's 'Lindenbaum'—the seductive subject of which is the appeal to death, and which Castorp sings as he rushes into the First World War. The extent to which Castorp is created, constituted, as an individual—as a romantic, with the twin goals of patriotism and love, service (involving death) and love similarly tilted towards it—is the theme of the chapter. The inadequacy of the emotions and their futility is demonstrated by Mann, exemplified by Castorp's rush on to the battlefield at the end, his having been 'interpellated' into the ideology of war by this music.[8] Its power to enchant is a deception, but it is regarded as a source of all inspiration.

What is at issue is the notion that the central operatic tradition, as mediated through the customary performances and presentations, may need questioning, and even refusing—this last being, of course, the option that the majority of people have selected, consciously or not: opera's appeal, however many the attempts to popularise it, remains highly specialised and elitist. Mann's suggestion in *The Magic Mountain* has to do with the destructive romanticism which is mediated through musical texts and which constitutes the subjectivity of Hans Castorp, a representative member of the German bourgeoisie: it is at least possible to argue that Castorp is created and ruined by a destructive tradition. Walter Benjamin's very radical insistence that 'there is no document of civilisation which is not at the same time a record of barbarism'[9] comes in here to suggest the limitations of high art, and that it is time to cease looking for universal values within the work. Art is not distinguished by its capacity to impart, or suggest lasting, permanent truths. The opera as film makes possible another way in, which, by removing the work from its auratic associations, it actually creates it afresh.

This liberation from the authority of the text gives a further freedom, which has to do with the recognition that texts themselves do not unify, that they are riven by 'aporias', i.e. points of difficulty between separate ideological statements, which the author must bridge as best can be done. Nineteenth-century opera, unlike the novel of that period, introduces the reader to fairly simple worlds, with people whose motivation can remain uninspected: Iago's non-Shakespearan soliloquy 'Credo in un' dio crudel' illustrated Boito's preciosity (as Baldini described it) but does nothing for understanding of the character beyond echoing some Goethean sentiments: nothing more inward is known of Iago by the end of the aria, and the music's lure prevents an analysis of the figure in dramatic terms: a musical analysis of the aria can yield no insight into character. Bizet marked the Toreador's aria in Act II of *Carmen* to be sung 'avec fatuité', but he need not have bothered: no one is likely to remember this or the point that Escamillo is all phallic swagger: the lure of the music prevents such a point being articulated, and the Rosi film goes far to make Escamillo (Ruggero Raimondi—playing the part with the same kind of dark melancholy that characterised his Giovanni) something heroic, by even showing him praying before the bull-fight— which has, of course, already been dignified by being made the very start of the filmed opera. The art-form allows for little interiority beyond that which can be suggested in musical terms, and then it is not clear that music is a subtle enough medium to suggest gradations of meaning: it is not for nothing that opera's affinities are often with melodrama (the Italian repertoire comes to mind), itself the least given to reflexivity, to discussion of itself and its own techniques. Not only does the evasiveness of music as language contribute here, but so does the remoteness of opera (what other art-form parades so insistently its removal from the nineteenth-century world in its determined historicising of plots?); so too does the size of the opera house, where few in the audience will be in a position to grasp a gesture, let alone the point that 'Toreador en garde' is being sung ironically; and so does the question of language, where it is far from clear that being able to follow, for example, the original Italian, increases awareness of what exactly the singers are articulating.[10] I would thus argue that far subtler opportunities are offered by the film: not only is there a re-accentuation permitted, but there is, virtually, another work of art.

What it seems necessary to emphasise is that there is no primary, authoritative text, and that texts remake themselves and are remade. It is what Julia Kristeva defines as 'inter-textuality'—'the transposition of one or more system of signs into another, accompanied by a new articulation of the enunciative and denotative position'.[11] That is, intertextuality implies that at each stage in a text's fissured and discontinuous history, it enters into new relationships, it meets other texts, it changes as it is placed in these new positions. And clearly the idea of the privilege to be accorded to the 'original' text comes in question. The dispute between the producer who under-stands this and the critic who does not is amusingly illustrated with Patrice Chéreau and George Perle apropos of *Lulu*. Chéreau writes on the Deutsche Grammophon recording of *Lulu* (taken from the Paris production of 1979): 'It may be objected that Wedekind (the writer of the 'original' *Lulu* plays) did not intend all this. In essence, however, that matters little: he *wrote* it. Without entering into pointless arguments about being faithful to the author, we may say that Wedekind in 1900 imagined a story, a narrative, which perhaps is not the same as mine, but that something of my tale has come from him, having emanated without his knowledge from the body of his text.' Perle, the established Berg critic, commented on the Chéreau production: 'Chéreau is only the most odious example in the current generation of a type whom Arnold Schoenberg characterised almost fifty years ago: "Producers who look at a work only in order to see how to make it into *something quite different*". . . In his memoirs Berlioz invoked a curse on the adapters of Mozart and Weber. His words are more eloquent than current taste finds acceptable, but I will nonetheless take the liberty of borrowing them: "Your crime is ridiculous. *Despair!* Your stupidity is culpable. *Die!* Be thou rejected, derided, accursed of men. Despair and die!" '[12] Perle's *angst* and his posture as a ghost out of *Richard III*, however, rather miss the point, which Chéreau nicely makes in pointing beyond Berg to Wedekind. Where does *Lulu* start? Investigation of this point would involve looking at much more than *Die Büchse der Pandora* and *Der Erdgeist* (1895); it would necessitate, probably, looking at Heinrich Mann's *Professor Unrat* (1905) and Sternberg's *The Blue Angel* (1930) as well as the Pabst 1928 film of *Die Büchse der Pandora*: thematically and textually, and in name, they are all quite similar, as the Fassbinder film of 1981, *Lola*, intimates. A director like Chéreau can hardly be ignorant of this history, and it fastens upon the point of intertextuality, for it helps to insist that there *is* no original: what is called the original is itself a modification of a previous text.

I would like to illustrate this point with a look at the way *Carmen* has been treated. It will be assumed that it is the Bizet text I am speaking of, but that in itself is not original: it rests upon the 'petite drolerie' that Prosper Mérimée produced in 1845, based both upon Mérimée's own visit to Spain and upon his reading of George Borrow. Intertextuality is present from the start, as it were, just as Bizet's working of the material (and through his librettists, Meilhac and Halévy) owes much to his readings of Scott, whose *Maid of Perth* he had set in 1866.[13] The opera of Bizet is a text written on, then, before it writes, and once written in 1875, it assumes its place amongst many examples of workings of *Carmen.* There is no original script: everything is a re-working. *Carmen* is an interesting example in the way it has been taken up by the cinema, with and without Bizet. Even when the screened versions have not used Bizet, that music of the Toreadors and of the bullfight has been at the back of people's minds, creating them as a particular type of spectator, who accepts certain myths about Spain (which Bizet never visited) and more particularly about women—especially when they belong to that further mythologised race, that of the gypsy. What is at issue is the history of a series of influences and reworkings of myth. To go through that history will do more than illustrate what intertextuality means, and suggest that there is no original to be faithful to; it will also open up the limitations and the possibilities of the workings of film.

Carmen has always proved popular with film-makers: its first treatment was in 1904, and by 1914 it had received some seven treatments, only one of which came out of Spain. Its popularity in the silent cinema had a lot to do with the availability of Bizet's music to act as background in performance—whether from phonograph or from live presentation. One of the films, released by Pathé, was called *The Cigarette Girl of Seville* (Seville being popular with composers such as Rossini, Mozart and Beethoven before Bizet, there may be felt to be an accretion of associations here). But it may be convenient to begin discussion with the Geraldine Farrar film made in 1915,[14] for here myth has taken hold. Farrar was a singer from the Metropolitan Opera House, and her importation to Hollywood was to advance the dignity of the motion picture, as it was put: the star-system, implicit from about 1910 onwards, was under way and actors were being wooed from the theatre. But to choose a singer implied two things—firstly, the dignity of opera, as something beyond the theatre, in ritual and respectability: the beginning of the process whereby so many films will aspire to the condition of the 'Met' by weaving stories around amateur singers who aspire to sing there. Secondly, the coalescing of life and ideological representation of life: though De Mille did not use the Bizet material, as copyright was too expensive, and the film was a reduction of the Mérimée material, the assumption is that a singer is best fitted for the role, remembering the Bizet text. It is not far from here to the idea that a Spanish singer (as Dolores del Rio) or actress (as Rita Hayworth) is best fitted to the part, as though on the assumption that the Spanish women are like Carmen anyway. Farrar moves from illusion to illusion: from singing *Carmen* to acting it in another version: the effect of this is to 'naturalise' the idea of a woman as a Carmen—or at any rate, either a virgin, or a whore (the Micaela/Carmen split that is instituted in the opera, not, noticeably, in the novella). And using an opera singer gives to the part that added glamour and exotic quality, which may also be associated with the European woman (and, increasingly, not with the American

one). Equally synthetic sultriness was provided by the Theda
Bara version in the same year for Fox: designed to run in
competition to Farrar's. Theda Bara, whose name was supposed
to be an anagram of 'Arab death', and was supposed to have
been born under the shadow of the sphinx, and to have been
weaned on serpent's milk: the publicity disguised her truly
American origins in order to create her as the vamp, which was
how she made her name, and how she played Carmen. Bara
played Carmen, Cleopatra and Salome as historic vamps alongside her 1914 debut in *A fool there was*. The title comes from
the Kipling poem to describe a Burne-Jones painting, and the
play, dealing with the moral wreckage of a man meeting a
woman on a liner on the way to Italy (American innocence
again corrupted by Europe) and her enticing him from his
wife, was written in 1909 by Porter Emerson Browne. 'Kiss
me my fool', as a line from this could only be said while
American sexlessness could also be conveyed by Mary Pickford:
the virgin–whore split is maintained there. What is instructive
about the Bara film is precisely its enlisting Carmen with other
fatal women; Carmen can no longer be understood without the
similarly mythologised Cleopatra, Salome, Mme Dubarry.
These European influences persist with Pola Negri, Dietrich and
Garbo, and the exaggerations behind the vamp have much to
do with the fascination accorded by the puritanical impulse to
the 'other', the self that is not the American male. The vamps,
according to Molly Haskell, 'are meant to represent demonic
natural forces that, like a cyclone, threaten to uproot man
from himself, but they are more like storm warnings than the
storm itself. Sagging under the excess weight of make-up and
jewels—the emblems of their wickedness—they are not likely
to seduce anyone unawares, but, with *Caveat Emptor* written
on their brow, are self-contained cautionary fables, like a
De Mille orgy sequence'.[15]

This note seems right and appropriate. The Bara *Carmen*
and the one of Pola Negri (1918, directed by Lubitsch, and
shown in the USA as *Gypsy blood* in 1921) belong to the
vamp tradition, whose function is to take away the sexuality
of the woman and the attendant personality, and replace it

with a kitsch kind of glamour whose function is minatory and evasive of any more engaged attitude towards sexuality. Sexuality is aligned to luxury, to idleness, to the exotic, and thus reduced. Rather than a stress being placed upon the otherness of the woman, she has her sexuality reduced: the differences from the Pickford model turn out not to be that different. An account of *Carmen* in terms of intertextuality suggests that there *is* no *Carmen or* Carmen: there are simply re-surfacings of a similar situation where the names encourage a false sense of continuity. Mérimée's *Carmen* is decentred: the emphasis is upon Don José, who is himself a figure within the text of an 'I' who comes across him first as an isolated bandit, and then meets her in another context, and learns to put the two figures together. On a third occasion, he hears José's story as a condemned man, and gets Carmen's story as José's text. Carmen, thus, is the result of two male discourses—the narrator's, and José's, both of which are held by a third, that of the directing author, who allows for no other possibility, but has forced a classic 'closure' on the text there. To that myth of the destructive and natural gypsy—which Mérimée tried to make more natural, less mythic, by his use of gypsy terms, and his last chapter, which is a discussion of gypsy culture itself, from the point of view of a Romantic, the 'vamp' films which have used the Mérimée text have added a further removal of Carmen —that is, they have made her clearly exaggerated and fictitious, a mythic figure in another sense (from Barthes's in *Mythologies*); made into an object by the male puritanical gaze which by its reification drives out any confrontation with the other. At the same time, the image of the vamp allows for male dominance as the male viewer is invited to think of his own ability to 'circumvent, dominate or propitiate' (Haskell) the female thus mediated to him.

Molly Haskell suggests that there are elements of self-parody about Pola Negri's performance as the vamp: certainly this Polish actress (supposed to be the daughter of a gypsy violinist, thus further encouraging a Carmen identification, and mytho-logising the woman even more thereby) played the standard roles of female seducer—Carmen, Mme Dubarry and Camille (as Bara had also taken this role—derived from Dumas–Verdi), but made her Carmen less the gypsy than the slattern.[16] *Carmen* had itself been parodied in its Farrar and Bara manifestations, by Chaplin, in 1916: parodying the latest movie hit being 'a staple of the comic shorts'.[17] That film ended with José ('Darn Hosiery') and Carmen (Edna Purviance) getting away together. These points suggest the recognition of the stylisation of the project: certainly by the 1920s the vamp figure could no longer survive: sexuality could no longer be set aside so simply: so the next Hollywood version, *The loves of Carmen*, made in 1927 with Dolores del Rio, was designed to emphasise sultriness rather than the vamp's coolness and sinister qualities. It is a more open and overt sexuality, as the title—perhaps suggested by Escamillo's words to José in the Bizet opera—'Les amours de Carmen ne durent pas six mois'—suggests: Carmen is becoming more an object for the delight of the male gaze, in the years before the Production Code of 1933–4 put restraints on the idea of female sexuality in the American cinema till the war years. The French cinema made a *Carmen* in 1945, with Viviane Romance in it: 'Miss Paris' of 1930, and a cabaret and music hall artist: the conception of character, of Spain and of the gypsy is here noticeably crude, but it was this film, shown in America in 1947, that inspired the next Hollywood version— Rita Hayworth's *The loves of Carmen.* (For completeness, the French version of Jacques Feyder (1926), the English *Gypsy Love* with Marguerite Namara, and the Imperio Argentina film made in Mexico in 1940 might also be mentioned at this point.)

The Hayworth film was made possible because of yet further changing attitudes to women licensed through the war—which sanctified the idea of the 'pin-up' in the barrack room, and thus made the female body object of more obvious fetishised significance.[18] With the end of the war, women's position becomes the more depressed in actuality (no Rosie the Riveter now), and the merely physical is what distinguishes Hayworth, Betty Grable and Esther Williams. Again filmed sans Bizet, this setting was billed as 'This is Carmen . . . creature of a thousand moods . . . whose arms were kind . . . whose lips were maddening . . . whose story is immortal'. Hayworth's eroticism was established in *Gilda* and the *Carmen* project was intended to bring her back to this sex-goddess status after *The lady from Shanghai* had disappointed, but it seems that—despite her part Latin-American background, which again was intended to invest her with exoticism—she looked too innocent, her face too clean, her nails too manicured. *The loves of Carmen* represents an exploitative kind of treatment of women, which itself in its inadequacy exposes the factitious nature of the attempt (just as it is often said about Bizet's opera that no one can make enough of the title role); the myths of universality of endless sex-appeal, of enduring erotic variedness are what begin to hang around the newer mediations of *Carmen*. Indeed in 1967 it can be presented quite explicitly for exploitative purposes, in *Carmen Baby*, directed by Radley Metzger, with Uta Levka playing the waitress in an unspecified port, whose seduction of a policeman (the José), of the head of a prison parole board (joining him in bed with his wife) and of Baby Lucas, a pop-singer—the new kind of Escamillo—allowed for plenty of nudity and for lines like 'she was a witch. Her kisses poisoned me but I couldn't have enough of them'.[19]

The absence of Bizet does not imply ignorance: in all the films discussed the opera is there, perhaps overtly as background, to give a sanction, by its status as high art (which also happens to be very popular) to these film creations. Art does not inspire, or exalt, inherently, as suggested earlier: its function here is quite other: to sanction projects that become more and more purely commercial in their aim. There is a significance in the absence of musical treatment while all the time being aware that it is there and that its authority can be invoked to give credit to fake kinds of projects: indeed, it is almost paradigmatic of the way the bourgeois use what is constituted as 'art' at any time. Further, it also asks the question, which could not, I think, be approached nearly so conveniently by another route, as to how the *Carmen* of Bizet differs from these exploitative uses of its and Mérimée's material. Why should the Bizet be privileged and be ritualised within the opera house? Is there a greater degree of authenticity in what it is handling? But then an approach to the opera cannot be made in the abstract, either.

It would be better done to survey two musical films which have done something with it—Preminger's *Carmen Jones* (1954) and Francesco Rosi's *Carmen* (1983). *Carmen Jones* represents a great move forward from Rita Hayworth's treatment of the material before it (though, of course, *Carmen Jones* was a stage musical on Broadway in 1943–4 before it was filmed, so it pre-dates Hayworth). It is another articulation of the *Carmen* plot, but where the influence of *Showboat* and its negroes ('Ol man river') has been felt (both works were scripted by Hammerstein), and the Carmen here (Dorothy Dandridge) works in a parachute factory during the war, somewhere in the South. She goes off with her José to Chicago, deserts him for a prize fighter, and is strangled at the end for her unfaithfulness. The Bizet plot and music are alike simplified: there is more spoken dialogue than ever the Bizet has. Its presentation of blacks is also created out of *Porgy and Bess* (1935—filmed by Preminger in 1959): historically Carmen has much to do with Gershwin's Bess, and the romance of that later work was deliberately inspired by the Bizet; but the effect of *Porgy and Bess* is to produce *Carmen Jones*: the similarity is evident in the heroine who leaves the good Porgy to go North to Harlem with Sportin' Life; both works similarly idealise the male: certainly Joe (Harry Belafonte), the GI about to go to flying school, is so presented as helpless, brought down before flight. And as with *Porgy and Bess* the necessarily external attitude towards the black prevents anything new being said: there is something inherently patronising in the pretence that the black can be handled by a white lyricist (with such numbers as 'Dat's love', 'Dere's a cafe on the corner', 'Beat out dat rhythm on de drum' and 'Stan' up an' fight' replacing the Habañera, the Seguidilla, the Act II Chanson and the Toreador's number) and in the assumption that a European music can handle black sentiment, or indeed could generate it. Despite its use of jazz idiom, the same point hangs over *Porgy*, despite Mellers's defence: 'the theme applies obviously to urban industrialised man whatever the colour of his skin: the plight of the Negro merely gives one peculiarly pointed manifestation . . .'.[20] That might well have served for ten years ago, as a critical comment, but it seems more import-

ant to stress difference now between black and white experience
as they have been constituted, and similarly, differences between
male and female, rather than eliding them in the name of something more generalised like 'mankind' (which, practically, turns
out to be male-based). Thus *Carmen Jones* is likely to seem now
nearer to caricature than close observation: exaggerated dialects,
the stress on hair-pulling fights between black females, the
comforting sense that the blacks know how to entertain themselves and have a spontaneity denied to the white (the mythology is an extension of what was said about the gypsy in the
nineteenth century) will ensure that, rather than the banality of
the dialogue, which remains tolerable for many musicals.
Dorothy Dandridge (who was dubbed by Marilyn Horne for the
singing, so that a European and 'art' texture in the voice seems
to be ensured: whatever the motivation, it seems a pity that
black experience is negated there), played Carmen Jones as a
woman of mixed race, thus with no fixed identity: the film
emphasises her as 'the jungle queen tied to the stakes'.[21]

The emphasis is on wildness and naturalness: the myth
persists, then, of the greater range of emotions in what has not
yet been civilised: the factory experience must be fought by
this representative of Nature—as it is fought in Mérimée and
Bizet. But it does not by that become the access to a social
criticism, for the impossibility of allowing the presence of the
natural is enforced right through the various manifestations of
Carmen. The factory is *accepted* as a way of life. At the time of
the original *Carmen Jones* there were plenty of women in US
munitions factories, and the government was pleased to let
them be replaced by men when they returned. No form of
criticism emerges of all this, which must have been a present
consideration in the 1940s and 1950s; just as the home values
that Micaela appeals to (strongly, in this film, through Diahann
Carroll) are left uninspected. In *Carmen Jones* neither black
experience nor urban conditions receive an authentic treatment.
Instead there is the mythologising of the dangerous black or
mixed race woman, and of her ambivalent 'nature', and there is
an acceptance of the status quo. The film remains pleasant for
all that, and it is arguable that it only replicates, in a different

way, the inability of the Bizet to ask important questions: those which would have to do with its failure to ask any questions about the nature of the cigarette factory—where Carmen is a strangely biddable worker until she has a private argument with another woman—or about the possibilities for a woman's experience to be authentic. Micaela, who is 'a standard by which to measure Carmen and a symbol of José's character and psychological environment before he met Carmen'[22] and José's mother are believed in by the Bizet opera: the most serious thing that the opera does is to marginalise Carmen by this, to refuse to see her as representative of a class or group. Keeping her natural, and a gypsy, or, as in *this* case, of mixed race, prevents the articulation of what she really is.

What the *Carmen Jones* presentation seems to do most interestingly is to question, by its status as musical, the position of *Carmen* as opera. The actors were dubbed, so there was no question of having authenticity in the singing, to go along with the physical status of the actors, but the work was re-orchestrated with a consequent simplification and addition of driving emphasis, and that it ran on Broadway rather than in the opera house, and that it succeeded as a film both make implicit comments on the artificiality of the Bizet, emphasise how far as a text it is created by its time, and that its music is a function of public taste and respect to public tolerance and readiness to pay. In Chapter 4 we shall return to the theme of the Hollywood musical relativising the conception of serious nineteenth-century opera, but it might be said here that the films discussed in this book have all been distinguished by a certain passivity in the face of the music: a readiness to accept it as beyond question. *Carmen Jones* does this, and thus echoes Rosselli's point that at the beginning of the nineteenth century, *opera seria* was regarded as more important than *opera buffa* because it cost more.[23] What is viewed as to be privileged in art terms turns out to be a matter of costs: the ethics of opera houses' costing, at least in the West, bears little inspection, and rarity value does much to make opera seem appealing. When that happens, as historically nineteenth-century opera became a matter of smart middle-class taste, criticism is likely to become the lackey of this establishment of taste, and to probe a text for endless subtleties and nuances. Film criticism, involved as it is so much with what is usually designated 'popular culture' rather than with high art, is able to be the more phenomenological about what it sees and to question *both* the art-types (which have been carefully separated out) as alike subject to ideological positioning and commercial pressures. *Carmen Jones* will appear a lesser work to those who accept the values of the opera houses: its radicalism, perhaps unintentional, its ability to question those values, to suggest that they are not absolute, but positioned.[24]

The question then might be raised as to how far the Rosi film, clearly being presented with political implications, following the lines of his career beforehand, succeeds in constructing a new reading upon the text. Rosi's work is the fullest and lushest treatment yet of the work, with a young American opera and popular night-club singer in the principal role: it comes as the culmination of four recent attempts to work on the *Carmen* material—the Peter Brook film *La Tragédie de Carmen* where the emphasis is provided by the title, the Godard film *Prénom Carmen* and the Saura ballet being the other three. Brook's is a minimalist version, thus is a strong contrast to Rosi's: it cuts down on orchestra (fifteen players), reduces decor and pares away a third of the narrative as well as working to erase the Spanish elements—which were always slightly factitious, of course. The idea is that here is a Carmen whose history is not mere melodrama, but capable of engaging a deeper sympathy than that, and to this end Brook fuses the ends of Mérimée and Bizet: in Mérimée, Carmen dies soon after the defeat of her Escamillo (called Lucas here) in the bull-ring; in the Bizet, of course, Escamillo is successful. Brook makes the Escamillo die, and so lets Carmen choose to face death because she now has nothing to live for. The change from the earlier texts is complete, and what binds Brook and Rosi is their sense that Carmen makes an existential choice: the freedom of the gypsy in Mérimée, who knows that her husband has the 'right' to kill her, though she will still remain free for all that, is replaced by a woman's freedom to choose. 'Jamais Carmen ne cèdera! Libre elle est née et libre elle mourra!' In the Bizet, 'mourra' is sung at precisely the same moment as the offstage chorus sings 'Viva': the ironic juxtaposition perhaps works against the merely tragic. Perhaps, too, there is a stress on death as rebirth: Bizet's work is not free totally from such mysticism. Brook aims at a personal truth about character in his film and its adaptation of the opera: Rosi suggests a social context and in that sense the paradigm for tragedy is not so narrow: we are getting out of ahistorical reflections of 'the human condition' that so dog discussions of tragedy.

The Godard and Saura films both use the *Carmen* material metalinguistically: Godard appears as Carmen X's uncle, enticed by Carmen (Maruschka Detruers—with shades of Anna Karina) to direct a film which will serve as a front for a scheme to kidnap a financier and his daughter. Beethoven quartets, rather than Bizet, provide the music, though the Habañera is whistled; 'If I love you, you're finished, you know', and the film quotes too from earlier Godard films, such as *Pierrot le fou*, so that the washed-up film-maker is being wooed by this Carmen, who seems to be also the muse of cinema, the inspiration for making movies, back into his old ways; as Don José is wooed by Carmen. The inspiration is tantalising, and simultaneously base. Gaumont's *Carmen*, the Rosi version, trades on the success of its *Giovanni* and provides the same formula in conductor (Lorin Maazel), faithfulness to the musical score, and use of internationally-known singers: Domingo as José ('his musicianship seems to homogenise emotion: his voice is majestically bland'— Pauline Kael in the *New Yorker*, 29 October 1984), and Raimondi; while the period is firmly that of the 1870s, and the settings are locations in Andalusia. The film expects to succeed by its colour and sound; Carmen (Julia Migenes-Johnson) raises her skirts in the Habañera and is pleased to be the object of male looking, the cigarette girls are idealised, and given an attractive dance for their first appearance (choreographed by Antonio Gaudes) where they are joined by an old peasant (Enrique El Cojio), so that it gains a folk-sense, contributes to a Spanish peasant myth of freedom. The contrast with Brook's sand-pit setting could not be stronger. Brook emphasises primitivism: the Habañera is introduced by drums, to give an African quality to Carmen, just as she is seen at the start crouched old and witch-like, trying to tell Micaela's fortune, and only being revealed as Carmen when José appears. Brook's version contributes as much to myth as Rosi's, only in an alternative direction: he believes in the tragedy as Mérimée wrote it, rather than as Bizet presented it, but does not wish to inspect what underlies the Mérimée text, to see where it is coming from; accepts it rather, and merely wishes not to romanticise a prostitute, as Carmen very clearly is in his Act II; rather wants to present her as she is, and to evoke pity and terror that way. Rosi's film, though so much more conventional, actually seems more rewarding.

Rosi makes the bull-fight, and the Church's attitude towards it, central: the film opens with a silent, slow-motion view of the now dying bull receiving the coup de grâce: the moment of death is the cue for the start of the Overture—no better contrast could be imagined, and the crowd-scene in the overture involves a procession bearing a statue of Mary: the dancing described in the first act works in significant contrast to this celebration of cruelty associated with mystification. Escamillo is dominant (he will be seen in the fourth act kneeling in prayer before going out to the ring, in order further to set out the Church's complicity in this celebration of the macho), and the bull-fight represents, for Rosi, a throwback to *Il momento della verita* (1965), an essay on the life of the torero, seeing that life as exploited for the benefit of mass commercialism and profit, where the exploited is the bull itself, as well as the torero, who has the choice of poverty in agricultural labour, or this. At the end of the film, the man dies, gored in the ring.[25] To buy a television set for his mother is the first goal of the fighter: an emptily material reward secured at the price of life: the title's cliché fulfils itself.

'The bull that is killed, is of course, Don José, a limited and stupid man, who is goaded and mastered by Carmen, and then destroyed by his helpless passion for her'—David Denby in *New York*, 8 October 1984. Certainly that reading picks up on the literal fight between Escamillo and José in Act III, and implies that it is the brutish Escamillo—played with perhaps too much nobility in acting and singing terms—who is life's winner; a reading Brook's film would destroy, of course. Yet does not this reading look wanton in its omission of Carmen? Is she not also the goaded and bleeding bull, whose hands are tied in Act I, and is at the mercy of the men, as the bull is; unable to escape, though perhaps destroying before death? Yet this reading too might be simplistic, if only because bulls are male, and another reason for the scene being privileged before the diagesis of the film begins seems called for. Philip French suggests that Rosi has 'accepted now that bull-fighting is a fact of Spanish life, a valid metaphor for the human condition (and not just class exploitation), and a fitting occasion for heroism' (*Observer*, 17 March 1985). Decent liberal notions, these. But 'the human condition' as a phrase still makes me wince as it wrings its hands before life, not recognising the processes of history; and though the film may move towards conventionality, especially in its reliance on fine, if a little antiseptic singing (though Julia Migenes-Johnson, more light in voice than the usual heavier stage mezzo-soprano, needs excepting from this), there is no need to see the film as anything less than robust. I read the bull-fight as a symbol of the male power at work in the film, deliberately excluding the woman—obviously Micaela (Faith Esham), but even Carmen, save as she watches on, at the end with Frasquita and Mercedes. That male power is what Escamillo and José both live by, in their different ways, and its image—finely done in this film—is the knife-fight between the two men in Act III. Escamillo counts on wooing women by making them watch him kill. 'Whoever loves me will come'— meaning, come to the bull-fight. The temporary success of Carmen is that she breaks that male power, firstly by her successful wooing of the soldier in Act I and secondly by her antagonism to his solidarity with the bugle and all it represents in Act II. His determination to go back to the men at the barracks excites her rage as nothing else does. 'In her rage and scorn speaks something more and larger than the moment and the personal: a hatred, a primeaval hostility against that principle which in the accents of these Spanish bugles . . .

called to the love-lorn little soldier. Over that it was her deepest, her inborn, her more than personal ambition to triumph'.[26] Mann reads that principle as 'duty' but in the light of the Rosi film, and its articulation of issues, it may be seen more as maleness—the oppressive spirit that in the first act of the opera manages to scare off Micaela—again, a very finely played little detail, as six or seven soldiers gather round her, and in the 'friendliest' manner, harass her. And José's killing of Carmen is the defence of a male power that has lost its ability to quell in other ways. It seems that the bull-fighting, far from rescinding any of the previous associations Rosi gathered around it, now deepens them, by presenting the ugliness of what this society likes and is prepared to call heroism. Heroism itself is erased as a blood-raising irrelevance.

This reading sees Carmen as victim because she is a woman, rather than making her a vamp, or seductress. Her freedom to seduce is a poor freedom in comparison to what the males do. The absence of an interior kind of music for Carmen becomes important at this point: she has no aria for herself, save perhaps in her solo within the card trio. What she sings—the Habañera and the Seguidilla in Act I, the Chanson and the solo with dance and castanet playing in Act II—is for public consumption: she is on display and she is presenting herself to men. What the Rosi film makes possible to see is that the inflammatory nature of her temptations does not come from her being, in any absolute sense, Woman, as the previous views of her, up to that of Hayworth, suggested, but rather Woman as constituted by the male, and by a particular kind of maleness, that which is attendant on soldiery and the cult of heroism. In that sense there is the genuine construction of a reading upon the Bizet and Mérimée texts. The Habañera—which begins with Carmen framed in a doorway, as though in a proscenium arch, is a deliberate staged response to a male question—when will she say that she loves one of them? The reply takes the form of a danced and sung display of herself. The words 'L'amour est enfant de Bohème', which recall the transposition of Bohemian life into the Murger novel, *Scènes de la vie de Bohème*, heavily influenced by Mérimée, and the source for Puccini, represent

C

her way of constituting herself as subject: she identifies with love, and makes the most of the mythic associations of the gypsy. She is only free to use a language that is given her. Perhaps the best use of the Rosi film is that its touches of naturalism show a Carmen who must live pragmatically, and in any way she can: opera in the theatre allows for non-naturalism in its slurring over details of ordinary life; opera on film need not be naturalistic at all, but if it chooses to employ naturalism, as Rosi does intermittently, then it demystifies the heroine; it makes clear that her appearance of being strange and unreachable—Woman in essence—is a creation. In this film, the contradictory ironies apparent in the officers arresting Carmen in Act I and then using her sexually in Act II are well stressed: the character emerges as formed through contrary types of discourse, mutually exclusive, and each constructing an alienated being.

Those different articulations of the *Carmen* material—from Bara to Rosi—suggest that the Bizet opera itself must be seen as something relative to a series of enunciations of the nature of the gypsy woman in the nineteenth century, and that it is a text which needs freeing from any placing within an ideological framework in which Bizet might have understood it, antipathetic though he might have been to the middle-class audience who saw it. ('So they want trash (*de l'ordure*)? All right, I'll give them trash'—his comment on the 'Toreador' song; 'Don't you see that these bourgeois have not understood a word of the work I have written for them?'—his comment after the first night.)[27] The point is that now any attempt to return to Bizet in absolute terms, to regard that as binding upon the opera house, is an imprisoning, and the Mérimée and Bizet workings of the material can themselves be seen as partially constitutive of the articulations of Carmen herself as essential, passionate, natural Woman, and thus creative of a myth of femaleness and of the place of the woman for the twentieth century.

The stress on 'intertextuality' is liberating in pointing to the work, not as a unified whole, a meaningful set of issues, but as a system of signs which are there to be taken in different ways, which can and have been read according to the ideology of the age. Rosi's *Carmen* will probably not be the last use of Bizet, though it is interesting that amongst the many versions of *Carmen* it seems to be about the first to go at the music 'neat'; but in returning to Bizet, it picks up, too, on work done since. Its new articulation of the sign-system that is Bizet's opera presents a possibility for film to pick up on newer readings that will treat that system as so much raw material. Whatever the compromises made by the Rosi film in terms of its concessions to traditional beauty, to local colour, to the obligation to be complicit in an actual bull-fight and death, and above all in its concessions to have the music uncriticised—presented beautifully and as if in the opera house in what will no doubt be hyped as a definitive performance—it does provide a perspective from which to read the ideological bases of previous *Carmen*s. And that ability to provide a standpoint for relativising seems to be a strength of film amongst twentieth-century arts.

NOTES

1. John Roselli, *The opera industry in Italy from Cimarosa to Verdi: the role of the impresario* (Cambridge, 1984), p. 170.
2. Walter Benjamin, 'The work of art in the age of mechanical reproduction', *Illuminations* trans. Harry Zohn (1970), p. 223.
3. For an overview of opera on film, see Jennifer Batchelor, 'From *Aida* to *Zauberflöte*', *Screen* 25 (May/June 1984), pp. 26–38. For details of opera in film and filmed opera, see *Music theatre in a changing society* ed. Jack Bornoff (Unesco publishers, Paris, 1968), chs. 8, 9.
4. Julian Rushton, *W. A. Mozart: Don Giovanni* (Cambridge, 1981), p. 80.
5. Roland Barthes, *Image, music, text* trans. Stephen Heath (1977), p. 143.
6. See on this *Whose music?* by John Shepherd, Phil Virden, Graham Vulliamy, Trevor Wishart (1977).
7. A critique of this argument (derived from Deryck Cooke, *The language of music* (Oxford, 1959) is in Alan Durant, *Conditions of music* (1984), pp. 10–15.
8. For 'interpellation', see Louis Althusser, *Lenin and philosophy and other essays* (1971), pp. 162–70. The work of art, by its hailing the reader as an individual creates him/her as a subject of its own discourse: as the reader who thinks in that text's values.
9. Walter Benjamin, 'Theses on the philosophy of history', *op. cit.*, p. 258.
10. See G. Baldini, *The story of Giuseppe Verdi* trans. Roger Parker (Cambridge, 1980), pp. 89 ff. for discussion of this in relation to *Ernani*. I return to the subject in chapter 3.
11. Quoted, introduction by Leon S. Roudiez to Julia Kristeva, *Desire in language*

(Oxford, 1980), p. 15.

12.   George Perle, *The operas of Alban Berg: Wozzeck* (Berkeley, 1980), p. xvii.

13.   See on this Jerome Mitchell, *The Walter Scott operas* (Birmingham, Alabama, 1977), pp. 259–60.

14.   On Farrar in *Carmen* see Cecil B. de Mille *Autobiography* ed. Donald Hayne (1960), pp. 126–34, Ethan Mordden, *Movie star* (New York, 1983), pp. 16–17 (also for Bara, pp. 3–10).

15.   Molly Haskell, *From reverence to rape: the treatment of women in the movies* (New York, 1974), pp. 102–3; on Bara, see also Alexander Walker, *The celluloid sacrifice* (New York, 1967). See in addition Sumiko Higashi, *Virgins, vamps and flappers* (Montreal, 1978). Larry May, *Screening out the past* (Oxford, 1980) quotes Bara saying 'women are my greatest fans because they see in my vampire the impersonal vengeance of all their unavenged wrongs' (p. 106): so the Vamp could also be taken as a force for liberation.

16.   For details of this film, see Herman G. Weinberg, *The Lubitsch touch* (New York, 1977), pp. 323–4.

17.   Gerald Mast, *A short history of the movies* (Oxford, 1985), p. 80.

18.   Marjorie Rosen, 'Popcorn Venus', in *Sexual stratagems*, ed. Patricia Erens, (New York, 1979), p. 26. Hayworth's *Carmen* is in the tradition of *film noir*, and the projection of woman there belongs to the fear of the aggressive woman worker created by the war.

19.   See review in *Monthly film bulletin* (1970), pp. 79–80.

20.   Wilfrid Mellers, *Music in a new found land* (New York, 1975), p. 393.

21.   Donald Bogle, *Toms, coons, mulattoes, mammies and blacks* (New York, 1973), p. 169.

22.   Winton Dean, *Bizet* (1975), p. 213.

23.   John Rosselli, *op. cit.*, p. 40.

24.   More critical accounts of the film are offered by Gerald Mast, *Film/cinema/movie* (Chicago, 1973) and James Baldwin, in *Black films and film makers*, ed. Lindsay Patterson (New York, 1975), pp. 88–94. Baldwin sees the film as representing three ideologies: that opera has nothing to do with the present day, and therefore nothing to do with blacks; that blacks' passion makes *Carmen* an ideal vehicle for their graduation into art; and these are exceptional blacks—American—and capable of interpreting lower class blacks. With these points it is hard to disagree, though see also Paul Mayersberg's review of both *Carmen Jones* and *Porgy and Bess* in *Movie reader 1-14*, ed. Ian Cameron (1972), pp. 47–9.

25.   For an account of this film, see John Francis Lane in *Films and filming* (December 1964), pp. 5–10.

26.   Thomas Mann, *The magic mountain* trans. H. T. Lowe-Porter (Harmondsworth, 1960), p. 648.

27.   Mina Curtiss, *Bizet and his world* (1959), pp. 390, 392.

CHAPTER 2

Film aspiring to the condition of opera

Film has shown, historically, a desire to be used by opera. At the beginning, it was Geraldine Farrar, a Metropolitan Opera singer, who could not go on tour to Europe in 1914, and was therefore available for film work, to which she lent prestige. There was a personality selling associated with her, as the woman in the most respected art form, stooping to conquer in film: she was a prima donna: she had had European associations: had been rumoured to have been involved with the Crown Prince of Berlin. And this status did much for film. When sound was introduced, use was made of Grace Moore—a 'loan from the grand opera stage', and of Lawrence Tibbett, the baritone from 'the Metropolitan Opera in New York, where beauty, wealth and fame gather to pay tribute to the world's greatest voices', so that Tibbett was marketed for film audiences as 'the greatest voice of the Metropolitan Opera now yours'.[1] Wealth certainly did pay its tribute at the 'Met' where income was derived from the sale of boxes for the whole season to either the socially prominent or the ambitious, and where in the 1920s financial help was provided by Otto Kahn, the Wall Street banker. Just as Harold McCormick and his wife, Edith Rockefeller McCormick, had made up the deficits for the Chicago Opera Company, and Samuel Insull built a skyscraper at a cost of 20 million dollars in 1929, the first five floors of which were to contain the new Chicago Civic Opera House. That was not to survive the depression, just as the 'Met' had to receive government help in 1932, but it was certainly to provide a model for *Citizen Kane*. No wonder that *all* opera was styled 'grand', with patronage on this scale, a patronage which persists as a dominant rule today, and ensures that the 'Met' has to rely almost exclusively on the box office, and thus ensures the endless round of Wagner, Verdi, Puccini, Donizetti and Rossini in performance.[2] And other opera singers have been associated with Hollywood: Gladys Swarthout, who was brought in by Paramount to rival Moore at Columbia; Lily Pons, similarly brought in by RKO, Nino Martini, Lauritz Melchoir, Ezio Pinza, Mario Lanza, who made *The great Caruso* (1951), Richard Tauber; the non-Italian tenor Beniamino Gigli, who sang in films from 1937 onwards, and Salvatore Baccaloni, who sang in comedy roles in the 1950s.

Perhaps Grace Moore's career was the most interesting; starting with the 1930 film on Jenny Lind, *A lady's morals*, intended to cement the myth surrounding the opera diva, which would constitute her the object of endless desire. The film was lightweight, with extracts from Donizetti's *La fille du régiment*, with 'Casta Diva' from *Norma* and with operettas from Oscar Strauss and others; where opera is only very imprecisely known about, its myth-making powers seem further ensured in terms of promoting images of taste and the good life. The 1930s are usually seen in terms of the dominance of the musical and operetta, with Jeanette MacDonald and Nelson Eddy as prominent figures, but side by side with the 'backstage' musical tradition, such as *42nd Street*, there is a line of 'backstage-opera' films, and the importing of opera singers assisted in this creation. Filming the prestige of one medium gave it to the other. Films with operatic topics encouraged audiences to come to opera houses during the Depression. And film had always aspired after the condition of showing opera: even Edison, himself an opera lover, thought in terms of the Kinetograph of 1889 being able to show operas with the sound added; and was to declare in the *New York Times* of 27 August 1910 that 'we'll be ready for the moving picture shows in a couple of months, but I'm not satisfied with that. I want to give grand opera'.[3] Evidently he felt he was on the edge of a breakthrough with sound by use of phonograph records: the storage fire of

Diva. Frédéric Andrei (Jules) and Wilhelmenia Wiggins-Fernandez (the *diva*). Courtesy Greenwich Film Production.

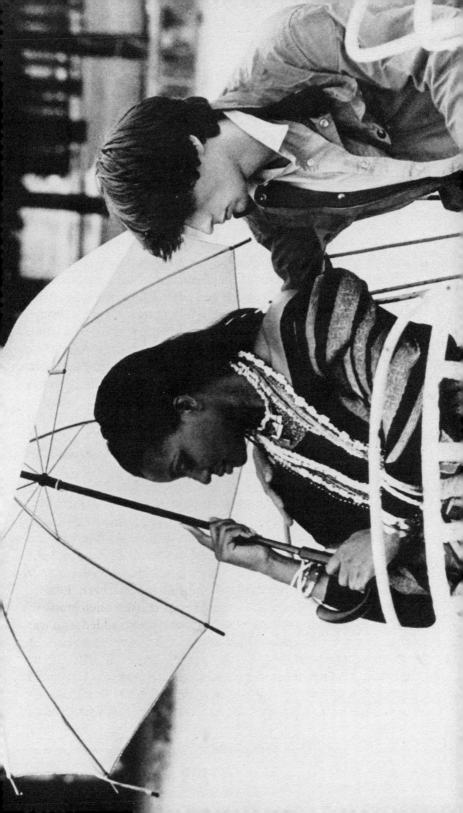

1914 put an end to the experimentation. And this American's American clearly felt that the moment of success would be when opera swept through from coast to coast on the screen.

Grace Moore, whose own career was to be filmed in *So this is love* (1953), with Kathryn Grayson, made her success with *One night of love* (1934)—the fourth most popular film of that year—directed · and with music by Victor Schertzinger—after some relatively unsuccessful films at the start of the 1930s. *One night of love* belongs to a whole genre of films that advertise opera as the accompaniment to romance. It deals with that Jamesian theme of the American innocent girl going to Italy, but there reversing the James plot by becoming a success—as an opera singer, under the influence of her impresario, played by Tullio Carminati. The corrupting influences of Europe make her become the temperamental star, whose rejection of the faithful love of the impresario nearly causes her to fail in the performance of *Butterfly* she is giving (note the reversal of sexual roles here, as between the Puccini art and this 'life'), but she is saved by the sight of her faithful maestro in the prompt box—useful places, prompt boxes. The end of the film comes with her singing 'One fine day' from *Butterfly* on the stage at the 'Met'—having come home again to American warmth and innocence. The climax of love is the putting on of the performance, and it would be perfectly possible to use Mark Roth's thesis about the backstage musical upon this: that the deep subject of the genre is the encouragement of collective activity in the time of the New Deal, that the individualist fails, while the person who is integrated into a larger whole succeeds: but there is, none the less, still the final authority of the director.[4] Clearly the film works by opposing America to Europe; a common trope. 'He was a hit in Vienna, Paris, Covent Garden . . . but *this* is the Metropolitan' says a character to a doubting soprano in *The great Caruso*, which so appropriated that singer that it even made him die onstage at the 'Met' (rather than in Naples). None the less, it is not American music that is sung (besides Puccini, there are extracts from *Carmen* and *Lucia di Lammermoor*). It praises upward mobility—as Moore herself began as a café singer—and the film's subject then is self-reflexive.

Grace Moore followed this with *Love me forever*, with Leo Carrillo; she a failed jazz singer who eventually makes it to the 'Met', he a figure who loses his fortune in gambling, but is redeemed by Moore's singing in *La Bohème*, which music, it is sharply implied, can only be appreciated by people of refined sensibility. (As if to indicate the depth of that delicacy, the film also rescores the quartet in *Rigoletto* for full chorus.) The ideological premises are only lightly subcoded; operatic music spells love, and the family; just as in the comparable *I dream too much* (1936), with the French—in life as in art—Lily Pons, who opens the film with 'Caro nome' from *Rigoletto* which defines how far the woman will go in terms of sacrifice. The plot involves her falling for a penniless American opera composer (Henry Fonda) who writes 'marvellous music, just like Schubert'. Her career is successful; his is not, so she turns his opera into a musical comedy (the triumph of American music over Europe), stars in it, and retires to motherhood! Jerome Kern provided further music, including jazz for the Paris cabaret where Pons works (the French singer marries the American composer, Europe is again subordinated). The film also includes a sequence from the Delibes opera, *Lakmé* (which has a plot identical to that of *Butterfly*, only set in India), and thus pulls at the ideology of the woman paying for the man—only here, the idiom is comic, rather than pathetic, and opera is assimilated to music of lighter quality. This is positive in implying a break-down of hierarchical distinctions—America the home of democracy—but also suggests that there is only a weak sense of anything marking out opera to make it worthwhile asserting as a form in its own right. Opera means schmaltz, only sanctioning a domesticated, home-consumption view of love as faintly mystical, in its non-rational association with music. 'Love, you have given me beauteous dreams', Lakmé sings at the time of her suicide (and hence the film's title); the role was crucial for Pons, and the words evoke the oneiric state that is opera and its ambience which is inscribed in the no less dream-factory conditions that the film's romance exists to manufacture.

These films went on with Jeanette MacDonald in *Oh for a man* (1930), about an opera star whose apartment is raided by a burglar with a saving love for singing (she marries him); *Children of dreams* (1931) (Romberg/Hammerstein II, Warner) about a girl taking up opera singing to save her father from being sent to jail, but eventually returning to the love of her childhood; and a number of films made around 1935. They included Warner's *Stars over Broadway* where the tenor James Melton begins as a hotel porter, but aspires to opera: there are extracts from *Aida* and *Martha* in it; *Here's to romance*, a vehicle for Nino Martini, playing a tenor whose rise to fame is assisted by a wealthy female patron, but who falls in love with a ballet dancer, and whose career consequently spells failure—he comes back from Paris to New York in poverty, having made a fiasco in his debut. The film also uses the contralto Ernestine Schumann-Heink, one of those whose rise from poverty and affairs with the aristocracy in Europe were the material of the American opera publicity machine. Then there was *Metropolitan*. This, from Fox, included a satire on the world of grand opera and on the 'Met' with Lawrence Tibbett and Alice Brady, an operetta singer, and included extracts from *Faust, The Barber of Seville*, the prologue to *I Pagliacci* (an opera which had been filmed by the San Carlo company in 1930), and *Carmen*. The list could be extended with MacDonald's romance films, *Rose Marie* and *San Francisco*, both released in 1936, and with excerpts from Gounod's *Romeo and Juliet*, and *Tosca, Faust* and *Traviata*; and *Follow your heart*, with extracts from *Lucia, Les Huguenots* and Ambroise Thomas's *Mignon*, all about an opera company being stranded in Kentucky. It is in the context of these that *A night at the opera* must be seen; equally 'screwball' comedy, its anarchy has nothing of the edge of the previous *Duck Soup*, but represents a concession to the ideal of love as operatic: the deconstruction of the set of *Trovatore* that Harpo performs is only to allow Ricardo Baroni (Allan Jones) and Rosa Castildi (Kitty Carlisle) to sing together. As a device, it bears a similarity to the downfall of the divisive blanket, the 'wall of Jericho', that separates Clark Gable and Claudette Colbert in Frank Capra's initiatory screwball comedy, *It happened one night* (1934). There the deconstruction marks the end of social and economic barriers: the collapse accompanies the lovers finding themselves in a new unity. The Marx brothers had previously used the 'Anvil' chorus in *The Cocoanuts* and *Monkey Business*, and had poked fun at the silly-solemn pretensions of the operatic singer, while no doubt it is relevant that Harpo plays on the boat free to poor people; but the satire is local, and the status of opera not finally questioned; only the means by which people come to sing in it. (Rosa is sacked by Rodolpho Lassparri, the tenor from Milan, for not being in love with him.)

The popular conservatism behind the New Deal was felt from 1934 onwards.[5] It makes these films on operatic topics what they are: statements that prioritise the money behind opera as part of the ideal that an urban working-class should aspire towards, and it stresses music as tuneful, as should be indicated by the extracts chosen, and inviting a bel canto style rather than having any connection with either drama—or even words. Italian opera is privileged precisely because of its short bursts of song, and thus it maintains its popularity: Wagner, more seamless, hardly appears. Hollywood's refusal to film operas but its willingness to plagiarise music and arias for stories of its own devising indicates its need to erase from even the sentimental Italian operas of the nineteenth century the oppositional elements that make up the conflictual drama of opera and require even Puccini to be taken seriously: the lack of interest displayed in opera as drama emphasises what is brought out by 'grand opera' as a designation: here is spectacle, static, so unquestionable. Music—the tune—is crucial. Opera is conceived of as consisting of short periods of song, no different, in other words, from the musical: indeed, bio-pics like *The great Caruso*, or *Melba* (1953), effectively were musicals, with their wide selection of tunes. The mystique of the singer who produces out of suffering is foregrounded. Duty, so Victoria (Sybil Thorndike) tells Melba (the 'Met' singer Patrice Munsel) means singing, and a career; Melba must not go home to her husband: if it comes to feelings, even queens have to suppress them: powerful ideology for the Coronation year. The same idea of what an opera comprises is seen in those films that use it as a background.

Thus the 1943 remake of *A Phantom of the opera* makes the diva sing a Chopin nocturne for her 'French opera', while Tchaikovsky is similarly adapted, and Schubert was so used in *The climax* (1945). 'Shadow operas'—sequences specially written as pastiches of nineteenth-century operas for films that required them—were quite popular.[6] The outstanding example is Bernard Hermann's *Salammbô* for Susan to sing while making her debut, in *Citizen Kane* (1941). There the intention was to want her to open in Massenet's *Thaïs*, since that opera had been written for Sybil Sanderson, Hearst's first love, and also one of Massenet's, but the fees would have been too great, so that Hermann, himself the composer of an opera based on *Wuthering Heights*, went in for pastiche.[7] Where music proves so easy to be imitated, with the assumption that no one will spot the inauthentic, opera remains an easy vehicle to evoke desire for the inaccessible. Susan was conceived of as being 'a cross section of the American public', and her wish to sing—she is seen practising 'Una voce poco fa' with the standard Italian teacher—is perhaps an interesting commentary on the myth of the opera in the American mind. Hearst's own interest was in Marion Davies, who made movies: the choice to use opera as a medium for the unfortunate starlet rather than the cinema makes a point about the elision of two glamour-worlds. The 'Met' is Xanadu, the dream palace in the films discussed, the place where a Rosebud-like innocence can be regained, if anywhere, and so the object of limitless desire. In the pursuit of this desire, reactionary, as has been seen, the actual details of opera must be excluded: all that remains is the tune and the voice.

This is all that is stressed, too, in the remade *Phantom of the opera* (1943). Like the 1937 *Charlie Chan at the opera*—which also used a 'shadow opera'—it stresses show business as the epitome of life, by its offering a 'backstage' sense of the theatre. The Phantom in Claude Rains's impersonation differed strongly from the 1925 Gothic fantasy; this one made the Phantom an arthritic musician, so about to be forcibly retired, and then disfigured by acid. The film stressed the grand nature of opera, by its innovative use of red, by its generally striking colours, by its use of song (e.g. *Martha*), and spectacular moments from

Russian opera: in these ways it traded on its setting, and on the aura associated with that: European (Paris), rather than the 'Met'. Susanna Foster and Nelson Eddy sang in the film, too, which ultimately is dedicated to evoking the power of music: the 'Lullaby of the bells' that the Phantom has written is declared to be a masterpiece, the piece of beauty that only extreme suffering can produce. The ugliness dies, but the music lives for ever, is the conclusion. Very comfortable in its sense of the rewards for squalor and poverty. Art belongs to an absolute world, and its aura and power surpass all individuals. Susanna Foster also appeared in *The climax*, as an operatic heroine menaced by an obsessional lover (Boris Karloff) who eyes her from a box, and who has killed an earlier prima donna, keeping her body embalmed in a back room in the opera house. The sacredness of music, which cannot be kept down, but surfaces in all the power of its own mystique, is the point, and George Waggner directed to promote operatic spectacle. In these films opera is kept as myth, awarded an aura by its associations with non-rationalism, with luck and mystery; art is privileged as beyond all human interference, and its sources clouded. It is all the same when the 1962 *Phantom*, set in an 1890s London, and including a 'spectacular' grand opera subject as the life of Joan of Arc, relies on the genius, the Phantom, being a starving musician, whose work was bought up for £50 by Lord Ambrose D'Arcy, a rake who wishes to pass himself off as an opera composer. But truth will out, in these cases. It sounds exactly like the plot of *Amadeus*, which, according to Peter Hall's Diaries, Milos Forman, the director, saw as embodying 'the problems of the creative artist in all ages'. Salieri (F. Murray Abraham) would like to colonise Mozart's music: Mozart (Tom Hulce) is impoverished and dies in squalor and ugliness, as his scatological references have also meant that all decent people must make a split between the man and the music. And the fiction demands that the unquestioned beauty of the music must surface without effort, or even without da Ponte.

Schaffer's script uses extracts from all the comic operas save *Così fan tutte* (not dramatic enough?), and builds in perfectly to the ideology of art discussed thus far: above all, the idea of beauty remains a privileged metaphysic, and is presented as an eternal issue as Forman suggests, precisely because the historical nature of Mozart's originality is never discussed, save that Salieri's own opera *Axur* is presented with much visual huffing and puffing from Salieri conducting, so that we are clearly meant to take it as clumsy and old-fashioned. Otherwise, the myths of the beauty of art, the non-rational basis of inspiration in the artist, the timelessness of the achievement, and the complacency this generates have not changed much since they were so forcibly presented in the 1930s. The marked difference, however, is that by the time of *Amadeus* opera had become much more a subject of relatively popular discourse, as the 1928 remake of the *Phantom of the opera* knew, with its study of fairly naked prima donna ambition, and so *Amadeus* uses very evocative, sequences from the Mozart operas, staged by Twyla Tharp: and has a fascinating demonstration of vaudeville, making up with authenticity here for the otherwise heavily mythologised subject-matter.

The 1970s and 1980s have seen a significant increase in the number of films that have used opera, perhaps for metaphorical purposes, and which have differed in this use from the 1930s genre films discussed earlier. Important here has been the recent appearance of opera films: the tone is more sophisticated, the assumption made that the discourse of opera is integral to a bourgeois audience: not an assumption that could have been made, for instance, with the 1951 Powell/Pressburger film *Tales of Hoffmann*.[8] Werner Schroeter's *Death of Maria Malibran*, Herzog's *Fitzcarraldo*, Beineix's *Diva*, Fellini's *E la nave va*, Bertolucci's *La Luna*, even Pasolini's film of *Medea* (1969) with the appearance though not the voice of Callas, *Atlantic city USA* with its use of *Norma* as the signifier of an ideal mode of existence, *Breaking away* with its use of Italian opera to express a spirit of optimism, Syberberg's work, both paying tribute to Schroeter, and possibly derivative in many ways from him[9] —all these belong to the same frame of reference which has relied strongly on a myth of the opera.

The prima donna interest evident in the films made for Grace

Moore, Lily Pons, and Gladys Swarthout—five films, for Paramount, including *Give us this night* and *Romance in the dark* (1936, 1938)—has its own genealogy behind it, and one that film has picked up on. The diva is still stressed: Schroeter made a film portrait of Callas in 1968, for instance, and the cult of the prima donna has meant the foregrounding of coloratura rather than dramatic works: again not Wagner but the Italian repertoire, where the voice becomes bird-like and ethereal, and wanders or soars through its range, Bellini-like. The extracts from Catalani's opera *La Wally* (1892), dealing with a romantic theme set in the Swiss Alps, and used in the film *Diva* are typical: the voice is allowed full rein, and what is stressed is not words but purity of sound. Now this differentiation between sound and message is the basis of recent French psychoanalytic thinking, and is worth further investigation.[10]

There is the distinction Roland Barthes makes between the grain of the voice and the signification that comes from its words: the materiality of the voice itself, the sense of the body in the voice as against its use as an instrument for communication purposes. The voice, when freed from the burden of signifying simply in the antiseptic way Barthes points to in discussing Fischer-Dieskau, attains a new semiotic value, potentially, in that it belongs, in Guy Rosolato's analysis, to something anterior to looking: something nearer the origin, nearer to the unbroken state of union that the infant, in its entry into the symbolic state, through the mirror-phase, intuits that it has enjoyed in relation to the mother. Looking presupposes separation and distance: hearing overcomes the sense of a gap in space, since voices can, for instance, go round corners, and in any case, a voice is internalised when it is heard in a way that contrasts with looking which involves no interiority: it is inside the body that reception takes place, so that the division of spaces is overcome there, too. There is a penetration of bodies: in psychoanalytic theory, the body of the child is possessed fully, the 'desire of the mother' consummated; that desire both for and of the mother.

The voice, then, belongs to the imaginary state, as Julia Kristeva would describe it, the state looked back to, before there was a division of experience implied in the child's insertion into language; that process associated, classically, with the father's authority. Insertion into language is associated with the symbolic order as opposed to the imaginary, and there are thus two senses to be held of the valency of the voice in singing straightaway: one which has to do with its use in, say, Schubertian lieder, where the emphasis is on the words, and so on the symbolic order, and one which might be associated with coloratura, where not the words but the sound is important, lulling, rousing, or meditative-elegiac. That last use has to do with the voice as something poised between body and language. If it only had to do with the first term of that dyad, it would mean the presence of full presence, the existence of that transcendent fullness connected with the imaginary state, and in touch with origins, for the lack of which the subject finds itself in the state of desire; if it only had to do with the second term, it would mean the complete surrender to the symbolic order, to the dominance of the terms of the law of the father.

Rosolato discusses harmony and polyphony in this light; in the movement of separate voices in polyphony is 'the entire dramatisation of separated bodies and their reunion which harmony supports'.[11] Romantic opera, coming as it does after the end of the castrato's dominance, founds itself on the symbolic order that belongs to the family: soprano, contralto, tenor, bass, evoke the family, fully constructed in gender terms, and suggest that the condition of the coloratura soprano, so frequently enacting a struggle against an oppression, belongs to the moment of the bourgeois insistence on the family, and registers the need, displaced in most operatic plots, to break free from that symbolic order and the law of the father; the conflict which is dramatised so fully in Verdi's work, for instance, as with *La traviata*. Song-cycles are less in touch with that sense of a struggle, one that will always end with the destruction of the heroine, anyway: they belong to either male or female voices, indistinguishably; the nostalgia they evoke being more generalised, a more complete sense of loss. The voice of the soprano in Romantic opera, by contrast, represents the pull that is made to bring everything within the domain of the symbolic.

It would be possible to extend this analysis in terms of the role of the castrato. It may be ambivalently perceived, as the asexual, unearthly voice that resists classification, but does so as the price it pays for its lack of placing within the symbolic order, its defeat, literally, in the Oedipal struggle. Here is the hermaphrodite ideal, copied fully not only by the trousers roles taken by women singers (effectively an obliteration of the woman)[12] but in the desire that the woman should also sing in a manner that would embrace and extend her vocal range. Coloratura succeeded the castrato. Maria Malibran (1808–36) played either of the roles of Otello and Desdemona in Rossini's opera and was thus either prima donna or primo uomo. The divine voice, pushed further and further and fetishised, just as the castrati had been fetishised, proclaims that death of the singer as woman: Malibran's demise, after an excess of singing at a music festival in Manchester, is symbolic for the displacement of the female and her replacement by the fetishised voice. This is certainly the stress of Werner Schroeter's film, *The death of Maria Malibran* (1971), which has as its central section a part devoted to Malibran's father, himself a famous tenor, and who was, anecdotally, supposed to have told his daughter while he was playing Otello and she Desdemona (strange inflection of the dominance of the Law of the Father, in Lacan's terms), that if she did not sing well, he would indeed kill her with his knife: fitting instrument of penetration. Repressive father and jealous husband in one, he becomes the symbol of that history which prioritises patriarchal authority and which appropriates the passion of the individual. The self is defined by a discourse which misnames it and forces it into its order: Michel Foucault discussing Schroeter's art with him says that it delineates a self which 'at its limits seeks to maintain itself only to disappear'—as Malibran does. Schroeter's reply to this description of the muted pessimism of the films he makes is interesting: he quotes Foucault at the end of his study of the human sciences, *The order of things*, that 'man is an invention of a recent date. And one perhaps nearing its end . . . if those arrangements [of the way knowledge of the self exists] were to disappear as they appeared . . . then one could certainly wager that man would be erased, like a face drawn in sand at the edge of the sea'.[13] In other words, the conception of 'man' held by the scientific–historical discourses of the nineteenth century is a grossly reductively naming and misnaming one, and Schroeter wishes for its abolition, rather than constructing an existentially authentic self within those conditions. And so the death of Maria Malibran is the death of life as excess, suggested by the music, a life which has already been defined and so misnamed. The *Liebestod* at the end of *Tristan* is a similar evocation of 'excess', equally fated.

The soprano voice in opera, then, becomes a rich source of meanings: both the reminder of that lost origin, of the imaginary state, and the source of pleasure in its invocation of that cohesive condition; and secondly an evocation of loss, of the effective abolition of the woman in favour of something 'unnatural', unearthly. Those scenes for the diva who is 'pazza'—mad (the description of Elvira by Giovanni)—become intelligible as the expression of a consciousness that is deprived of its own passional integrity. For the voice will also suggest the power of interdiction; the power of the patriarchal: the traditional medieval picture of the Virgin conceiving through the ear receives a new emphasis in Rosolato, who is quoting Ernest Jones, of the alternative power of the voice to suggest the phallic law of the Father, whole and total. In one mode, the voice, situated between body and language, is a trace of that presence recollected in nostalgia, in another it speaks of loss, pre-eminently in the case of the castrato, the occlusion of the woman, and may be considered a reaction to the law of the father, just as the tenor, residual reminder of the soprano and feminine register, is reduced: Siegmund by Wotan, Alfredo by Germont, Otello by Iago, brought under the sway of the law.

But further, the feminist critic Luce Irigaray suggests that a patriarchal culture invests more in looking than in hearing, and Christian Metz finds the primary stress on the visible as crucial to Western European cultural production. A voice in the theatre or the cinema may be said to be 'off', when its source is not visible: but there is no off: a voice is audible or not, and does not depend on seeing: it is defined by being mis-described, subjected to the visible. Opera interestingly works to reinstate the neglected: grand opera may rely on spectacle, and the voice become one component in an unfocused total *mise en scène*, but as its own history suggests, with its castrati, its trousers roles, its hysterical heroines, its sopranos who die, breathing out their last in singing fortissimo, its very make-up, aspects of its discourse, speak the dominance of the oppressive, registered in the space left for the voice. Stephen Heath refers to the potential excess within the voice in film, similarly, and sees this in *Questions of cinema* as implying a possible 'heterogeneity in and against the image'. It is the reinstating of this auditory force that inspires Straub and Huillet's films, and which needs to reverse the terms of the position that prioritises the visual over the aural. The voice in opera film, so often pre-recorded, and coming out with the total force of the Dolby system, set against the more relaxed images of the singers appearing on the screen, generates its own sense of the power of sound, that subconscious, archaic force that is allowed to rise up as a challenge to an order that is inherently cruel, or repressing.

There seems to be an interest in the voice for itself in film's use of opera: just as the figure of the diva could be mythologised so easily partly because of these associations with loss and nostalgia and oppression that I have discussed, so it became important that she should appear in Hollywood, with that excess in the voice tamed yet again in the symbolic order of American 1930s romance. The voice ('God doesn't come with a gun, he comes with the voice of Caruso', says Fitzcarraldo), is made the object, fetishised, as the whole of *Fitzcarraldo* (with an initial opera house staged scene, directed by Werner Schroeter) may be said to reflect the fetishised nature of opera in bourgeois terms and its availability to act as a source of power. In *La luna* Bertolucci specifically connects the voice with the mother, the figure that induces the Oedipal reaction. *Diva* (1981) is a text of baroque-like involution, but it too functions as a conscious and intelligent study of the desire for presence.

In *Diva* there is the connection between the older opera

singer (Wilhelmenia Wiggins-Fernandez), black American, to
define her as a figure of loss, somehow not at home, and the
young Jules, the postboy messenger on the motorbike (Frédéric
Andrei) whose yearning for the purity of the voice, and for the
fetishised object—the dress—proclaims the Oedipal fixation; the
fetish serving, as in Freud, as a substitute for the absent phallus
of the mother. The plot of *Diva* centres on the way the singer
refuses to have her voice mechanically reproduced, though Jules
has pirated a tape at one of her concerts (it is significant that it
is a concert, not an opera performance: the emphasis is off the
spectacle, and on to the purity of the voice). At the same time,
a tape is dropped into his bag by a woman about to be picked
off by a Parisian drugs gang whom she has exposed in the tape
she has made. The confusion generated by the existence of
these two tapes, which Jules has, and both of which the gang
knows he has, provides the action. At the end, the singer,
thinking about Jules, whom she has met once, since he came to
return her dress which he stole from her while getting her auto-
graph after her concert, wanders on to the stage. She is thinking
about the loss of the boy. She thinks of the loss of the aura of
her voice now that, Benjamin-like, it has been mechanically
reproduced; only to hear it coming over, amplified, from the
tape that Jules is playing. He walks on to the stage for reunion
while she expresses delight at the way her voice sounds, caught
up by that into a myth of 'presence', as Derrida would say,
confirmed in her status by the mirror that her voice is: no
longer defined by that loss of the voice, by that sense of
betrayal. The end of the film is the triumph of the Imaginary
state. Just as the screen acts as the mirror to objectivise the
spectator's narcissistic looking, in Christian Metz's terms—a
looking which will confirm the ideal sense of self that was
attained in the mirror stage, when the infant saw itself as a
united, perfect, whole being—so the reconciliation between
singer, her voice, and the boy is a moment of filmic pleasure
intended to catch the spectator in an emotional complicity, to
confirm him/her as Metz's 'transcendental subject'.[14] It also
confirms, to the characters in the diegesis, in its glimpse of
the ideal, a condition of wholeness. Mechanised voice over

tape and camera figure each other: the film comments on the way cinema ministers pleasure to the self.

Diva began life as French crime fiction: in Beineix's film it celebrates the evocativeness of the voice, healing and creating nostalgia in the midst of life considered as male melodramatic violence. The women are defined in terms of loss: the deserted and betrayed singer, who is also Caribbean in origin; the prostitute killed with an ice-pick, the Vietnamese gamine who acts towards Jules as a substitute for the singer while she is absent from the screen. The film even finds a visual equivalent for coloratura in the famous Metro sequence where Jules rides his motorbike up and down the stairways in an attempt to get away in a chase sequence: that careering up and down becomes the very image of the singer's freedom over the scales. In one way the gangster sequences become rites of passage for Jules by which he reaches to the singer, beyond the realm of the fetishised object, such as the tape; in another sense, the film's existence, as well as its celebration of the fetish (Jules's garage, with its decor, the records shoplifted by the Vietnamese woman, with her interest in photographs) emphasises the importance of mechanical reproduction for its demythologising value, which enables the singer to accept her voice on tape finally. Yet the film is itself more nostalgic than that, so its end is operatic in the reunion of lovers that it provides, while it suggests that the existence of the fetishised object—here the two tapes, which both lock up the secret to the appropriation of money—entails degradation of the woman. Singer and barefoot prostitute are brought together in an alliance of being exploited, and opera is as much big business as drugs, the only difference being the clientele. The singer's voice evokes a double loss now: the first the psychoanalytic, the second that displacement which occurs from the voice, with its 'grain', being laundered, lost, by being separated from the body, and made more bird-like and non-human by its having been reproduced, objectified. The film's nostalgia is seen in its desire for presence: in what seems to be its regret that the voice has been mechanically reproduced.

For Metz, using Lacan, the spectator's impulse is scopic, voyeur-like (as in Jules's capturing of the voice on tape), and in its auditory aspect, it involves the 'invocatory drive'.[15] This desire to hear involves a narcissistic desire to have the self confirmed, by its ability to return to the imaginary state; to be authenticated as a primary presence. As with the cinematic look, it receives its pleasure from absence: for there is no singer, just as the screen is flat, with nothing behind it, in opera film, and the sound is artificial. In this sense, mechanical reproduction affects nothing. The basis of desire is that it will find no satisfaction in an object: opera on film relies on the invocatory drive, and on its only illusory promise to satisfy it. Just as, in the opera house, the performance of the diva will always disappoint: that is structural to the nature of desire, not to her performance.

There is an interesting contrast between the films of the 1930s in Hollywood and those recent ones mentioned here, in the contrasted uses made of opera. In the first case it is imbricated with romance, in the second with melodrama—which certainly characterises *Diva*. An example of this connection might be given from Fellini's 1976 film *E la nave va*, which also has to do with the fetishised artist, beginning with the voice of the deceased operatic heroine, Edmea Tettua, whose funeral ship is being taken out to deposit her ashes on some remote Mediterranean island. The voice is still played over by her demented former lover in his cabin, while he watches photographs of her as the ship sinks down, not sails on, shot down by the Austro-Hungarian warships at the start of the First World War. The ship sails to music from *La forza del destino* with everyone on board, from the present reigning diva (Barbara Jefford) with full supporting operatic company, to the young Grand Duke of Harzock, with his entourage: with Freddie Jones as the journalist covering the events, and a rhinoceros down below, seasick—though such is the force of the discourse of romantic opera that the company think it must be lovesick.

E la nave va functions in several ways, some playfully, as is suggested by the rhythm of the title; some seriously. It is a 'ship of fools' that sails: the title recalls Stanley Kramer's film about

World War Two: this work has to do with the complicity of the complacent bourgeois-aristocratic in a spirit of indifference that prevented the seeing of Serbian nationalism for what it was: Serbian refugees come on board half way through, to the horror of the beau monde on deck and though later they enjoy the peasant dances, they let the refugees go to their fate indifferently when the Austro-Hungarian warship arrives. The ship is called the 'Gloria N(azionale)', and the title suggests the spirit of 1914, one that is ministered to by opera, that high and grand art form that sustains ruling ideologies, and that, by providing a title such as *La forza del destino*, allows for the idea that history is somehow ahistorical, that events just happen because they do, because of destiny, not because certain events produce concomitant circumstances. The reduction of life to the simplicities of operatic and melodramatic discourse is cheering in the way it enables responsibility to be evaded.

The film is also about the history of cinema: it begins as a silent, sepia portrayal of people going on board ship, and points up the artificiality of film—and by implication, of opera too—by its use of plastic waves and an obviously studio moon: the end of the film reveals clearly that the action is set in Cinecittà, as the whole ship is photographed, including the machinery that has enabled the ship to appear to roll, and thus has allowed for the simulated sinking. At the beginning, a spectator keeps wandering in front of the camera and thus into focus, not comprehending the newness of what's happening: the artifices of cinema are not natural, but mystifying, and the point holds for opera too. At one point, the various singers wander on to the balcony above the vast and cavernous boiler room, a perfect echoing chamber, and are asked to sing by the stokers below: after some hesitation, they compete with each other to produce the most florid and full bell canto. With duties done towards the lower orders they can march off, and resume their quarrels, apart from the time when the basso profondo entertains everyone by hypnotising a chicken with his voice.

There is a connection between the showing up of the artifice of film and that of opera: the fading polite world of 1914 is parodied for its failure to live outside the realm of artifice, and Verdi and Fellini combine to render up an account of 1914 that is operatic melodrama. Nothing is underplayed in Fellini's film, and the reliance on the exaggerated, the deliberately heightened, in both his work and Bertolucci's, may well have to do with a country whose cultural construction is much more linked with opera than, say, Britain's, or the United States'. The opera films of Carmine Gallone, since the 1930s, emphasise a direct popularity, of opera in Italy. His film of *Tosca, Davanti a lui tutta Roma tremava*, the title deriving from Tosca's words over the Scarpia she has just killed, made much of anti-Fascist resistance, just as Rossellini's *Roma, città aperta*, made the year before, in 1945, with Anna Magnani, used the *Tosca* plot, with its Republican sympathies, by having a group of Italian singers defy the Nazis while performing *Tosca*: the singing of Cavaradossi's 'Vittoria' (on hearing that Napoleon has been triumphant), is delivered to Allied troops in the opera house, who have just liberated Rome. Gramsci argues in the *Prison notebooks* that Verdi's music and libretti are 'responsible for a whole range of 'artificial' poses in the life of people, for ways of thinking, for a 'style'.'[16] In saying this, Gramsci may sound patronising towards the people that he finds by melodramatic feeling, and in any case the argument cannot be made solely about Italy, since—as he himself recognises—the melodramas that Verdi set were of a broad European provenance, often not specifically Italian texts at all. None the less, what is interesting is Gramsci's possible linking of melodramatic opera and film: for him Verdi is the type of the popular artist, akin to Eugène Sue in the history of literature in terms of status. It is an interesting emphasis, and might suggest that Verdi is ill-served by trying to resurrect him for 'serious' rarefied musicianship, that this attempt to give formalistically difficult accounts of his works only deracinates him, separates him from his popular place, one which might be best described by suggesting that he wrote the nearest thing to the equivalent of the popular film, in the nineteenth century. And Gramsci indeed speaks of sound films of his own day being done in 'an operatic style'.

The melodramatic emphases in recent film are, however, different from the earlier heavily rhetorical and emotionally

generalised texts of Gramsci's period: they rather draw attention to melodrama as a conscious signifying practice, emphasising
that the distinction, often invoked in discussion of melodrama,
between artificial and natural emotion is not sustainable: all
displays of emotion are already coded, are products of textual-
ity, and deliberate ways of signifying. Whereas modernism had
to do with the difficulties apparent in interpreting reality, in
knowing it at all through the artificiality of signifying practices,
post-modernism, within the cinema and without, is bound up
with the problems of saying whether anything can escape the
status of being mere text, mere artifice. In such circumstances,
the present popularity of opera, in so far as it is not merely
produced by economic taste, is not hard to account for, since
here are textual practices that make no pretence to naturalness,
but that flaunt their artifically produced status: as all discourses
are similarly produced, but most prevent themselves, by their
status as ideology, from being seen as that. The erosion of the
concept of nature is important: it is not surprising that Werner
Schroeter should have expressed dislike of Losey's *Giovanni*,
particularly for its use of the open air setting. I think his view
wrong, as it seems that there are solid advantages to be gained
from the attempt to site the opera in a firm narrative, and in
any case, melodramatic accentuation is not far away from the
high-tension quality of Losey's film, but Schroeter's point is
still well taken. The use of opera in *Diva* or in Fellini or
Bertolucci acts as a metalanguage to suggest the extreme,
baroque ornamentation that is a part of all cultural production,
and *Diva* certainly advertises the element of baroque fantasy
within it.

Baroque, as an adjective, may well be applied to opera,
remembering the time and circumstances of its birth, while
nineteenth-century melodrama certainly provides a basis for
considering an inspiration behind film: the two terms may be
thought in the same breath, Bernini along with Bellini. 'Melos'
means 'song', of course, and Thomas Elsaesser suggests the
importance of this motif in suggesting that melodrama is
'characterised by a dynamic use of spatial and musical categories, as opposed to intellectual or literary ones'.[17] It is

significant that Bertolucci's 1976 *Novecento* begins with the announcement of the death of Verdi: nineteenth-century melodrama is to be replaced with a Mussolini-inspired more baroque one that is Italy's history up to 1945 (and true to Verdian inspiration, the plot of *Novecento* begins with the birth of two boys on the same day, one to be favoured as the member of the bourgeoisie, Alfredo (Robert de Niro), and the other into the peasant class—Olmo (Gerard Depardieu). It is as though the two infants of *Il trovatore*, opposed to each other as Manrico and Luna, though in reality children of the same family, are coming back again, in stronger and more antagonistic form, as their personal fates replicate—indeed, are, political fates too). *Trovatore*, which crosses romantic and forbidden love with the politics of war, and was used as the opening sequence in Visconti's *Senso* (1954), itself about adulterous love for the enemy, is archetypal melodrama, and acts importantly in Bertolucci to suggest the importance of excess, of the transgressive, to break what is socially codified and accepted.

Bertolucci makes full use of the Verdian register: Kolker in his study of the director points out that only four of his nine films are without some reference to Verdi. In *Prima della rivoluzióne* there is a performance of Verdi's *Macbeth*, and *Strategia del ragno* uses one of *Rigoletto*.[18] But it is *La luna* that imbricates the experiences of an opera singer, Caterina (Jill Clayburgh) with a difficult son (Matthew Barry), with Verdi. The son is fixated on the moon, and in *Il trovatore* performances, where she plays Leonore, she stands under a stage moon, bathed in the eerie whitish blue light that the son remembers from his infancy, and which emblemises her unreachability. But *Trovatore* contains its own Luna, the figure to whom Leonore must give herself in order to save Manrico, whom he loves. The word 'luna' thus evokes both mother, easily and traditionally identified with the moon, and the male: hence the father, in the Oedipal conflict. The stepfather has died, thus giving the son the victory, but the actual father, Giuseppe (Tomas Milian) is still alive, and the end of the film will bring all three together. She sings 'Sempre libera' (*Traviata*) as she packs in America to go to Europe to sing: then Joe wishes to go too. Being no Violetta, she refuses, but then on the death of her then husband, she accepts, and they both go to Rome, which is to be the setting of backstage sequences of *Trovatore*.

Not only is the boy fixated—in a way which suggests the use of Deleuze and Guattari's thesis in *Anti-Oedipus*, that the Oedipal conflict is imposed on the child by the parents who thus codify and channel young sexual energies towards themselves, and thus keep the family as the prime site for the production of the gendered subject—but the mother is similarly distorted in her incestuous desires after the son, so that he is to be understood as the Manrico of her agon in *Trovatore*, the Duke to her Gilda in *Rigoletto* (as the aria 'Tutte le feste' from Act II suggests)—the figure the woman must love in a transgressive way despite the interdiction of the father—and the Riccardo to her Amelia in *Un ballo in maschera* (the opera which closes the film, and the one which most explicitly of all Verdi operas, makes transgressive love its whole theme: it is the nearest thing to Verdi's *Tristan*).[19] The film alternates between an objective account, and one where these accentuations of Verdi are to be seen as subjective interpretations by the characters. Caterina leaves her son to go to Parma, where she seems to recover her roots, and the departure is done to the opening of the last scene of *Traviata*: the boy is cast, thereby, as the lonely feminine. She herself declares that Verdi was like a father to her: Parma, full of Verdian associations, was where Bertolucci originated, and this only stresses the defining role of the father, and the way that Verdi, the patriarch, dying in his late eighties, at the end of the nineteenth century, provides the way in which familial and therefore emotional existence has to be expressed, having been first produced through this agent of the Father. All the Verdian heroines can be run together: all in different ways recall the dominance of the father, so that a constant theme emerges: the soprano's sense of loss and near-hysteria, evoked crucially in the coloratura, is the voice of an oppression and a driving to the edge, a position characteristic, of course, of melodrama. Violetta, Gilda, Leonore, Amelia—they can be thought together, as caught figures of deprivation, whose sexuality in its painfully attenuated form is not accidentally related to their mode of existence, as sopranos.

At the end of the film, while a rehearsal of the finale of *Un ballo in maschera* plays, Giuseppe finds his son, watching in the audience (the setting is the Baths of Caracalla), and strikes him: he had previously understood, from his son, whom he did not then recognise, that he was dead. The moment of recognition is analogous to what is happening on stage. The killing of Riccardo (tenor) by the husband Renato (bass: the semiotics behind these registers are, of course, relevant) whose wife, Amelia, Riccardo loves, is reaccentuated into the Oedipal conflict where the husband/father takes possession again. Giuseppe strikes his son, and this reassertion of patriarchal authority replicates the reassertion of the normal familial set-up in the opera. It is true that in *Un ballo* the transgressive love of Riccardo for Amelia has been of the most innocent kind, and the death of Riccardo is really an appalling mistake, but this discovery is only made at the end, so that the last line of the opera has everyone singing 'Notte d'orrore' (an interesting contrast to the film's title). But the point is that the passions figured by the opera allow both for the entertaining of the transgressive, as the inevitable product of the familial structure, the necessary opposition to the law of the Father, and then the reassertion of this law as something ultimately too strong to be threatened, save only in marginal ways. Thus the ideology of the family is preserved in the Verdian melodrama: it is something that cannot be challenged to its ultimate damage. But the interest is in the fascination with transgression, and it may be that melodrama provides a vehicle for reducing its potential threat, accommodating its subversive possibilities within a deliberately ornate and elaborate structure, that by its excess actually looks less dangerous, more artificial, able to be thought about as entertainment.

La luna is aware of that presence of ideological design, by its quotation of Verdi to reaccentuate the nature of the familial oppressions that obtain in each of the operas. Verdi indeed takes on a mythic dimension, as Bertolucci has said: mythic in expressing the conflicts apparent within the setting up of the bourgeois family, with its attendant oppressions mirrored within the very structure of opera. But equally, the film uses melodrama itself as a principle of excess, to create an operatic cinema, one that deflects attention from realism and naturalistic presentation. Bertolucci's film was heavily criticised, and Kolker's analysis of it leaves little room for praise, but the idea of freeing Verdi from a passive historical role as just the shaper of so much thinking about the family, was, at the least, important.

There seems a fit between the operatic voice, which itself draws attention so much to its way of signifying, and gives the principle of excess, however much subject to loss through the bringing in of the symbolic order, and the very excess involved in a cinema that celebrates melodrama. Eyes, ears, the sense of rhythm, the physical senses are all invaded through film: it is part of the larger than life sense that pervades vision and sound on the screen. Bertolucci refers to his belief in pleasure, with regard to this film, setting himself in contrast to Godard, and quotes Barthes's phrase and title, 'the pleasure of the text'.[20] The symbolic order is to be subverted through pleasure—the text is to yield an erotic sense, felt on the body, the site of reception: *jouissance*—the principle of pleasure that is not reducible to the formal and formulaic. Both melodrama and opera itself belong there, because both have to do with the power of heterogeneity, and elaboration, foregrounding, of formal devices, to take the spectator out of mere complacent watching into something more like excess. Bertolucci's invocation of Barthes, after Marx and Freud, is still intellectualising, speaking only about *jouissance*, as talk can only do, and in any case is special pleading about *La luna*; but limited as it remains, it brings opera, melodrama and cinema into a constellation where they work analogously in terms of pleasure, and in the return of an ideal excess. The medium of film stands to gain from the operatic, then.

NOTES

1. Quoted from *The movie musical*, ed. Miles Kreuger (New York, 1975), p. 145. On the subject of the prima donna, see Rupert Christiansen, *The prima donna* (1984) and for the opera star in film, see Roi A. Uselton, 'Opera singers on

the screen', *Films in review* (April–July, 1967) and David L. Parker, 'The singing screen', *American classic screen* (March–April, 1983). See also Ethan Mordden, *Movie star: a look at the women who made Hollywood* (New York, 1983).

2. See Rosanne Martorella, 'The relationship between box office and repertoire: a case study of opera', *Sociological Quarterly* 18 (1977), pp. 354–66.

3. Part of the patent of 17 October 1888 from Edison himself says: 'By gearing or connecting the Kinetograph by a positive mechanical movement, a continuous record of all motion is taken down on the Kinetograph and a continuous record of all sounds are taken down by substituting the photograph recording devices on the Kinetograph for a microscope stand . . . it becomes a Kinetoscope and by insertion of the listening tubes of the phonograph into the ear the illusion is complete and we may see and hear a whole opera as perfectly as if actually present although the actual performance may have taken place years ago' (memo dated 8 October 1888, part of the patent caveat, no. 110). For this information about Edison I am much in debt to Professor Jay Boyer of the Film Programme at Arizona State University, in a letter.

4. Mark Roth in *Genre: the musical*, ed. Rick Altman (1981), pp. 41–56.

5. Ralph A. Brauer in *Movies as artifacts*, ed. Michael T. Marsden, John G. Nachbar and Sam L. Grogg, jr. (Chicago, 1982), pp. 25–43. See also Andrew Bergman, *We're in the money* (New York, 1971), and Robert Sklar, *Movie made America* (New York, 1975) for treatments of the Depression.

6. See Francis Rizzo in James L. Limbacher, *Film music: from violins to video* (Metuchen, New Jersey, 1974), pp. 166–72.

7. For background information on the making of *Citizen Kane*, see Pauline Kael in 'Raising Kane' in *The Citizen Kane handbook* (1985).

8. This film, English libretto by Dennis Arundell, conducted by Beecham, using ballet sequences derived from the earlier success of *The red shoes*, using dubbed actors (Moira Shearer, Robert Helpmann, Pamela Brown), and with Robert Rounceville as Hoffmann, is discussed interestingly by Thomas Elsaesser in *Powell, Pressburger and others*, ed. Ian Christie (1978). He sees the work as using romantic archetypes to criticise romantic cinema, and argues that Powell belongs to a European Expressionist tradition that sees the artist as marked by moral perversity and psychic cruelty: hence the film's working with the fantastic.

9. For discussion of Schroeter, see Gerard Courant, *Werner Schroeter* (Paris, Goethe Institute, 1982). and Timothy Corrigan, 'On the edge of history: the radiant spectacle of Werner Schroeter', *Film Quarterly* (summer, 1984), pp. 6–18. I regret that I have not been able to see his earlier article, 'Werner Schroeter's operatic cinema', *Discourse* 3 (summer, 1981).

10. See Roland Barthes, in *Image, music, text*, trans. Stephen Heath (1977), pp. 179–89; Barthes, 'Le chant romantique', *Grammar* 5 (1976), pp. 164–9; Roger Lewinter, 'Le genre aigu', *Nouvelle révue de psychoanalyse*, no. 21 (spring 1980), pp. 155–9; Felicity Baker, 'Singing and the song: a note on Barthes and Callas', *Paragraph* 3 (April 1984), pp. 83–93; Catherine Clement, 'Le rire de Demeter', *Critique* (April 1974), pp. 306–25 for further developments on this material.

11. For Guy Rosolato, see 'La voix' in *Essais sur le symbolique* (Paris, 1969), and Mary Ann Doane, 'The voice in the cinema: the articulation of body and space', *Yale French studies* no. 60 (1980), pp. 33–50: the quotation from Rosolato is on p. 45. See also Stephen Heath, *Questions of cinema* (1981), pp. 202–3.

12. This discussion the minimising of the female through the trousers-roles should be compared with Lisa Jardine, *Still harping on daughters* (Brighton, 1983), chapter 1, where she discusses the boy-actor in Elizabethan drama as evoking a homoerotic response, again occluding the female.

13. Michel Foucault, *The order of things* (1970), p. 387. Courant prints the interview between Foucault and Schroeter.

14. Christian Metz, *The imaginary signifier: psychoanalysis and the cinema*, trans. Celia Britton and others (Bloomington, 1977), p. 49: see all the section 'Identification: mirror'. For the mirror stage, see Jacques Lacan, *Ecrits: a selection*, trans. Alan Sheridan (1977), pp. 1–7.

15. Metz, *op. cit.*, pp. 58–60, using Jacques Lacan, *The four fundamental concepts of Psychoanalysis* (1977), pp. 180, 195–6. For desire as always deferred, that 'what I look at is never what I wish to see', see *ibid.*, p. 103; and for a useful commentary, Elizabeth Wright, *Psychoanalytic criticism* (1984), pp. 107–22.

16. Antonio Gramsci, *Selections from cultural writings*, ed. David Forgacs and Geoffrey Nowell-Smith, trans. William Boelhower (1985), pp. 377–80.

17. Quoted from 'Tales of sound and fury: observations on the family melodrama', *Monogram* 4 (1972), in Charles Affron, *Cinema and sentiment* (Chicago, 1982), p. 174. See the interesting discussion of melodrama in Affron, pp. 12–16, where he also invokes the operatic analogy, comparing the extreme in range displayed in arias to the close-up.

18. Robert Philip Kolker, *Bernardo Bertolucci* (1985), p. 8.

19. G. Baldini, *The story of Giuseppe Verdi*, trans. Roger Parker (Cambridge, 1980), p. 250, makes this point. Baldini also draws attention to the homosexuality in the original of Riccardo (Gustav III) and Renato (Ankarstrom): not used by Scribe in the libretto. Baldini says that the Covent Garden production in 1960 used this motif; and if Bertolucci was aware of it, it adds to the liability of sexual and gender roles in the film: as, of course, in Bertolucci's use of *Trovatore*, it does to the relationships between the unknowing brothers; Luna: Manrico: Renato: Riccardo; Giuseppe: the son stand in similar relationships, which have to be broken at the end.

20. Interview with Bertolucci, 'Luna and the critics', *Cineaste* 10 no. 1 (1979–80), pp. 27–29.

CHAPTER 3

The work of mechanical reproduction in opera

There is a two-way movement between opera and the cinema: not only has opera been built in film to serve an ideology in Hollywood and elsewhere, but film has imposed itself on twentieth-century opera writing: not perhaps radically, but certainly significantly. In considering this, it will be remembered how post-modernist composers such as Stockhausen or Zimmermann have used film—the first in *Originale* (1961) or *Donnerstag aus licht* (1980), where musical theatre wishes to produce sound as a theatrical event, and mobilises electronic music, tapes and photographs as part of the instantaneous occasion: the second in the opera *Die Soldaten* (1965) where events from an earlier part of the work are played back as in a dream sequence. And film becomes part of a multi-media event which breaks down categories that might exist in musical terms, between the opera and the concert. My intention in this chapter, however, is to give an impression of one use of film, almost as a thematic device, in much more conventional operas. In so doing, I would like to start with Schoenberg.

Schoenberg himself provides a film vocabulary to consider his operatic work by, with, perhaps, the exception of the one-act comic opera *Von heute auf morgen* (1929), which is in any case unusual, within his own terms, in its use of a modern plot. But *Erwartung*, the monodrama written in 1909, was 'to represent in slow motion everything that occurs during a single second of maximum spiritual excitement', while in *Die glückliche Hand*, completed by 1913, 'a major drama is compressed into about

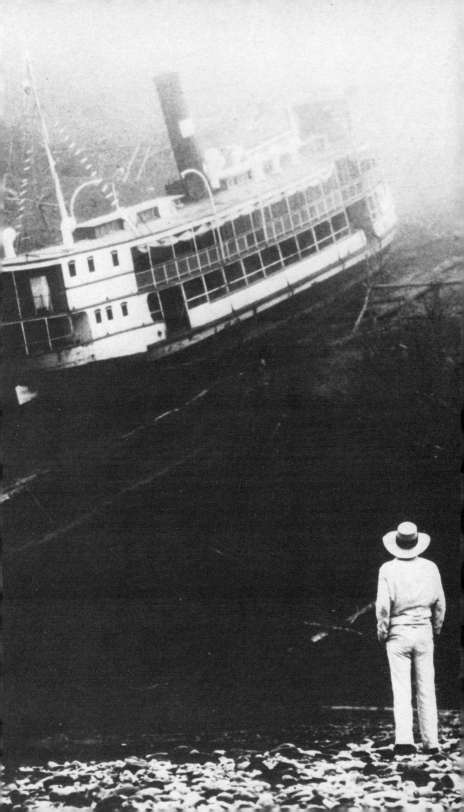

20 minutes as if photographed with a time exposure'.[1] Neither
of these works, perhaps, will seem conventional, though
Erwartung has received ordinary production in opera houses
steadily enough, often with the use of back-projections for
decor. *Moses und Aron* is altogether more familiar in form,
though I shall be drawing attention to its oratorio-like qualities
when commenting on the Straub and Huillet film of the work,
in Chapter 7. And it may be argued that there is something
film-like in the work, as though Schoenberg had picked up on
the inspiration offered in his *Begleitungsmusik zu einer Lichtspielszene* (Accompaniment to a cinematic scene) of 1930.
Thus Rognoni suggests that this film music was testing 'the
dramatic-musical dynamic device of paroxysmal crescendo
which he was then to adopt in the "Dance around the Golden
Calf" ', he adds that Schoenberg had considered introducing a
film sequence into this scene of *Moses und Aron*, and that at
this very time he discussed it with Berg apropos of *Lulu*—
which, of course, does have a film sequence in it.[2]

The first two of these works belong clearly to Expressionism.
Erwartung comprises three short scenes, leading into a final
longer one, and the events that the woman sings of are ambivalent in their questionable objectivity: at the end, the woman
seems to see her dead lover coming towards her: 'Oh bist du
da . . . Ich suchte'—'oh, are you there? I was looking'—and the
music fades out on a chromatic scale, upwards moving, as
contrary to her conclusion, as though the narrative could not
be end-stopped, but must continue, like a looped tape, never
ceasing: the end of *Wozzeck* provides a similar feeling of non-
completion, of a cycle about to begin again. The extreme
emotional state of the *Liebestod* at the end of *Tristan und
Isolde* repeats itself in this text which comes only ten years
before the *Cabinet of Dr Caligari*: another Expressionist piece
which frames the discourse of the narrator within a setting
which reveals his status as a mental patient: relativising the
status of his text to something that may or may not be objective, but which is certainly liminal, on the edge of extremity.
(That *Caligari* was not originally to be so framed, but that the
suggestion for this was made by Fritz Lang, who was at first

to direct it, and was continued as an idea by Robert Wiene, who did work on it, does not actually make any difference to the point: *Caligari* as an Expressionist film exists as that kind of text because of the treatment it received in the making.) It may seem over-easy to insert the Schoenberg of *Erwartung* and *Glückliche Hand* into the Expressionist mode, if it is argued that music is in essence anyway expressionistic and the reflection of an interiority of feeling, but the mode of thinking behind the latter, at any rate, with its Baudelairean interest in correspondences, in synaesthesia, in the bringing together of colour, light, sound and motion, certainly reflects the .discourse of Expressionism, and it is no coincidence that Schoenberg considered Kandinsky as the right kind of artist to work on the decor for a possible film production of *Die glückliche Hand.* Film, so undeveloped in pre-war Germany, was to become the new *Gesamtkunstwerk* that Wagner had wished for: the unreality that was to underlie Bayreuth—the invisible orchestra—was to find its fulfilment in film's potential to project a state as if removed from the everyday, abstract, marvellous. So Schoenberg, writing about the possible film, in 1913, says, 'My foremost wish is for something the opposite of what cinema generally aspires to. I want *the utmost unreality!* The whole thing should have the effect (not of a dream) but of chords. Of music. It must never suggest symbols, or meaning, or thoughts, but simply the play of colours and forms.'[3] What is apparent is the move into the abstract realm, into the avoidance of an image with clear signification. The cinema provides the possibility for a return to a lost plenitude, a fullness that language, images and signs are desperately trying to catch up upon: as in *Moses und Aron*, the opposition is between a God in his fullness who cannot be represented without dropping into banal reality.

Die glückliche Hand belongs to the moment when theatrical setting in Vienna, in the Court Opera, under Alfred Roller, was tending away from the realistic and towards the expression of emotion direct: Wagner was presented with light crescendos to accompany climactic moments: *Tristan* was differently lit for each act in a way that would stress the dominance of mood and

feeling over specific setting.[4] That intensification of responsive-
ness of theatrical technique moves towards the cinematic sense
that may be felt to underlie Schoenberg's opera, so that it
would, indeed, prove hospitable to the methods of film. The
four scenes of *Die glückliche Hand* go through, in their twenty-
three minutes, a series of light changes—red, yellow, blue,
violet being the dominant: the man whose 'lucky hand' is
focused upon almost literally as he repeatedly raises it—his
'fingertips lighted bright blue from above' at one moment in
scene 3; virtually a cinematic direction, rather than a theatrical
one, is the artist whose searching for the ideal is compromised
by his demand for the erotic. Green-lit faces, six men and six
women peer at him through a violet curtain at the beginning
and urge him to a Schopenhauerian rest and quietness: the
number six is replicated in the six-part wordless chorus that
begins *Moses und Aron*: here is a compassionate presence that
suggests, perhaps, the fullness that the artist aspires towards,
though he is held down by guilt—an animal has sunk his teeth
into his neck—and he craves the woman, and on possession of
her seems to move into another status: that of the bourgeois
gentleman who appears as his alter ego. The man's achievement
fails as he fashions a diadem, for it cannot be understood: the
workers who have been shown striving in their grotto like so
many Nibelungen try to attack him; his erotic inspiration fails,
and he is left at the end as he was at the beginning: prostrate
on the floor, with the animal upon him, and the chorus com-
passionating him. Schoenberg seems to have envisaged the
whole opera being acted on the screen to designs by Kokoschka
or Kandinsky or Roller and with the hand-tinted colouring
being supplemented by coloured reflectors casting light upon
the scene within the theatre, and the chorus and the solo male
singer giving performances live in relation to the obviously
silent, mimed film.

The detailed stage-directions, the small proportion of singing
to action, the requirement for magic effects—such as the appearance and disappearance of the goblet in the man's hand—given
to him by the woman, with clear echoes of the potion in *Tristan
and Isolde*—point to an interest in the visual that is itself cine-

matic. Yet interesting though it would have been had the music-drama been filmed, it would have been too monologic in its stressing romanticism: I agree with Henry A. Lea's assessment of the work that the composer 'imposes expressionistic music upon a romantic text',[5] so that there is a split: the artist is thought of in romantic terms as doomed and damned though possessed of the lucky hand, and that inspiration demands a denial of the workers who are, perhaps, the only other humans who appear on stage with him—the status of the woman is questionable: for she is the romantic eternal feminine. The artist is made absolute, and to have filmed the work would, as Schoenberg conceived it, only have increased that sense of the artist being unique: his vision beyond question. For the abstract-ness would have meant more of an exclusion of anything that would obtrude on the world of the artist: his vision would have been seen and declared to be the only one. In that way, an insistence by Schoenberg on the unreality of the film is beside the point: reality cannot be excluded without it having some meaning, even though Schoenberg might have wished for no meaning to be present: the absence of a definite image proclaims that another form of reality has been selected: one that disengages from the public and takes refuge in the private—as it is the argument of Kracauer and Lotte Eisner that German expressionist cinema in the years after the war involved a perpetuation of the private, irrational, and perhaps escapist yearning.

Schoenberg's own movement is away from that acceptance of the artist's position as sole and single: *Moses und Aron* sets up a dialectic between the artist and the representative of the people, and the people are visible, too, in that opera: reality returns, even though there can be no resolving the issue of how an ideal vision can exist in the public realm without its corrupt-ion. There is still something wrong with that kind of argument, as we shall see in Chapter 7 when we look at the Straub and Huillet film: it still savours of an elitism that privileges the original artist's vision *as opposed to* the people: none the less the change is strong. And it is Jean-Marie Straub and Daniele Huillet who have enabled this point to be made more efficiently, in a fifteen-minute short made in 1972 called *Introduction to Arnold Schoenberg's Accompaniment to a cinematic scene*, the 'agitational film' as Straub called it,[6] which was to be the third of three films made as a television documentary introducing Schoenberg's opus 34, the *Begleitungsmusik zu einer Lichtspielszene*, which Schoenberg, in his turn, had made for a small orchestra, using twelve-tone composition, at just the time when sound could be added effectively to film. There is nothing abstract about the titles of the movements Schoenberg used: 'Danger threatens'—'Panic'—'Catastrophe': they evoke, inevitably, shadows of the third Reich and the Jewish holocaust, and are taken by Straub and Huillet in this way.

Schoenberg's score was one of a group commissioned by a German music publisher—the actual titles reflect his own thinking. In just the same way, Straub and Huillet's film followed on two others which had as their purpose to introduce the Schoenberg score in a documentary manner. The first was by the Swedish Jan Martenson, the second by the French Luc Ferrari; in contrast to their conventional treatment, Straub and Huillet leave out the ordinary aspects of what the score is like, and use it to comment on Schoenberg's progress through the 1920s, as the conviction of his Jewishness as something positive is borne in on him, and as he dissociates himself from Kandinsky in two vital letters of 1923, written in response to the anti-semitic Kandinsky, who wanted Schoenberg to come to the Bauhaus to become director of music there. The correspondence is fascinating,[7] and revelatory of the distance travelled by Schoenberg from the time of previous association with Kandinsky at the period of Die Blaue Reiter, around 1911: Kandinsky had continued to aspire towards the transcendental and the abstract, non-factual world; while Schoenberg's sense of 'utmost unreality' in *Die glückliche Hand* had been replaced with a sense of what was politically possible: he refers to 'that man Hitler', which is fairly prescient for 1923, and his appeal to the value of the individual can only be seen as a political stance, though he himself dismisses politics, since 'official talk is all lies'. Furthermore, a depressed attitude towards the possibilities of collective action is evident in the second of these two letters: he accepts that life is a vale of tears. The letters have a strong poignancy about them, especially when set against Kandinsky's 'I reject you as a Jew', though he declares that he would wish to discuss the 'Jewish problem', that of 'the possess-ed nation' with him. These letters are read out in the Straub and Huillet film.

Schoenberg may be caught in the liberal–humanist dilemma of thinking that the individual is not already determined by politics, and he may wish to think of art in terms of the individual's expression of personal autonomy, but none the less it is possible to think of the difference between *Die glückliche Hand* and *Moses und Aron* as having to do with the re-insertion of the political into the world as something that is what art must be about: thus he moves forward and Kandinsky does not and that abstractness is bought at too heavy a political price. It is not surprising to find that Schoenberg was asked by the UFA in Berlin to record himself in picture and sound to welcome in the talkies: it reveals the desire to reconnect the artistic self to the popular, to wider communication. Nor is it incongruous to know that in 1935 he was approached to provide a score for Irving Thalberg's film of *The good earth*, a project which failed since he wanted 'not a single note of his score' to be changed. Along with the other musicians in Holly-wood in the 1930s, he was discovering the point that Vaughan Williams was to make in 1948, that 'the film contains potentialities for the combination of all the arts such as Wagner never dreamed of'.[8]

Die glückliche Hand works by breaking up separate, self-contained scenes that belong to nineteenth-century operatic forms: *Rheingold* with its continuous development might be something of an exception, and so might *Parsifal*, which Schoenberg thought would film well because it 'renounced the unities of time and space'—Schoenberg comments, interestingly, on *Von heute auf morgen* as 'using only the customary *theatrical* methods of condensing and expanding time' (my emphasis).[9] The atonal operas of Schoenberg, and the works of Berg are cinematic in this insistence on the continuous, with the disruption of what Krenek called 'the concept of self-contained,

static systems': a breaking up he saw as analogous to the method
where 'film sequences are cut and combined'.[10] To come to
Wozzeck (1925) after Büchner's *Woyzeck*—unhewn though that
work is—is to feel the strong interest in tautness of design, in
mathematical precision. Hans Eisler comments that it was as if
Berg composed with a stopwatch in his hand, and added that
'complex stage situations are often accompanied by complex
musical forms, such as fugues, in order to make them articulate',
which methods strove 'towards a type of technical procedure
that might almost be called a musical close-up'.[11] From the
liberation from closed theatrical sequences in *Erwartung* and
Die glückliche Hand to the tightness of control superimposed
on that liberation in *Wozzeck* or *Lulu* is a leap that suggests
that the moment of twelve-tone technique is also the moment
of the cinema: Strauss-type romanticism is subverted by order
and precision in both art-fields, potentially. *Wozzeck* is un-
thinkable without the two earlier Schoenberg works, and the
Büchner text, first staged in Munich in 1913, becomes an
Expressionist text almost by the fortuitousness of its performance: these predecessors to *Wozzeck* are fairly romantic, of
course. In Berg, the mechanical devices of the music, its retrogrades, inversions, passacaglias, its symmetries of musical
form—five character studies, symphony in five movements, and
six inventions, devices not to be heard consciously in the
theatre, but sustaining the work as something objective, provide
something else. They countervail the tendency towards mere
Romantic subjectivity—Berg identified Wozzeck with aspects
of himself—and they provide a dry irony to fasten on the
various *idées fixes* (not just the Doctor has one: they all do,
in this opera) that rule the characters' lives. The concentration
of thinking involved here, which far exceeds the looseness of
planning allowable in the theatrically easy and general forms of
nineteenth-century opera, does indeed imply that everything
has been seen in close-up. Indeed, Reich reminisces about Berg's
speaking of 'his pet idea of having *Wozzeck* filmed . . . he
pointed out how the formal arrangement of his first opera
corresponded almost exactly to the technique of film, and that
a film would be able to realise certain details to perfection by

means of close-ups and long shots . . . details that never emerged with the desired clarity in the theatre'.[12] The example given was of the street scene in Act II scene ii. Here the Captain and the Doctor are in conversation, and then Wozzeck walks past, to be twitted by the Captain with the Drum Major's affair with Marie, Wozzeck's wife. It is set out as a fantasy and fugue on three themes. The first theme is the Captain's, from I.i.; the second, the Doctor's, from I.iv; the third, Wozzeck's, from the previous scene (where he was also seen in contrast to two others—Marie and the child: the symmetry is important). The fugue begins when the Captain and Doctor mock Wozzeck ('Ja richtig . . . ') and the repetition of their themes as they do, reveals their obsessiveness, their crazed subjectivity. Berg's idea, if made filmic, would give an opportunity for the identification of theme with character, and for the revelation of the connection of obsession to musical structure: a fugue is both objective—as the torture of Wozzeck is—and also crazily involuted—as these figures are.

What emerges from Berg's interest in film is the sense that conventional opera actually demands too little of the audience in the opera house: Italian opera—Verdi, Puccini, Donizetti, Rossini, Bellini—can be listened to quite easily by people who have not a word of Italian but who just have a sense of the story—not that the requisite knowledge of the Italian would always make that much difference, since the relationship of words to music is so often, there, imprecise if not minimal. Everything of subtlety is done away with in the sense of swathes of emotion cut out by the singers and orchestra: the same point could well be made about Wagner: the attention that needs to be paid is too general, and translation of a libretto is only likely to make more crude, by necessarily simplifying, the sentiments of the original. Not the least of the benefits of opera on film are subtitles: the generalised appeal of an operatic episode is translated into a specific set of significations. Berg and Schoenberg require far more from the spectator, as does Britten, and film suggests the way to make that requirement become a possibility.

The film in *Lulu* (first performed in 1937, two years after Berg's death), may be seen as the continuity of Berg's thoughts about the way opera should go. In this truly twelve-tone work, where each character has his or her own tone-row, order is again preserved, and the opera has strong symmetries and coolness in that: if the character of Lulu recalls the eternal feminine, the use of the twelve-tone method, Krenek suggests, was to 'legitimise the fact that he was lingering in the familiar philosophy of an earlier generation';[13] to which it might be added that the modernism of technique goes much further than that in ironising the whole romantic image: like Adrian Leverkühn in *Doctor Faustus*, to whom everything appears as its own parody, Berg shows the limitation of representation throughout, and signalises this in at least three ways. Firstly, by having Lulu's portrait a feature of each scene, its fortunes both reflecting Lulu's, and pointing out the distance that she travels from the time when it was painted. Secondly, by having the musician Alwa—whose name, though from Wedekind, aptly suggests 'Alban'—think about writing an opera on Lulu: as he thinks it, so the orchestra plays the opening from *Wozzeck*, and representation is placed as something necessarily to be ironised. The third is through the device of the film sequence, which occurs at the end of Act II scene i, and marks the end of the first of the two Wedekind plays that Berg is adapting: *Erdgeist*. The film bridges the gap leading to the action based on *Die Büchse der Pandora*, and records the sensational events connected with Lulu's arrest, trial and escape from prison. The whole thing might well be seen as a parody of the cinema's taste for the glamour of action. Rognoni says, on Helene Berg's authority, that Berg went to see Pabst's *Die Büchse der Pandora* (1929) several times while working on the film, and Pabst's film, for all its brilliance, relies on an emphasis on glamour which softens the edges of what needs to be said about poverty or crime. It will be remembered how Brecht and Weill sued Pabst over his version of the *Threepenny Opera* (1931): the radical qualities of the Brechtian vision are conventionalised, the sets are grand: no beggar's opera this; and it works up pathos. Lotte H. Eisner quotes the view that Pabst translates his fondness for psychological subjects into the most popular idiom possible, and finds a facile quality there.[14] My suggestion would be that the film sequence in *Lulu*, while functional and important in that sense, is also anti-Pabst, if only in its readiness to use so freely the apparatus of that kind of easy, action-filled drama. Representation is challenged through the portrait, the idea of opera and the film: each medium imposes its own ideological slant, its tendency to soften and romanticise, even when trying to affect a naturalness, and the imposition is particularly marked when it comes to the representation of women, defined either as eternal feminine or as the sex-object of unmitigatable desires. What Berg's opera presents is the impossibility of knowing: Lulu escapes from definition although she may be the focus of much—principally male—discourse about her: the text that Berg offers refuses to enter the mythology that was already being licensed by such stars as Pola Negri, Louise Brooks, Garbo and Dietrich in the German cinema.

This does not imply that Berg simply ends with the equivalent myth of the woman as strictly unknowable: it has, as a point, only to do with the deconstruction of the idea of some essential femaleness within her. She may not even have a name: after Nelly and Eve, and 'treasure' and 'bird of Paradise', there seems no need to take even Lulu—a name which teases by its banality and pantomime associations—as real: 'Ich weis es nicht' is her response to all questions. She has no reality. Alwa may call her, romantically, 'Eine Seele, die sich im Jenseits den Schlaf aus den Augen reibt'—just a spirit, in the next world, and rubbing the sleep out of its eyes—but this is pure subjectivity, and Lulu brings him back to earth fairly strongly, firstly by reminding him that she poisoned his mother (II.i) and then that they are sitting on the sofa where his father (shot by her) bled to death (II.ii). Though she may triumph over the males in the first part, the third act, with the degeneration and the murder by Jack the Ripper indicates that this woman can achieve no final victory; just as the very casual murder of her lesbian lover, the Countess, by Jack emphasises further how it is the woman who must be hurt. The opera removes from Lulu any sense that she has qualities of her own, essential or otherwise: she is a cipher, as indeed the name, with its repetitious triteness suggests: a mere object to be represented in ways that mock: the cinematic being one.

The use of film sequences to bridge scenes in plays was familiar: Berg may have been influenced by Otto Falkenberg's 1928 production of the two Wedekind plays which did exactly that, as Mosco Carner suggests,[15] and Piscator and Brecht both introduced film into the theatre. Brecht speaks of Piscator's innovations in the 1920s in Berlin, that with film 'the setting was thus awakened to life and began to play on its own, so to speak; the film was a new, gigantic actor that helped to narrate events'.[16] What seems interesting about the increase of setting and action by means of film is the eliding of difference between the humanist–romantic sets of concepts, incarnated in the actors who are on stage and whose presence suggests something of a human potential, and the mechanical: they move together: the mechanistic lends itself to acting, and the result is that the humanist vision receives its sharp questioning, is relativised in terms of status. Just such a thing is occurring in the film sequence in *Lulu*: after the singing, which allows to the singers in their parts a sense of autonomy, of personal presence, comes the passage where no voices are heard: only the silent screen and the accompanying music. Life is turned into mechanism: or is more properly seen as that after the illusion of freedom offered before. The sense of being caught as a mere cipher is given effect to in this urgent manner.

And this explains why the music acts palindromically: it runs forwards then backwards as a retrograde, taking up the various basic series that have been heard in accompaniment to each figure, and the whole called an ostinato, because of the prevalence of semiquaver figures that go through it as if intensifying its sense of mechanisation. The visual also works like a palindrome: there is the arrest of Lulu for having shot Dr Schön, the detention pending trial, the trial and the prison: the actual point of turning occurs here, where first the portrait of Lulu is seen as a shadow on the prison wall, and then, after a year, when her face is seen reflected in a shovel; then there is the medical council, which is trying Lulu's illness, the isolation ward, and then the liberation, corresponding to the initial arrest. Rognoni quotes Berg as wanting a complete correspond-

ence between these two halves: the revolver and the stetho-
scope, the bullets and the phials, the Justice and the Medic, the
handwriting and the bacillus of cholera, the handcuffs and the
bandages, the prison uniform and the white smock, and the
prison corridors and the hospital wards. These matching pairs
may do more than make a Foucault-like point about the
identical nature of justice and medicine in terms of social
control: they point also to the interest Berg has in reversal as a
structural principle. The men in Lulu's life turn up as reversals
of their earlier selves in Act III, and Lulu's own statements
show that sense of an empty equivalence. In the *lied de Lulu* in
II.i she sings:

Du hast so gut gewust, weswegen du mich zur Frau nahmst, wie ich gewust
habe, weswegen ich dich zum Mann nahm . . .
   Wenn du mir deinen Lebensabend zum Opfer bringst, so hast du meine
ganze Jugend dafür gehabt . . .

(You know the reasons why you wanted to be my husband, and I know
my reasons for hoping we should be married. . .
   Though you are giving me your later and riper years, from me you've
had my youth in flower as a fair exchange . . .)

They are comments which mean nothing: Baudelairean *corres-
pondances* which correspond to nothing. The sentences come
out as mechanical reproduction.

Douglas Jarman suggests that the interest in palindromes,
and in retrogrades, in *Lulu* and *Wozzeck* belongs to a pessimistic
determinism on Berg's part—a spirit that consorts, indeed, with
Schoenberg's pessimism in the 1920s, as revealed in the letter to
Kandinsky. Jarman refers to the circles and all the imagery
associated with them, in *Wozzeck*,[17] and refers, interestingly,
to the Captain's obsession, in the opening scene of *Wozzeck*,
with the mill-wheel as a symbol of eternity, and with the
emptiness of time. Such a sentiment would fit in well with the
Expressionist interest in destiny: Fritz Lang's film *Der müde
Tod* (1921) comes to mind. And the reduction of life to film so
that it can be played backwards, or forwards, but is equally
fixed whichever way it goes is perhaps a potentially depressing

image for Berg. Something metaphysical enters analysis of poor folk ('wir arme Leut') in *Wozzeck* and his sense of the position of the woman in *Lulu*: she will be destroyed by some destiny independent of anything in bourgeois society. The determinism is part of a vestigial romanticism and part of its attractiveness is the fact that it prevents a thoroughly materialist explanation being found for the domestic tragedies that Berg depicts in the two operas.

The palindromic sense is used, too, by Hindemith in the one-act opera *Hin und Zurück (There and back)* which was written in 1927 and has been frequently revived, though not often in Britain. The text was provided by Marcellus Schiffer, a writer of revues and songs: indeed, *Hin und Zurück* began life as a revue sketch in England. It works as a skit on Teutonic Expressionism, where the passion of the husband who jealously murders his wife because he has seen a love-letter in her possession is satirised by being put into reverse by a deus ex machina— an old sage who descends to say that 'seen from above it does not matter whether human life runs from the cradle to the grave, or whether man first dies and then is born again. So let us reverse destiny and you will see that there is the same strict logic and that everything will be as before'. At that point, the music goes into a retrograde (nearly), and the action is reversed, on the lines of a film being played back, where the person who has thrown himself through the window reappears through it. And Hindemith referred to this as a film sketch, and so it is, though it is really parodic of film method for opera; and though it may make incidental criticisms of family life, with the family and the old mother who sneezes all the time, it is essentially a cabaret piece, written for wind, piano and harmonium, and an aspect of *Gebrauchsmusik*, functional music. Hindemith belonged with Weill and Eisler and Krenek and Brecht himself to the movement to free music from high romantic fervour and to make it serviceable to the consumer, and film music was an essential inspiration here as something that could only be said to have a utilitarian value, rather than one on its own account, yet where its voice could be an important method of providing a new accentuation for the action of the film. *Hin und Zurück* began life at the 1927 Baden-Baden festival that Hindemith ran: the 1928 and 1929 festivals were to feature film music, and the spirit of optimism that characterised these experiments sounds very different from the determinism that has been attributed to Berg by Jarman. There is the conviction that the mechanistic is not for shunning, can be used for utility purposes, and this emphasises the social reality that music is a part of, however much its use in high-art terms may disavow its connection with people, may make it an absolute within itself.

Thus though Jarman's thesis may have positive features about it in so far as it is attached to the Romantic in Berg, the argument that he is preoccupied with the idea of being caught up in an endless cycle of events, and that this is displayed in the palindromes, the symmetries and numerologically important motifs in the music seems to rest too much on a determination to find something personal within these devices: he does not consider them as reflections of the use of the mechanical elsewhere—film being a crucial instance of the insertion of the mechanical into humanist art-forms, such as novel or drama. In any case, too, he is in danger of attributing the sentiments of the Captain in *Wozzeck*, obsessed with the need to go slowly, and preoccupied with the idea of eternity, to Berg himself, as indeed Wozzeck's own tortured, expressionistic imaginings about rings and circles must become Berg's, in this reading. But these are not even elements that are specially devised by Berg: they are Büchner's, and become, by this, part of a traditional apparatus of Romanticism. Personal obsession is rather questioned by objectively constructed, ordered music that foregrounds its own nature as artefact rather than as spontaneous outbreathings in Schopenhauerian manner, of the will or of the soul: the music that finds its analogue in the idea of the mechanical—and which uses, in *Lulu*, film to image that artificial nature—is only by a Romantic criterion being trapped, or tragic: in terms of the 1920s, and the ideology that is being made available by film—one that permits *Hin und Zurück*, however light-heartedly to backtrack on its pessimism—it ironises, very drily, Romantic conceptions. In the *Lulu* film, which is similar to *Hin und Zurück* in the way both film and music follow a palindromic pattern, the convergence of two art forms, music and silent film, within a third, opera, ironises the sense of narrative continuity in each. It is a parodic point: the elements of the film, like the music, can go forwards or backwards: like Lulu's name, which is mindlessly repetitive, it reduces the separable elements into so many signifiers, incapable of suggesting a progression through narration. It is not the idea that nothing happens that is being emphasised, but rather it is as though narration itself is being questioned as a mode, one that is fundamental to nineteenth-century opera, of course, but undermined in all modernist texts. The shortness of the music, in *Lulu*, which compels the film images to hurry by in more than indecent haste, increases that sense, as it happens: there can be no definite sense of a narration being told out, except to those who already know the plot. The recent Covent Garden production made the point finely. A narration which looks as though it is offering itself in pellucid clarity, turns out to be opaque, and Berg's text questions its own power of representation the more completely. In *Wozzeck* the plot has a potentially cyclical nature. The last scene, following what Perle and Donat have suggested is something like an overture (the invention on a key—the device of an overture before the final scene is reminiscent of *Fidelio*) seems to suggest the possibility of a return to the beginning. It is a circular movement indeed, as the GDB chord sounds on repeated quavers, never ending, entirely analogous to the close of *Finnegans Wake*, but there is no need to get trapped in the idea that Berg thinks that tragedy is simply inevitable. That tragedy has been all too foreseeable, in terms of the exploitation of Wozzeck (for the Doctor's medical research) and in terms of the family's poverty, where morality, as the first scene indicates, is not affordable. Berg's criticism is sharp and focused.

Berg's music is radically new in its ability to move with mechanical precision, in a way analogous to film. Britten, whose studies of tortured innocence owe much to *Wozzeck*, provides a more conventional instance of an opera composer whose technique owes much to film, the medium for which he wrote much of his work in the 1930s.[18] While there is nothing in Britten of the stress on music's independence from film action, such as Brecht contended for, and his music is more likely to move along in imitation of that action, rather than separate from it, his film music belongs to the same moment as *Gebrauchmusik*'s stress on the liberation of music from speaking the language of the composer's obsession and Romanticism. The price of its not being thus Romantic is that it is a little bloodless; the only partial response to European modernism, however, makes it a little too comfortable, too easily fitting its social function. Both qualities seem evident in *Billy Budd* (1951), which while very beautiful, does not seem to me to be quite striking enough: a little too undisturbing. But there is also a strong originality in the work, and I feel this comes from its organisation, constructed as it is most cinematically. Tendencies apparent in Britten's operas from *Peter Grimes* on to stress continuous composition, and the abolition of the curtain are developed here by the use of the flashback technique, beloved of the cinema in the 1930s. Though E.M. Forster, who provided the libretto (with Eric Crozier), had wished to make Billy Budd the centre of the work,[19] Britten had thought of Captain Vere for that part, and the whole opera is structured around Vere as an old man, reminiscing about the days in 1798 when he commanded the Indomitable. Herman Melville's original novella had described Vere as killed in action, and had assigned the narrator's voice to an 'I' dispassionately observing events.

Vere in Melville's *Billy Budd* acts as a morally ambivalent figure within something that is constructed as a mythic encounter of innocence and darkness: Charles Olson argues that Melville's surrender to Christian values in the work after *Moby Dick* (thus including *Billy Budd*) *is* total surrender and necessitates a denial, so that Budd is 'epicene' and a manifestation of the way Melville became 'all balled up with Christ'.[20] In these circumstances homoeroticism, the displaced fascination in *Billy Budd*, must be rendered devilish (Claggart's interest in Budd), yet of course the entire narration makes 'Baby' Billy Budd's homoerotic appeal something that could only be eliminated—painfully—by condemning him to death, to hanging where he has—significantly—no erection, no 'muscular spasm': innocence remaining thus inviolate, if not preserved by death. With a plot that has so little to do with the social actualities as this has, where every issue can be dissolved into quasi-metaphysics of Good and Evil so easily, the opportunity of writing an opera based on it should be pretty dangerous. And Britten's opera does have elements of trying to allegorise: it is 'the endless sea' that Vere and his men are lost upon, and Billy Budd is cast as the figure who 'blesses' and 'saves', who eliminates, in the final aria of Vere, those descending fourths that were heard in the very beginning as Claggart's motif as a sound to disrupt the opening serene, if ambiguous (in terms of key signature) phrase.

To turn from *Wozzeck* to *Billy Budd* is to feel how nostalgic and dreamy the latter work is, more than the former: the flash-back technique works to license this ability to let the mind dally and become preoccupied with its own loss and sense that it cannot quite justify any action that is performed. Whereas *Wozzeck*, while fully as tortured, is so with a dry sense that this is the way poor folk must be. Britten's opposition to Romanticism—so that in 1950 he could speak of the 'rot beginning with Beethoven', the rot being that of music becoming 'intensely personal' as opposed to involved with the life of the community[21]—implies the thinness of response that might be said to cushion British culture and to make it safe and untroubled. Not for nothing did Britten so soon catch on. Despite his early socialism and strong pacifism, the foregrounding of Captain Vere means that the centre of attention is on the liberal who finds refuge in the past, in the wisdom of Plutarch, and considering, in the Prologue, that he has 'served his King and country at sea'. The injustice of the verdict passed on Budd may be felt as such, and even he may advert to it in his final aria, ('I could have saved him'), but the F major chords that sound after he has walked off the stage to tell Budd that he must die, and which thus eliminate the tragic and foreboding sense recorded in the F minor with which he sung of his decision ('I accept their verdict') allow him off the hook far too easily, and construct his sense of being trapped as something existential, from which he is to be saved by someone dying for him ('Starry Vere, God bless you') and thus rendering him, in his turn, finally innocent. That kind of plotting threatens nothing, because it side-steps all the questions that should be asked about duty and the rights of man. Not for nothing has Arnold Whittall, in his essay on the opera, been able to speak of the pacifism in the work being modified by the then currently waged Korean war, as though Britten was moving back to a more Establishment position.[22]

So the work remains safe in the ideology it assumes, and the flashback ensures a classic distancing from the events of the Indomitable. Vere's memory sequences do not work to ironising effect, as they would do in Berg, questioning the status of the memory, of the objectivity of the events, and assuming instead a temporal flow that is easy and regular, not problematic and bound up with questions of representation. It is true that Vere finishes by thinking of the events of 1798 as being 'long ago now, centuries ago', but that only endorses the production of myth that is going on in the opera—as in the novella: the hanging (compare crucifixion) of the innocent and good. None the less, the flashback and the cinematic technique it suggests is structural and original: the prose of the libretto, by reducing arias and melodies alike, ensures a firmer narrative-line, which is more analogous to the cinema than to the threate, and though there is no Wagnerian 'endless melody', the original four-act version did allow for a sense of the symphonic,[23] with the second act (Vere in the cabin, and the sailors below) as a series of nocturnes whose dreaminess at times allows for a considerable cinematic overlap. Vere sings in his cabin of the need of light to guide, which recalls the strained sense of the searching of memory in the prologue scene: the fog episode that opens the third act in the original version (Act II in the revised) again works by recalling the flashback sense: memory is confused and troubled, and what is at issue turns out to be more interesting than the simple operation of recalling what took place; it is attached more to the issue of Vere discovering what he is. The gap between words and feelings is expressed in his 'Mutiny? Mutiny? I'm not to be scared by words' when Claggart accuses

Budd within the cover provided by the mist: the words may be definite, but the *forte* tone reveals his passion, and Peter Evans points out how the presence of the 'mutiny motif' in the bass also makes him protest too much.[24] There are dawning consciousnesses at work in the next cabin scene, where Vere sings of the mists vanishing, and discovers that he is on trial, and to Claggart's motif, inverted, sings that he must destroy goodness: the correspondence with Claggart's earlier soliloquy being very marked. It is the discovery of an ambiguity in the self that makes him both Vere (truthful) and veering, that means that he initiates the motif, in 'O what have I done?' which with some variations speaks of oppression and mutiny, and that justifies the cinematic overlaying in the work. Vere becomes more James-like than Melvillian, caught in a sense of his own compromise, like Coyle in *Owen Wingrave*, a fascinated figure who is in danger of becoming a moral fool by standing outside action and decision: so often in Britten, the interest is focused there: even with Aschenbach in *Death in Venice*, the stress is on the trapped spectator, frozen by a self-imposed inability to act.

Billy Budd was given a television production on BBC2 on 11 December 1966, by Basil Coleman: it was a studio production the success of which was to lead to *Owen Wingrave* being commissioned; and the version made much of Vere as central: the *Times* review spoke of the 'meaningful cutting back and forth between Vere on board and Vere recollecting in partial tranquillity the same events' during the interludes. The rebellion at the end concluded with a long shot going up to the bridge and to Captain Vere, for the final postlude. It was the first Britten opera to be filmed for television—*Peter Grimes* followed in 1969—and a tactful response to an opera which works like a film.

None the less what is discovered about Captain Vere seems, though interesting, simple, and at the service of a thesis. The use of ambiguity in the key centres—with shiftings between B flat and B minor at the beginning, with the motifs that form so crucial a part of the score available for inspection—these things are interesting, but they all go to emphasise a single point about character and motivation that is being made in

Billy Budd—however finely stated that point may be. The very deliberateness of the recurrence of the motifs as the trial concludes, and Vere is left alone, for example, prevents any other voice being heard: what takes place in the orchestra only confirms, like an authorial intervention, what is said in the text. Here is the equivalent, in opera, of the nineteenth-century classic realist novel—which has its definite sense of the author bringing his/her own bearings to stress the way the action of the novel should be accentuated. A film soundtrack depends on the voice and music being disjoined. In *Wozzeck*, the music in the orchestra may provide a comment on the action—but a comment is no more authoritative than the action itself—but it does not really act integrally, as part of that action. The distanciation is an important aspect of the text being offered for the reader's/listener's interpretation: in that way the possibility of an interesting contradiction emerging from the deployment of words and music together arises. Britten's music believes in no such contradiction: all is to be, seamlessly, the expression of the author's point of view, and that leads to a poverty: where the work can be assumed to be univocal and untroubled by fissures or contradictions, it prevents the knowledge of its own status as artefact and as product of a particular kind of ideology being made known: reifies that ideological position, indeed, into something natural and everlasting. The idea of using film within opera remains an ideal still, not much taken up, but Berg's operatic texts point the way the contradictoriness could indeed be a real hope for film and opera.

NOTES

1. Schoenberg, *Style and idea*, ed. Leonard Stein, trans. Leo Black (1975), p. 105.
2. Luigi Rognoni, *The second Vienna school*, trans. Robert W. Mann (1977), p. 279.
3. *Arnold Schoenberg, Wassily Kandinsky, letters, pictures and documents*, ed. Jelena Hahl-Koch, trans. John O. Crawford (1984), p. 100.
4. See Alan Philip Lessem, *Music and text in the works of Arnold Schoenberg* (UMI Research Press Ann Arbor, 1979), pp. 100–3 for details of this background to the interest in colour.
5. In *Passion and rebellion: the Expressionist heritage*, ed. Stephen Eric Bronner and Douglas Kellner (1983), p. 324.
6. A complete account of the making of *Introduction* is given in *Enthusiasm*,

no. 1 (December 1975). Martin Walsh's chapter on the film in *The Brechtian aspect of radical cinema* (1981) is excellent.

7. It is reprinted in full in Hahl-Koch's anthology. She blames Alma Mahler for souring relations between Schoenberg and Kandinsky (p. 139), but though this may be right it seems inadequate to explain the terms of Kandinsky's anti-semitism.

8. Quoted in *Twentieth century music: a symposium*, ed. Rollo Myers (1960), p. 75.

9. Schoenberg, *op. cit.*, p. 105.

10. Ernst Krenek, *Exploring music* (1966), p. 108.

11. Hans Eisler, *Composing for the films* (1961), p. 34.

12. Willi Reich, *Alban Berg*, trans. Cornelius Cardew (1965), pp. 101–2.

13. Krenek, *op. cit.*, p. 119.

14. Lotte H. Eisner, *The haunted screen* (1969), p. 295. Eisner gives a useful analysis of the *Dreigroschenoper* lawsuit, pp. 343–5.

15. Mosco Carner, *Alban Berg* (1975), p. 233. See also Norbert Weiss, 'Film and *Lulu*', *Opera* (September 1966), pp. 707–9.

16. *Brecht on theatre*, trans. John Willett (1964), pp. 77–8.

17. Douglas Jarman, *The music of Alban Berg* (1983), pp. 237–41.

18. See on this William Mann, 'The incidental music in Benjamin Britten', in *Benjamin Britten, a commentary on his works* (1952). On film music in general, see Roger Manvell and John Huntley, *The technique of film music*, 2nd. ed. (1975).

19. Philip Brett, in *The Britten companion*, ed. Christopher Palmer (1984), p. 135.

20. Charles Olson, *Call me Ishmael* (California, 1947), pp. 13, 104.

21. In 'Britten the eclectic', *Music Survey* (spring 1950), p. 247.

22. Arnold Whittall, *The music of Britten and Tippett* (Cambridge, 1982), pp. 124–31.

23. Eric W. White, *Benjamin Britten, his life and operas* (1970), p. 157.

24. Peter Evans, *The music of Benjamin Britten* (1979), p. 181. I have also found Patricia Howard's *The operas of Benjamin Britten* (1969) very useful.

CHAPTER 4

Musicals,
opera and film

Though his name did not appear on the title-page, T.W. Adorno
was the co-author with Hans Eisler of *Composing for the films*
(1947), and Eisler quotes him with reference to the significance
of the climactic moment of *A night at the opera*: 'the Marx
brothers demolish an opera set as though to express allegorically
the philosophic insight into the disintegration of the opera
itself . . . or smash a grand piano and seize the framework and
strings as a sample of the harp of the future . . . The main
reason for the tendency of music to become comical in the
present phase, is that something so completely useless should be
practised with all the visible signs of strenuous serious work.
The fact that music is alien to industrious people reveals their
alienation with regard to one another, and the awareness of this
alienation vents itself in laughter'.[1] The Marx brothers' deconstruction of a production of *Trovatore* suggests a debunking
of those opera-romance films discussed earlier, and a refusal to
allow any work to take itself so 'strenuously seriously'; while
Adorno is also implying that it is a high-water mark of alienation
under capitalism that music should make so little difference,
and therefore need such a constant overemphasising in order
to mean anything at all. Barthes sees the same episode as one
example amongst many in this film of 'the logical subversions
performed by the text',[2] so that Harpo and Chico's actions
only exemplify the tendency of one part of a discourse to deconstruct another, to reveal a discourse to be such, showing,
involuntarily, how it has been constructed, brought into pro-

duction. It is appropriate to the Marx brothers, whose humour depends on a straightforward onslaught on all types of discourse whatever as fake: so Chico's constant mistaking—'There ain't no Santa Claus' when told to look for a (spurious) 'sanity clause' in a legal document; and so Harpo's dumbness so that he never understands or works by metaphor: when the password is 'swordfish', he produces one; so, too, Groucho's constant flow of deflationary rhetoric. Operatic discourse may well be particularly fake: in *Horse feathers* Groucho warns the audience to leave before the soprano begins to sing, but if Barthes is right *A night at the opera* captures discourse in the process of deconstructing itself, and opera is one mode of utterance that perhaps needs a helping hand to show its artificiality, as well as, in this film, its connection with snobbery, greed and European selfishness. The target was less radical than *Duck soup* with its anti-militarism, but it was worth going for. This subversion of opera mimes an equivalent tendency to parody operatic procedure that has been conducted through the musical film. The pluralising of musical possibilities (jazz, *Gebrauchsmusik*, operetta, the musical) that takes place in the beginning of the twentieth century (though operetta, of course, has an older ancestry, and, along with more satirical and self-aware revue, produces the musical as a form) belongs to the period when grand opera is being deployed most consciously for its culinary properties, and opera is becoming most aware of the need for a change from its nineteenth-century form. So Krenek's opera *Jonny spielt auf* (1927) opposes jazz to late Wagnerian Romanticism: America's music in preference to an etiolated European tradition. It is an opposition that seems meaningful in the context of the direction of European politics between the wars; and it is, significantly, the very moment of the production of the classic American musical, as an alternative, with its energy and its parodying and sceptical attitude to the serious, and above all its interest in fantasy. Weill, after listening to *Porgy and Bess*, not then presented as opera, said 'If there will ever be anything like an American opera, it is bound to come out of Broadway'.[3] The musical—American term—may be historically America's music, and so attractive to Weill, though

A man like Eva. Eva Mattes (Eva). Courtesy Blue Dolphin Film Distributors Ltd.

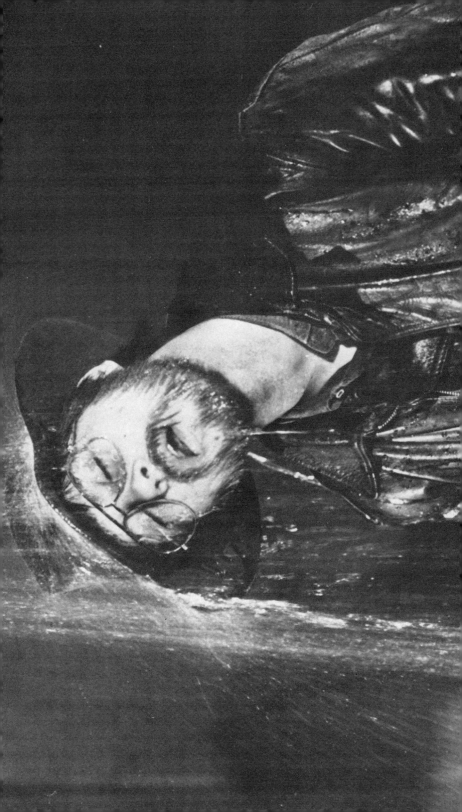

in strict musical terms it received more from Tin Pan Alley than from American jazz, and the desire to do something with it made Weill adopt it, admittedly in works that represented a loss from the modernism apparent in collaboration with Brecht, and the refusal of conventional musical-operatic tastes there, though *Street scene* (1947) and *Lost in the stars* (1949) have been performed both on Broadway and in the opera house. What does seem American is the film musical, with its dance, its stress on the visual, its volume and its move towards integrating these things in production.

Brecht's satire against opera is most fierce because he sees it as indefensibly artificial, always opposed to the popular, and elitist. 'The irrationality of opera lies in the fact that rational elements are employed, solid reality is aimed at, but at the same time it is all washed out by the music.' This artifice has nothing to do with an alienation effect, or with the Russian formalists' insistence on *ostranenie*, the idea that a work of art should defamiliarise, should induce a sense of strangeness, so that a conventional (bourgeois) viewpoint could be overthrown; rather, the composer, via his music, wishes to invade the opera-goer's consciousness, and to interpellate him/her as a willing and unfree-to-resist subject of his own discourse. Instead, the music simply overpowers the listener, and breaks down resistance: the more so as it is difficult to discuss music: it is only possible to bring it into discourse in the most general way, and there is no other art form which is so capable of lending itself to mystification, to a deploying of terms not easily challenged. That does not mean that the listener is passive: people choose the music that they wish to be swayed by, and become willing subjects of the type of discourse offered. So Brecht adds, on the subject of the emotional effects of music, that a Parisian restaurateur claimed that his customers place different orders under the influence of different types of music. 'Specific drinks were always drunk to the work of specific composers.'[4]

This implies that different forms of music are simply produced to cater for people's previously formed tastes, for created subjects of a prevalent discourse. And perhaps a society needs both those types of music it can brand as serious, or art, and those it calls popular. The distinction between serious and popular music is often made to distinguish musical types according to their independence of or reliance on the society they work within: can this distinction be fairly maintained? Adorno may stand as the example of the critic who thought it could, and the point is the basis of his disagreement with Benjamin's essay 'The work of art in the age of mechanical reproduction'. For Adorno, the crisis, in considering music in capitalist society, is that it is all reduced to the status of commodity and fetish. His criticisms of jazz—which seems to be his generic name for all popular music—are familiar: he sees it as passive, unaffirmative of subjectivity, and created by its need to sell itself to a large audience. But this critique—which includes the sense of popular music's appeal to arrangement rather than dependence on composition, its heavy use of colouristic effect, nostalgia for older musical forms—does not define itself as a Leavis-type attack on 'mass civilisation', which has to be opposed by a 'minority culture' (the terms recall the title of a pamphlet written by Leavis on this topic in 1930): for Adorno sees art music as similarly caught, with many of the earlier criticisms applicable to it, too. Thus there is, in the *Philosophy of modern music* (1948), the careful distinguishing between Schoenberg and Stravinsky. The latter is dismissed for his objectivism in his writing: his return to older, non-Romantic, musical forms: he is passive, puts up no fight against social pressures that would make the artist conform to the demands of the culture industry, and the primitivism that issues from his work rings all too truly in the atmosphere of Fascism, since there has been no attempt to define the self as other in its mode of writing. Whereas Schoenberg's twelve-tone technique is a triumph of subjectivity, the more so as Schoenberg writes as though there were no such thing as the twelve-tone method: in other words, he has deliberately put a barrier between himself and achievement, and then surmounted it, in his own dialectic. And that transcension is the model for the artist: since capitalism, and the culture industry objectify all forms of human subjectivity, so that art must work away from that objectification, into a subjective response as Schoenberg does. But the ability to achieve this dialectic is increasingly frustrated: the Devil who is also Adorno tells Adrian Leverkühn, the composer in *Doctor Faustus* who wishes to break into the new, that 'composing itself has got too hard'.[5]

For Benjamin, mechanical reproduction, such as film, and recordings, allowed the consumer a freedom from the loss of the aura surrounding the work of art: it need no longer be defined by its rarity value, by the price the singer can command in the opera house, for example, which will fetishise the performance, make it seem the more wonderful in proportion to the number of people unable to go to it as a result of its being out of their price-range. Adorno's response, besides his correspondence with Benjamin, was the essay 'On the fetish-character in music and the regression of listening' (1938), where not only is the fetishism in the production of music stressed (music has to have instant appeal, it must achieve effects crudely and loudly), but so is that which is involved in its reception: the cult of stars, of the maestro—Toscanini, for example—of instruments: all ways in which objectification spreads. Adorno returns to the classic work of art in effect, and is alarmed by Brecht's influence on Benjamin, so that the latter can 'transfer the concept of magical aura to the "autonomous work of art" [this would mean Schoenberg], and flatly assign to the latter a counter-revolutionary function'.[6] It is clear that Adorno wishes to defend the autonomous work of art in an absolute sense, and he contests Benjamin's position on mechanical reproduction by suggesting that the new modes of production must be inserted into a wider sense of the social relations of production: in other words, into the whole range of what is allowed for within a society's production of culture; the manufacture of it for social control, and for the licensing of certain meanings. Just as *42nd Street* belongs to the economism of the New Deal, and celebrates the idea of working together under a firm leader—Julian Marsh (Warner Baxter), who has himself lost out in the Stock Market crash. (All Americans together.) The spirit of optimism here, as in *Gold Diggers of 1933* and *Footlight Parade*, the other Warner musicals of 1933, is crucial.[7]

Adorno's argument is a strange mixture. It is stronger than

Benjamin's in its critique of the mystificatory power of Hollywood, or the whole culture industry, and in its sense of the passivity this induces: so too it is more sensitive, less terrorist, in its desire to reinstate the 'autonomous work of art'; Benjamin in contrast, 'under-estimates the technicality of autonomous art and over-estimates that of dependent art'. That is, he does not consider how far art music employs techniques in order to deform and defamiliarise a conventional sense of reality: these techniques have been 'conformistically dulled' in modern popular music, and 'technical development'.[8] None the less, the stress on the artist's autonomy is itself a cultural myth: Adorno acknowledges the claim that 'art' makes, and assumes that it makes its appeal in a culturally transcendent manner: that it has its being in itself, having successfully surmounted the social context that produced it. The question that needs to be asked of Adorno, as it does not of Brecht or Benjamin, is why he feels that art music—say Schoenberg—has an absolute claim. Is there not something deceptive about the argument that finds it—popular music that is—not worth attending to, even though in theory, Adorno is committed to a view that sees popular and serious music as the two halves that should add up, when put together, to a freedom? As in 'The fetish character', he begins by seeing in *The magic flute* a moment where 'the utopia of the Enlightenment and the pleasure of a light opera comic song precisely coincide', but after that 'it was never again possible to force serious and light music together'. The point is that the terminology reveals a separation in his mind: a prioritising of Mozart's serious music over the popular, and this binary opposition needs deconstructing: it already reveals a disposition to assume that the first term of the pair has some metaphysical claim to superiority over the second, since coming from the autonomous artist. There is already a covert preference: and this crosses over into the distinction he is making between music which is critical, and that which is merely reflective, of the society it issues from.

Though Adorno may be critical of nineteenth-century music, as with his work on Wagner, the angle of attack is more personally polemical, and has no such view as Benjamin has of the possibility of redeeming the work, rescuing it from its producer, the key utopian position of Benjamin, his way of denying the kind of progress history displays itself as having. Adorno remains with the author, and this lonely position, which has as its corollary the necessity that the audience should follow the composer, leads to an *avant-gardism* which denies a public to itself, in practice. Eisler, who declined Schoenberg's style of composition in favour of a more popular one, associated with Brecht, complained of Adorno's 'metaphysical, blind belief in the "development of music" . . . If Adorno would only once understand that music is made by people for people—and if it also develops, this development is not abstract but somehow can be connected with social relationships!'[9] It is true that Adorno was responsive to strains of the popular within serious music: with Mahler, Satie, and Kurt Weill, for instance, but the praise was from the standpoint of the modern requiring difficulty, demanding the production of a music to defy the dominant system. Weill seems more radical than that: his *Mahagonny* music ironises conventional tastes and also the idea that music means something, that it can be said, outside of a context, that a piece of music has feeling. 'Denn wie man sich bettet, so liegt man'—Jenny's aria about the choice in this life either to lie down and be kicked, or to stand and kick, has a love-song tenderness in its lilt, but the sentiment belies it, as it also mocks the idea of the love lyric. No essential meaning can be ascribed to a piece of music: nothing has an inherent sense; all is dependent upon the part it plays within the total signifying system.

Eisler's music for Brecht, affirmative and popular in orientation, Adorno would deny status to as an 'art form'. Not because of its propagandist intention, but because he would see it as competing with a successful bourgeois production, with its ability to control ways of listening, and unable to separate itself from that and at the same time remain popular and authentic. Thus Adorno's position is within a closed circle: authentic popular music is virtually impossible to write. He denies Benjamin's possibility that the ideological meaning of 'mass' culture may be decided in the process of its consumption, not by its production; that argument which has been used so much in defending rock's radical possibilities: and since, though he may wish to speak of music within the context of the state of bourgeois society, he is really contaminated by the desire to see it as something having absolute value, he cannot face popular music at all. Now in possible answer to this, something more is needed than Brecht's witty dismissal of bourgeois agonisings over the precise deep meaning of a complex text: 'Depth doesn't get you anywhere at all. Depth is a separate dimension, it's just depth—and there's nothing whatsoever to be seen in it.'[10] The absolutism of Adorno can be replaced by a semiotics that sees different types of music belonging to differing signifying systems: a musical text is not inherently serious or popular; it receives that inscription within the whole field in which it is named, the name itself precluding other types of music. Popular music becomes serious when it is part of *The magic flute. Porgy and Bess* becomes opera when it is presented in an opera house: labels are labile. The serious will be defined by its difference from the popular: and this effect of difference does not create any essential definitions.

Thus it may be fashionable to argue that Sondheim is 'really' an opera composer, and that *Sweeny Todd* should be presented with the resources of an opera house, just as *Kiss me Kate* has been presented in opera houses in Europe: but the issue is otiose, only exchanging one form of essentialism for another: maintaining a strict definition of what makes an 'opera' that, and a 'musical' the other. Keeping those definitions, so that opera is allowed its privileged place as the first term of the pair, while musicals sport in blissful supplementarity as the second, only keeps opera houses as temples of culture and tradition, lets them remain unquestioned in their terms: the possible inclusion of a Sondheim will only demonstrate their consumer-friendliness; nothing else will change. Film, I have argued, following Benjamin, has the potential to change the grounds within which the two signifying systems of music-drama and cinema work; to the mutual benefit of each, though particularly for opera's benefit: for there is everything to be gained from its exposure to a wide public through film. When it appears thus, the comparison with the Hollywood musical becomes irresistible, since it is made on two counts, both the filmic, and the musical itself.[11]

Musical films work within a fairly defined structure, which has been given some analysis recently, though the genre has been under represented in film studies. Within their modes of signification, they stress fantasy and non-naturalism; the opera-films discussed later (with the exception of the Schoenberg and Wagner) have worked within a tradition of narrative, but the musical tends more to the foregrounding of spontaneity and the production of a celebratory spirit, for which the 'backstage' tradition is crucial. Jane Feuer has stressed how many musicals are, characteristically, about putting on a show: not a film, because a show assumes, as a film does not, an active, present spectator,[12] and the musical film works to interpellate that spectator into its own mythology: to close the gap, and make the audience feel that they are part of the fantasy world that is on the screen. Thus the aura is replaced: mechanical reproduction disguises its mode, and magicks the spectator. From *Show boat* to *A chorus line* the effect is the same: the final ensemble number of *A chorus line*, 'One singular sensation', is cathartic in its intended effect: after all the waste and possible tragedies that have been implied or spoken of in the auditions, there is the sense that the personal is irrelevant: is merged in the community of identically dressed dancers, multiplying more and more (the effect is analogous to the pulling back of the camera to show more and more wooden crosses at the end of that other Attenborough musical film, *Oh what a lovely war!*). The chorus line provides a strong sense of solidarity by that to offset the earlier sense of isolation. The mask has been taken away during the course of the film, before a voyeur-like producer and the film audience, constituted as no less voyeur-like by the film: now the vulnerable members of the chorus can retreat into the affirmative chorus which restores them to blissful non-differentiation (while the chorus number, none the less, affirms the reality of the unique individual girl). The performance heals the pain of being individualised, and identified as that, and the film audience, by being made the theatre audience, is similarly invested with a role: inserted into a community, whereas before it too had watched as a collection of voyeur-like individuals. The ultimate creation of the chorus line is also the ultimate creation of the audience, and part of the fantasy world of the musical, which, in itself, sets the form apart from opera.

There is, too, a continuity between the sense that life consummates itself in the auratic atmosphere of the stage: a feeling noted in the 1930s films of Grace Moore and others, and inscribed in the dance, which is the distinguishing mark of the musical from the Hollywood operetta, as also from opera.[13] Astaire's and Rogers' dancing, for example, poses as the celebration of energy spilling over into excess: the self is most perfectly expressed by it. Music in the genre is the embodiment of excess: it suggests that life cannot be contained in its ordinariness, but must spill over into it, and into rhythm, singing and movement. It may become strained: as Michael Wood suggests happened to Gene Kelly's professions of self-confidence in the 1950s,[14] but it suggests, as much as the breaking with high art traditionalism, an excess of energy to be paired with the *immediacy* of sound. Steve Neale refers to the musical as the genre that 'renders sound spectacular', as opera never does, and quotes Jean-Louis Comolli on the importance of clarity of sound in abolishing the distance between the listener and the sound-source.[15] Film aspired to the condition of sound, and silent cinema was genuinely operatic in its use of musical backing: 'our actors are transformed into silent opera singers', according to Brecht.[16] Opera may invade the ears in the theatre, but operatic writing also separates listener and work by its complexity of created sound: opera-film, and even more so the musical, which lays all the stress on easy intelligibility, not out of indifferent musicianship, but out of this movement towards total involvement of the listener, foregrounds sound as a sensuous experience in itself, desires immediate contact with a listening audience by its facility in music. It is no coincidence that the first film to have made significant use of sound was *The jazz singer*: the miracle occurs: the gap is closed, and both sound and cinema receive a justification. The most popular, if anodyne, musical, by being called *The sound of music* draws

E

attention to sound as a thing it itself, the yearning for which (discussed earlier, in Chapter 2), needs to be satisfied. The director to have been attracted by this non-naturalistic form was Rouben Mamoulian, significantly an opera producer in New York in the early 1920s, and attracted to cinema by its sound, since he was 'seeking a theatre that would combine all the elements of movement, dancing, singing, decor, lighting, colour and so on'.[17] Hence the 'symphony of noises' that started his production of the play *Porgy* (1927), which became a part of *Love me tonight*, and the fittingness that he should have produced *Die glückliche Hand* in 1930. That interest in sound (and experimentation with mixing), goes with the related visual sense of rhythm. Mamoulian becomes symptomatic of the 1930s movement towards integration of filmic elements, and the musical proves a figure of that.

But though there is a dominant attitude in the classical musical that the world is romantic, and epitomised by physical movement and song, in an atmosphere where New York is the promised land, though also the place of sharpsters and crooks, yet it inevitably introduces a harder self-reference into its form, both by the characteristic 'backstage' tradition, which draws attention to the artifice within the genre—though the idea of showing a rehearsal may explain 'naturalistically' why people should be singing, as people do not do ordinarily, it also inscribes the notion of life as art, as deliberate signification into the form—and it uses its music as excess. More, the dancing is frequently metaphorical in function: evoking the sexual, both conflictually, and resolving opposition. In opera, music is the normal mode, and has little of excess about it: since the whole is a display of excess already; and it uses dance as something separate from singing: in the musical, rhythm and sound become inevitable: a utopian space is opened up: music and song offer a possibility that changes existing reality.

And this utopian space itself can be ironised. In the MGM Freed–Minnelli musical *The pirate* (1947), with Cole Porter music and Kelly working on the dance numbers as well as performing with Judy Garland, the heroine begins as a romantic on a Caribbean island desiring to be carried off by the fabulous

Black Macoco the pirate: at an open-air performance she submits to mesmerism and in this mood dances with Serafin (Gene Kelly) while thinking she is in the arms of her pirate. He woos her successfully, and exposes the real pirate as the man she would have married, and whom she loathes for his every grossness, and she ends up with him in his acting troupe, and singing the finale number 'Be a clown'.[18] Romanticism is subverted from within; and the conclusion, sung within the context of a show, so that again, the whole musical has turned out to be the preparation for an onstage performance, not only ironises the former dreams but comments on the artificial nature of what has been presented: reveals Kelly and Garland as both characters and as outside the partially naturalistic context of the diegesis. In the meanwhile, the hypnosis is the revelation of her displaced desires: she repudiates the actor–singer consciously while fantasising about the pirate: in the event, she repudiates the pirate—indeed, identifies him publicy as Macoco—and marries Serafin. Putting on the show is analogous to putting on a marriage: Serafin earlier 'stops the show' with his acrobatics on the morning of Manuela's wedding to Macoco; just as she later stops *his* show by throwing the props at him when he thinks he has gained her as an object, for marriage to her. Jane Feuer discusses interestingly the importance of dreaming in musicals: the dream sequence leads, characteristically, to the actual fulfilment of the desire, and the dream resolution, the end of the film, and the audience leaving are co-incidental events. And that combination implies the dream nature of the musical: its kinship to the lifting of repression: which is, significantly, felt to weigh upon the woman.

This dream sequence, which integrates singing and ballet, as *Oklahoma!* did (Broadway, with Mamoulian directing, 1943, film 1955), is like the one in *Oklahoma!* (the musical that makes building a Territory analogous to putting on a show). Laurey sings 'Out of my dreams and into your arms' before leading into the dance that ends the first act, where she is faced with both Curly and Jud on her wedding day: and where both men represent aspects of the self that must be confronted: the result being she 'makes up her mind', Jud having been exorcised through the dream. In both sequences, the woman lifts the repression, and subconscious state and musical form entirely relate to each other: the utopian sense and the pleasure principle come together. The song-title implies the modulation of the musical form from daydream to dream: the spectator is included in this, as the use of the pronoun 'you' suggests, is caught up in the fantasy: identifying and identified with the absence that is at the heart of cinema: there is looking, but no finding in the cinema: everything is recorded.[19] The musical on this basis is an apt figure for cinema itself, declaring, as ordinary fiction films do not, the way the spectator is inserted into its discourse. At the centre of the musical form is the realisation that any enacted fulfilment of the dream is itself fictional: that beyond these bright lights and rhythmic creations is a loss, an absence, that is inscribed in the very screen character of the cinema, and which the viewer must internalise.

The quasi-psychoanalytic use of dream in these musicals may reflect America's particular appropriation of Freud for the concept of the construction of the self, in a self-confirming way, but it exists within a signifying practice which is always, implicitly, self-referential: pointing to the cinema as itself the dream and the producer of it, evoking a surreal atmosphere in decor, to back a world instinct with rhythm and non-specific music and movement which can be discovered by a shift out of the ordinary realm of discourse. Jeffrey in *The band wagon* (1953) says 'we enter with naught but a dream, but when we leave, we'll have a show', and the film 'show', though it *is* characterised by absence, is still a metaphor for the possibility of a dream becoming substantial, evoking another possibility. Hence the importance of the ironising quality: while fiction-films disguise the gap between them and the spectator, musicals, though they interpellate the spectator strongly as subjects of their discourse, also keep a difference: keep the spectator aware of the utopian nature of the proceedings.[20] The conditions of Bayreuth are designed to conceal attention to the artificiality of the signifying, while the musical film does the reverse. It is the musical's capacity for self-reflectiveness that makes its distinction: the dream is ironised by Garland and Kelly at the end of *The pirate* singing 'Be a clown', just as, at the beginning, Garland says, 'I realise there is a practical world and a dream world. And I shall never mix them'. Licensed folly, for a holiday, cathartic in its implications, however, and because it opens up a new set of possibilities, not to be despised, has taken over for a while only. It relativises the romance, accepts the absence at the heart of desire. Though acting in the troupe at the end may be equally a fantasy, yet the number becomes an apt figure for Hollywood's mode of existence. It proclaims that the self-parodying ironising is all there is even within the provision of the dream from the dream-factory. That could hardly be a sentiment from Vahnfried: though something like it may just be heard in the Hans Sachs of Act III of *Die Meistersinger*, when he tells Walther that poetry is no more than the true interpretation of dreams (Wahrtraumdeuterei), thus giving poetry a solidity and substantiality above the dream (the show as proposed to the dream), and privileges 'Wahn'—madness, folly, illusion—as a supreme good; and this tone is, significantly, heard at the end of a career in the finale to *Falstaff*.

Opera and musical film work both as artifical modes of signification; opera on film as in the theatre, has tried, characteristically, not to reveal its connection with a set of signifying practices. Opera singing, for instance, is self-consciously beautiful, and it takes itself completely seriously: so much so that it is the singer as much as the opera that attracts the regular opera-goer; once this process of foregrounding the singing starts, there is no need for it ever to stop: voices become fetishised and interpretations of set arias create mystificatory distinctions in minds that respond to this sort of thing. Opera here might learn something from the musical, which early on replaced some of its Nelson Eddys, Ezio Pinzas and Mario Lanzas with a singing and manner more self-aware, less immaculate and professional, as its use of Jeanette MacDonald could produce a singing and dancing both deliberately sophisticated and sceptical about itself.[21] Mechanical reproduction problematises the operatic voice: as it makes recordings better, technically, than ever live performances could be, since it relies neither on one rendition of an aria, nor on mere ears to receive the sound before it is purified, the mystique attaching itself to the rare tenor or prima donna could, it seems, be allowed to disappear, as an example of the way the opera house, as a institution keeps cultural elitism going. And elitism is hankered after with the musical: it is capable of aspiring after that laundered style of singing: as with the recent Te Kanawa and Carreras recording of *West side story*: it has not learned its independence from that discursive mode, still sees itself as gaining from the cachet of having international singers, not to say, in the case of Kanawa, media personalities, with their unique combination of film-star-like reputations, and depth of interpretation. So *West side story* can be reclaimed as 'serious' music: nothing has changed since Mellers wrote about it in *Music in a new found land* as approaching the category of serious music, when not tarnished with Hollywood sentiment, or unrealistic ballet-dream sequences.

It seems a matter for regret when the musical sees itself as a poor colony of opera; more crucial that its own method of signifying should be enabled to question that of the imperial power. Musicals *have* used the motif of stressing the value of popular song over serious, as Jane Feuer suggests; and film has done so repeatedly, as even with *I dream too much*, and certainly with René Clair's film *Le million* (1931) where operatic techniques are on display as artifices.[22] Live opera and filmed opera, or the musical film, stand contrasted in Benjamin's formulation; and mechanical reproduction should have the availability to challenge the pretensions of the former, privileged category: but the question that remains to mute Benjamin's temporary optimism is, under what circumstances can the mechanical reproduction work to change perception? It might have the power to do so, but all depends on the opportunity to use that power. And in this sense, artistic production remains a site of contest: certain meanings can be licensed, and certain not made available to thought, often enough under the screen of artistic worth, which is defined by the users of these modes of cultural production. It is not evident that the musical film can be seen to subvert, or to question, the absolute values of opera.

With its variations, the musical is a recognisable genre, with use of techniques that may be ironised from one particular version to another: and the type has effectively defined itself as middle-class consumer culture of the twentieth century, thus taking over, partially, ground once occupied by opera, and no doubt, giving some of its audience to opera as well. Thus its existence asks whether nineteenth-century opera was anything else, really, in its effect. *Singspiel* and number operas, such as *Carmen*, begin to look more like musicals. The differences—far more ensemble work than the musical usually tolerates, and more developed finale work—are crucial, but musicals have not gone in that direction since the criterion for the musical has never been the complete musical score, but the individual number, which is what is designed to stay in the memory. Movement towards continuous music has only therefore been gestured towards. And that lack of integration has entailed a corresponding counterpointing of interest between text and music, a separation between the two, as Roth argues, in *Genre: the musical*, obtains in the contrasting ideologies of the individual (seen in the words) and the community (whose importance is demonstrated in the music) in *42nd Street.*

There is no clear division between the audiences for opera and those for popular music, in practice, but there is a marked difference in the ascription of value to these forms, none the less. Opera, now rarely topical, or satirical—no Verdian fears of the censor now—and certainly not tuneful—no 'La donna e mobile' today—has been made into a fetish. That process, of reifying cultural artefacts, as Lukács termed it, in his *Theory of the novel* is the expression of what happens historically, as the process of change empties out the meaning and inner life from aesthetic forms. For Lukács, the epic, drama and novel epitomised changing and successive moments in consciousness: the changing form fitted different perceptions of the self, and for both Lukács and Adorno, the danger was the persistence of writing in older forms after the possibility of that form actually meaning something had gone. The argument is not free from a residual idealism that assumes it knows exactly what is implied by those forms; none the less, the question of outmoded types of representation is important. For Adorno, the necessity of music to be difficult was premised on the basis of the easiness of accepting worn-out forms, and it can hardly be denied that the presentation of opera internationally has been conservative and self-confirming; resolving itself into revivals that offer perhaps varied bits of business to go with a different production, but which have the function, none the less, of reifying the work as it stands. The promise of finding 'depth' and complexity in the score licenses this, but that, too, is self-confirming: to look for these things is a mark of the way high art has been defined. Art need not be defined in terms of ambiguity and complexity: as Verdi's art was not, historically, till quite recently. To define it in those terms is tantamount to saying that a certain education is necessary to understand it at all: which is a convenient way of policing culture, and making sure it is kept as the property of an elite.

The boundaries are drawn up, in discussing art, in ways that favour the concept of the genius, who produces out of sheer inspiration: auteur-theory in the cinema replicates this in the medium of mechanical reproduction: it foregrounds the director, as possessed of a unique vision. Whereas Benjamin's point about the non-auratic nature of film holds to deny the point, and, indeed, to make the musical film the best example of his contention: here professionalism counts, and each element is separately produced. Indeed, if there has been a decline in the fortunes of the musical film, it has a lot to do with the loss of the studio system, which guaranteed that ready professionalism in all departments. So the composer is not the same as the orchestrator; even Sondheim hands a piano score over for arranging; and there is a keen relationship between writing and production, which no doubt obtained equally in Shakespeare's theatre, and which guarantees the integrity of the work, and emphasises that the easy availability of the mechanical means that the life-expectancy of the work is shorter: the concept of the enduring work of art proves to belong to a different episteme. Where this holds, talk about complexity and depth as absolute concepts shades into metaphysics: and indeed the conditions under which operas have been produced, historically, are illuminated, and themselves seen as less pure, more improvisatory.

From this, two gains emerge: the distinctions between the complex and the simple is seen to be a matter of a choice of signifying practice, not a method of classifying into serious and popular; and then those two terms offer themselves for re-definition. It might be added that depth and complexity become ways of justifying a non-affirmatory sense of life. Opera has characteristically been nostalgic, embracing a pessimism or tragedy: opera which is comedy, unless it is Mozart, or the wistful humour of *Die Meistersinger*, or *Der Rosenkavalier* (though again *Falstaff* is the exception), becomes 'comic opera' and is thus marked out as trivial, or merely tuneful. Cultural pessimism endorsed, and unironised, indeeed reified, by being proclaimed as high art, and implicitly condemning anything affirmatory, (though not necessarily optimistic) has become the characteristic of opera at the present, and it leads to the imposition of a conservative, even reactionary, ideology. The other modes of signification discussed here—film, which potentially redeems opera from that closure within the re-actionary, and the musical which, despite its own period of conservatism in the 1960s and 1970s, has continued its own possibilities of renewal, through rock idioms, continued self-parody and through its modernism of technique—*Cabaret, Nashville, The rocky horror picture show, Tommy, New York, New York, All that jazz, Hair*[23] suggest the need to see that pessimism itself as a meaning produced, the construct of a mode of signification, and thus creating a way of seeing, not in any way a description of things as they are, or as they might be.

Rock music may take the emphasis off dancing in pairs, and put it on to the solo dance, and thus contribute to the 'decline of the musical', as Delameter puts it,[24] as a genre having to do with fantasy (while musicals taken from the stage versions have frequently had little fantasy, only straight narrative in them), but Robert Altmann's *Nashville*, satirical about both show business and politics, and the dance sequences in *A chorus line* (by Jeffrey Harnaday, who choreographed for *Flashdance*), do not imply a deadness, however much *A chorus line* might have remained literally theatre-bound. There are strong possibilities for the integration of drama and music and dance still, and perhaps the opera-film might learn a lesson from the way that Hollywood musicals were better and better to the extent that they freed the material from the theatre, and cut and moved around music and words, and were not passively replicating the earlier theatrical experience. Opera on film, in other words, should lay hold much more of what is potentially filmic, and lose its ultimate dependence—even for its singers and actors, on the (mythically) original and superior opera house.

NOTES

1. Hans Eisler, *Composing for the films* (1951), p. 132.
2. Roland Barthes, *Roland Barthes* (New York, 1977), pp. 80–1.
3. Douglas Jarman, *Kurt Weill* (1982), p. 136.
4. *Brecht on theatre* trans. by John Willett (1978 ed.), p. 90. The sections on pp. 33–42 and 84–90 are both of interest in this context.
5. Thomas Mann, *Doctor Faustus*, trans. H.T. Lowe-Porter (Harmondsworth, 1968), p. 232.
6. For the Benjamin–Adorno debate, see Martin Jay, *The dialectical imagination* (1973) and Susan Buck-Morss, *The origins of negative dialectics* (Brighton, 1978), Gillian Rose, *The melancholy science* (1978), and Eugene Lunn, *Marxism and Modernism* (1985). The correspondence between the two is contained in the New Left Review, *Aesthetics and politics* (1977), quotation p. 121. Martin Jay, *Adorno* (1984) is useful.
7. See the discussion of *Gold diggers of 1933* in Bruce Babington and Peter William Evans, *Blue skies and silver linings* (Manchester, 1985), pp. 46–72.
8. See 'On the fetish character in music and the regression of listening' by Adorno in *The essential Frankfurt reader*, ed. Andrew Arato and Eike Gebhardt (Oxford, 1978), p. 296.
9. Quoted by Susan Buck-Morss, *op. cit.*, p. 42. For further discussion of Adorno on music, see *Whose music?* by John Shepherd, Phil Virden, Graham Vulliamy, Trevor Wishart (1977), pp. 233–41, and Max Paddison, 'The critique criticised: Adorno and popular music' in *Popular music 2: theory and method*, ed. Richard Middleton and David Horn (Cambridge, 1982). For discussion of Adorno's general position, see also Simon Frith, *Sound effects: youth, leisure and the politics of rock 'n' roll* (1983), pp. 41–8.
10. Quoted, *Aesthetics and politics*, p. 90.
11. For the musical, see John Russell Taylor and Arthur Jackson, *The Hollywood musical* (1971), John Kobal, *Gotta sing, gotta dance* (rev. ed. 1983). Music has been inadequately treated, but see Wilfrid Mellers, *Music in a new found land* (1975), pp. 371–437, and 447–9. See also Alexander Faris, 'Opera and the musical', *Opera* (May 1961), pp. 295–300, which provoked a magnificent discussion in the July, September and October issues, including Bernard Keeffe's 'is not the appreciation of works of art of all periods and styles a matter of an

unusual sensibility', and the interest in musicals implies 'a desperate seeking after novelty . . . more characteristic of a child than a mature adult', while Rose Hill contended that 'those who flock to the musical would be out of their depth at the opera—any opera'.

12. Jane Feuer, *The Hollywood musical* (1982), p. 23.
13. Jerome Delameter, *Dance in the Hollywood musical* (UMI Research, Ann Arbor, 1981) discusses dance as the prime distinguishing quality of the musical film.
14. Michael Wood, *America in the movies* (New York, 1975), p. 150.
15. Steve Neale, *Cinema and technology* (1985), pp. 101, 100. He quotes Comolli, 'Intervention', in Teresa de Lauretis and Stephen Heath, *The cinematic apparatus* (1980), p. 57.
16. Quoted by David Bordwell, Jane Staiger, Kristin Thompson, *The classical Hollywood cinema* (1985), p. 34.
17. Tom Milne, *Rouben Mamoulian* (1969), p. 13.
18. For discussion of *The pirate* see Joseph Andrew Casper, *Vincente Minnelli and the film musical* (Metuchen, New Jersey, 1977), and Dennis Giles, in Rick Altman, *Genre: the musical* (1981), pp. 93–6.
19. See Christian Metz, *The imaginary signifier*, trans. Celia Britton and others (Bloomington, 1977), especially part 3, 'The fiction film', on film and dream.
20. Metz discusses Benveniste's distinction between story and discourse, *ibid.*, p. 91, and argues that the traditional fiction film is the first: it 'obliterates all traces of the enunciation, and masquerades as story'—i.e. as pure realistic narrative. Discourse draws attention to its signifying devices. Jim Collins, in Altman, *op. cit.*, pp. 137 ff uses this distinction to suggest that the musical is story that disguises itself as discourse; and that the backstage musical device is a device which conceals art to produce art—it gives 'the illusion that the work is a *discours* in the process of creation'. But while agreeing with this, there does seem room in the musical for the enunciation to show itself.
21. See Ethan Mordden, *Movie-star* (New York, 1983), pp. 97–8, and the discussion of *The merry widow* in Babington and Evans, *op. cit.*
22. See the discussion of this film in Gerald Mast, *A short history of the movies* (Oxford, 1985), pp. 200-1.
23. For discussions of the musical in the 1960s, 1970s and 1980s, see Russell Taylor, *op. cit.*, pp. 93–9; Babington and Evans on *Hair* and Thomas Schatz, *Old Hollywood, new Hollywood: ritual, art and industry* (IMI Research, Ann Arbor, 1983).
24. Delameter, *op. cit.*, chapter 8 discusses the 'decline of the musical', as does Casper, *op. cit.*, pp. 167–73. For Delameter, rock music means that musicals are no longer written in the most popular style: part of the conservatism of Broadway, as of Hollywood. For Zeffirelli, this putative decline would be opera-film's opportunity.

Owen Wingrave and television opera

Britten's *Owen Wingrave*, first screened on 16 May 1971, was not the first opera to be commissioned from television: Menotti's *Amahl and the night visitors* was written for NBC in 1951, and Arthur Bliss wrote *Tobias and the angel* to a libretto by Christopher Hassall for presentation in May 1960. Bliss was, like Britten, an important composer of film music: his 1935 score for the H.G. Wells text *Things to come* had been turned into a concert suite, and he writes in his autobiography of the usefulness of composing for the films in teaching compression and the avoidance of sentiment. But both the Menotti and Bliss works were intended for the opera house eventually, both composers regarding television writing as being very ephemeral, and something of a quantum leap is involved in considering Britten writing specifically for television. He had previously recorded a production of *Peter Grimes* at the Maltings in Snape in 1969, refusing to work in a BBC studio which might necessitate the conductor being in a separate room from the singers, and it seems likely that the experience of putting on *Owen Wingrave* was less than ideal for composer and BBC alike. Myfanwy Piper, the librettist, speaks of the effects department wanting to spray the set of Paramore with artificial cobwebs when they heard that it was a ghost story that they were dealing with, and that absurd type of realism (akin to that of the critics who complained that the ship in *Billy Budd*, when televised, did not appear to be moving) appears to have led Britten to a rather antagonistic attitude towards what he called 'realism', preferring that his work should stress the artificiality of opera. There was, he said in an interview with Donald Mitchell, to be a preference for arias and ensembles over perpetual recitative, and the audience was never to be led into forgetting the point that here was opera. The interview, though interesting, deals with largely commonplace ideas in a grandly solemn manner redolent of Pseud's Corner—Mitchell: 'I think this really is an extraordinary interesting discovery or conclusion to have come to as a result of the *Grimes* filming';[1] the discovery being that of the need for realism to recede. But realism here means very little, and certainly *Owen Wingrave*, though it does move into the atmosphere of a ghost story in its Act II, is nothing if not realistic: precisely rooted in class, in London, in a specific milieu of time and place, and with interior scenes that, particularly at the beginning, are strongly natural-istic—as they would be in material drawn from Henry James. There seems to be little enough theory at work in Britten's thinking in the interview.

The filming at Snape Maltings does not seem to have been a complete success: Britten objected to the cameramen being the bosses,[2] and most critics who reviewed it found it interest-ing but dull, and certainly not inherently suited to television. It was transferred to the opera house, opening at Covent Garden on 10 May 1973. No doubt Britten had intended it for the stage ultimately, but there was something disappointing about the way that television let it go, and then the opera house failed to pick it up: *Owen Wingrave* has never become a part of a stand-ard repertoire. That may have an extra-musical reason lying behind it: the work is a pacifist piece in a way the *War Requiem*, which rather stresses the pity of war, is not. Harold Rosenthal said of the stage performance, in *Opera*, July 1973, that 'Britten's anti-war feelings are no longer as effective or as necessary as they were at the time of the *War Requiem*, if only for the reason that almost everyone now accepts his point of view', which is revealing, even if it is reflected that the Vietnam war had ended that year as far as the United States were con-cerned; and evocative, too, of the hermetically sealed world opera enthusiasts seem to ask for, when it is considered how,

Owen Wingrave. Benjamin Luxon and Janet Baker. Photo: Reg Wilson. From a Royal Opera House production based on the original production.

while people accept, supposedly, Britten's point of view, the present arms build-up seems massive on a scale even Britten might have found hard to visualise. I would not be surprised if it could be shown that a lot of the motivation behind quietly forgetting *Owen Wingrave* had to do with a sense that its pacifism meant a little too much: and certainly I would assert, having re-seen the film at the BBC, in a sealed-off room in the archives section, that it works splendidly, and seems one that requires some growing into. It was produced by Brian Large, who worked further with opera in the 1970s at the BBC, with Colin Graham, a more familiar collaborator with Britten.

The martial, percussive prelude begins with the camera focusing on each portrait of the Wingrave ancestors, a musical portrait and a visual one going together, the eleventh focusing on Wingrave himself (Benjamin Luxon in the film), impassive and thoughtful: as the camera pulls away from a close-up of him, he is seen to be at a distance from Coyle (John Shirley-Quirk) and Lechmere (Nigel Douglas) in the study where Coyle is explaining military strategy with chess pieces. That the portraits have been seen already both establishes the importance of both house and ghosts, providing the necessary link to the beginning of Act II, and indicating what the ghosts point towards: the Oedipal weight that hangs upon Owen himself: the house and its presences must be destroyed, for even the women at Paramore act as agents of the Father: Kate locks Owen into the room with the phallic key that proclaims her masculine power over him: the part is not given to a contralto for nothing; its register suggests the way she has excluded anything specifically feminine from her nature. (Thus, though Janet Baker might not have seemed right on paper for the part, and at thirty-seven too old, the sense of maturity and hardness conveyed is absolutely right.)

At the end of the first scene Coyle's soliloquy 'Oh! I thought I knew them all' is sung as he moves out of his study and into the hall, and the first interlude follows with its series of flags. Owen is then seen in the park, reading Shelley, while Coyle speaks to Miss Wingrave (Sylvia Fisher—looking as imperious as if she were playing Gloriana still) in a set with a picture of a cavalry charge on the wall, which merges with the actual gallop by the Horse Guards, seen in a double exposure, with Owen's head seen before them. There is a strong sense, in the movements of this film, of presences coming out of darkness and then receding: so it is here, and the effect adds to the sense of military punctiliousness. The second interlude, with Owen reading, and only tattered flags appearing as if to point up the reality of the military enterprise that has come and gone and which is imaged in the cavalry charge, returns the action to Coyle's study. Mrs Coyle sings of Owen—'Is he my favourite' while going over to her mirror and looking into it, while the action around her seems to freeze, and the lights dim: her speculation on her relation to the young man that she mothers looks like narcissism and reveals the ambiguity in her relationships. (It is more pointed in the James: 'Coyle had already accused the good lady more than once of being in love with Owen Wingrave. She admitted that she was, she even gloried in her passion, which shows that the subject, between them, was treated in a liberal spirit'.)[3] The part is sung by Heather Harper, who had recently performed the part of Ellen Orford, the motherly figure, in the television *Peter Grimes*, and the memory emphasises the mother-nature, which is a displacement of the real feelings for the young men, whose going out to war becomes a way of her being able to rationalise the sexual feelings felt, and being able to look at herself in a mirror and so create an image of herself. In this opera the Coyles take the centre: they are under trial, which is another meaning of the looking in the mirror, but especially they are being tried in their readiness to look at what is happening between Owen and the contestants he meets at Paramore: unable to make a moral decision themselves about the rights and wrongs of Owen's case, they are reduced to the status of spectators, which is itself a condemnation. Coyle himself, with his name 'Spencer' recalling the proto-military figure of Gloriana's reign, looks like a priest in his high collar, and that further emphasises, near-satirically, the way that moral judgement is looked for from him, and is not there, save in the most blandly liberal of ways—'I even feel for them, you know'.

The third interlude gives views of the house, Paramore (rather obvious models) and introduces Kate (in yellow: the colour seems appropriate), with her mother (Jennifer Vyvyan) and Miss Wingrave: the film nicely points up the haunted-house motif by playing on the way Owen comes to what seems to be an empty house: the device is out of any horror-movie, and appropriate as a reminder of the artificiality of the genre. Owen's entry soon brings him into contact with Pears as a Sir Philip Wingrave with a shock of white hair. The sequence of scenes that follow is written like a miniature four-movement symphony, where each 'How dare you' brings each face into full view by itself as an introduction: the camera here takes the place of Owen. The second movement—'They'll never stand for it' is a scherzo-like movement set in the garden, where the voices of all four, seen together in the shot, appear in fugato manner. (Sir Philip's frailty, symbolised by his dressing gown, adds to the emotional battery directed against Owen.) This ends with a soft-focus shot, and the third, slow movement in this barrage which is supposed to last a week, begins with Kate's 'I used to love, admire you', and is an interior, with Sir Philip weeping on the balcony. The last scene, after 'how disappointing', is done as an interior with the family having coffee, and then there is a return to the opening scene, with each head isolated, and ending with 'How dare you' again, with the anger accentuated. Here structure in musical terms and filmic technique are at one. 'I'm in a state of siege' Owen declares in the next scene, and it is tempting to think that only the ability to use close-ups would permit that feeling to come across so powerfully. At the same time, the vocabulary in Owen's mouth is redolent of the war-talk of his adversaries, and a fit reminder that he cannot dissociate himself from their martial spirit; to be peaceful he must fight them. In the James novella the realisation of this leads Owen to say 'Ah, we're tainted—all!' (p. 35) and it underlies his death and defeat, dying 'like a young soldier on a battlefield' (p. 51): in the Britten there is more interest in inspecting the reasons for the need to be martial. As the contrast with Lechmere shows, and as the choice between being a soldier and sleeping in the haunted room indicates, the issue is that of facing the Oedipal conflict, of exorcising the father, and asserting the right to self-determination, or of becoming a soldier and so accepting that domination from above and behind; evading the issue. For it seems clear that Britten locates the war-spirit as linked to the oppression of the Father: 'But the old man would not so, but slew his son/And half the seed of Europe one by one' is the end of the 'Parable of the old man and the young' in the Offertory section of the *War Requiem*: the same happens in *Owen Wingrave*, as it does too with Peter Quint and Miles in *The turn of the screw*.

The last interlude is played with the dinner table being laid, and the dinner party follows, with the camera tracking a full 360 degrees to give the thoughts of each person as they brood on the situation. Sir Philip walks out at the end: the victory temporarily Owen's, though the situation is to be reversed at the conclusion of the next act. The shorter second act is introduced with Pears singing, to the accompaniment of boys, the ballad, which is acted out in slow-motion, in sepia tones. This ballad of the 'Wingrave boy', contrasting with the 'Minstrel boy' that Lechmere sang about in the first act, establishes a cinematic flashback by its probing further the nature of the house that Owen was to 'listen to'; the opera involves a deepening knowledge, a penetration. Its first shots are of the ancestral pictures (with shades of the importance of portraits in *Der Freischütz* and *Der fliegende Holländer*), but from these façades at Paramore the shift is to the interior of the locked room, which, with its Freudian associations as the place of the primal scene, the place where the father's power is finally to be located, justifies the solution of a mystery model of narration that the libretto adopts. As said before, there is the motif of the traditional ghost story close to the surface: and the ghost has to be laid, as in all films of the type. Thus it seems well thought out that the ballad should intervene to deepen the analysis of what has happened earlier in Paramore, and that the music should be using motifs, now understood and precise, that were first heard in the third interlude, where Paramore was shown on the outside. More than that, it seems right that Pears should sing the ballad, for the effect is to recall Sir Philip, and to invite a double exposure of that character in musical terms: the archaeology of his character, if the point may be so put, is revealed: the Oedipal conflict finds its home in him, the grand-father of Owen Wingrave. The device is analogous to the way Pears sang the opening recitative in *The turn of the screw*—which introduces another cinematic flashback—*Billy Budd* is not unique in its use of that device, in Britten—and then sang the role of Quint. The dignified narrator and the hysterical pederast are identical, beneath the dissimilarity of their music. Further, the effectiveness of the device depends on the voice being recognised as the same: easy to do in Pears's case, though not necessarily easy to replicate in other productions.

The sepia colouring of the action of the ballad foregrounds the conscious use of the cinematic flashback, and leads into the darkened atmosphere of Act II, which is set at night, as Act I belonged to the day. The figures of the old man and the boy have turned into their portraits: Act II opens with a dissolving of this into the scene of Wingrave explaining the significance of the ballad. The first part of Act II, which requires virtually all the cast to be in the hall—with the exception of Sir Philip, who 'will not reappear tonight'—the irony of 'reappear' is nice—is a little static in the television production, though it produces fine effects: the aunt in imperial purple, Kate in a red that discloses both her sexuality and its alliance to martial passion. Hence the pun on 'Paramore' and 'Paramour', and the significance of Lechmere's name: soldiering is a kind of leching, and a substitute for it. Kate flirts with Lechmere while looking at Owen: the associations of manhood–soldiering–love-making are asserted, but the text indicates that as links they are only apparent, not real, for soldiering is a displacement of the sexual urge, and leaves out entirely the issue of how a person faces his or her sexuality, both in terms of the self's realisation, and acceptance, and in terms of public validation. These two things cannot be brought together: Owen faces his grandfather's disgracing of him, and then sings his soliloquy to peace, walking around the dimly-lit area at the back of the stairs in the hall, then, coming to rest at the foot of the stairs, see the move-ment of the portraits of the old man and the boy at the stairs' head. That seeing unsays the earlier confidence: he has won nothing, despite his bravado: for the ghosts seem to epitomise his own troubled psyche, with its sense that the Oedipal struggle has not been fought through yet; indeed, can never be. Thus when Kate returns, to find the jewel from her brooch—the excuse might well recall the very lovely setting of 'And I have found Demetrius like a jewel/mine own and not mine own' in *A midsummer night's dream*, and thus suggest how far Britten has moved from that sense of reconciliation—he is ready to begin the conflict again. He will sleep in the haunted room. In function, that action will fuse, ideally, the need to bring together private and public validations of the self and the course chosen by which his manhood is to be defined. As an action, it will fail. All he can *win* is his *grave*, and while 'Owen' no doubt means in Scottish 'the young soldier',[4] it also suggests 'owing', in contrast to 'winning'. The self is always in that position of desire, not attaining to a position where its energies are not displaced, thrust away from it endlessly.

That the whole struggle between Kate and Owen has to do with his sexuality seems evident in the way Lechmere eavesdrops, as a rival, who should be beaten off, as the boy in the ballad should not have accepted insult. (Owen is aware of this register, as he sings 'And with his friend young Lechmere played' to the tune of the ballad.) Kate taunts him with cowardice, to which Owen replies in words that indicate that soldiering is the development of an emotion which is 'to amuse the gaping ladies'—a way of short-circuiting the more fundamental issues of sexuality, simply to win the woman: and notice 'gaping', which is both anti-feminist in tone, and also revelatory of the castration-fear. Kate retorts by demanding that he should sleep in the haunted room (which Lechmere had volunteered to do), but the significance of that is lost on her as on Lechmere: it means something else as a rite of passage for Owen. He must attain manhood as opposed to becoming a soldier through this: as he goes in, Kate asks, 'Why was I not a man?' to which Owen's response, 'Come turn your key' is the only fit response, as the presence of the key describes her as male. It is a climactic moment: the trumpets sound and the martial rhythms that began the prelude return to establish the male force of the Wingraves—'the horrible power that makes men fight'. Owen confronts maleness in its fantasised forms, and centrally in the woman, aligned with the power of the Father. The opera seems to suggest that the struggle cannot be resolved positively. From an opening that looked simply like a credo for pacifism, the work has become a study in the sexual basis of violence. The attempt by Britten to use percussive instruments to accompany the sense of peace that Owen has in his solo aria, is to break the connection between energy (including sexual energy) and violence: and the opera itself seems to imply its impossibility.

The penultimate scene is set in the Coyles' bedroom, where the fading lamps and the movement of the clock-hands indicates the passing of time through the night: Coyle and his wife are separated, she in bed, he by the fire: the distanciation emphasising that there can be no tenderness, or sexual contact where the prevalent—and partly unconscious—discourse is violent and tuned to the martial spirit. Never was there an opera so consciously anti-female in the way it sees the women as partaking of that male discourse. The sense of barrenness, of lack of sexual fulfilment is strong: the only mother is the farcical Mrs Julian, and I take it that the casting of Jennifer Vyvyan for the part is crucial here, since she played the Governess in *The turn of the screw* initially, and it is the Governess there who—with the ghosts—destroys Miles. 'What have we done between us' she sings: words reminiscent of Vere's equivalent, 'What have I done?'. The mother-figure annihilates the child, and the motif returns in this other Jamesian novella, casting another light on *The turn of the screw*, reaccentuating the character of the Governess, no longer seen as heroic. The scene of tension and waiting again belongs to the horror movie and leads into the quick resolution, where the characters fling open the door of the room, and the camera circles round Owen dead, and finally cranes down on him. It is a commonplace of criticism of this opera to comment on the excessive brevity of its ending, and the way that the reprise of the ballad fails to compensate for lack of musical development here. Perhaps the silence of the text reveals uncertainty in the composer about the status of Owen's death: it may be interpreted, as it is by Donald Mitchell in his sleeve notes to the Decca recording as a triumph, but in terms of the agon over sexuality that may be its displaced subject matter, the opera can endorse no sense of triumph at all. The desire to find a resolution is a fine example of liberal–humanist criticism to wish to suggest that the author of a text can solve some crisis in his/her art: thus suggesting that the terms in which the author sets up the debate are the appropriate ones to resolve it in, as though those terms could be complete. *Owen Wingrave*, more interestingly, shows, by its reaching after another subject, that the ideological givens of the text are not complete, involve a displacement, and that the work can be seen as indeed opening up fissures, areas where the text differs from itself.

As a work for television, *Owen Wingrave* works by its use of shorter scenes than are customary in the opera house, by its confidence in making a second act much shorter than the first, by its ability to isolate one character from another by use of soft focus—which explains the strong use of arias—and by its intensity of argument: the opera is about something and the debate is strong within it. Little use was made of voices out of vision, and the presentation was perhaps too studio-bound: a fault that came from Britten's desire to stage the whole work at Snape. In contrast to nineteenth-century operas that have been filmed, the work presents few opportunities for virtuoso singing: arias are scaled down, reflective, which comments both on Britten's technique, and the fittingness of the opera for television. Within its short length, less than two hours, the opportunities for televisual effects were not great, and were, wisely, not taken up: what remains is the impression of tact, of functional photography, and of music that fitted the production as surely as the production worked for it. The quality of sound could be criticised,[5] and could be given as a reason for wishing to see the piece in the opera house, but it seems an insufficient reason for taking against television opera and ultimately a mere elitism, where it is assumed that only trained musicians would either wish to or ought to hear the work while the rest of the large audience is denied.

Though I have suggested in writing about *Carmen* that the concept of an original is for radical questioning, it could be stressed that the television presentation of *Owen Wingrave* has a force behind it that no later production can match, and not just because the camera can track through corridors to the haunted room in a way that cannot be done in the theatre. The commission enabled Britten to write for specific singers, and the advantage of this I have shown in terms of the way singers he had worked with before play their part in the personal autobiography of Britten that is being written at the same time that the operas and other works are being set on paper. A degree of precision is attained that could not exist elsewhere, and the opera, by being written for television, ceases to make its claim to be some trans-historical human document: it becomes rooted to time, that of the composer, and that of the audience. Those critics who were pleased to see the opera on the traditional boards of the opera house are inserting it back into the mythology of high art, where 'human values' triumph, and where specific questions of history—which include the composer's own history—can be avoided. The work of art exists here *for* mechanical reproduction, and so emphasises its own part in a changing discourse within society. The work ought to be screened again, and another version of it made in due course, but already Britten has shown that there is no need to consider opera as something that must escape transitoriness: it seems a pity that he lost faith in the medium as the work progressed. It also seems a shame that he took against 'realism', wishing to emphasise more the operatic. For the dichotomy is, of course, false: there is no realism in art; only a series of signifying conventions that sometimes advertise their artificiality, as does opera, characteristically, and some that conceal themselves and prefer to imply their profound naturalness. Opera-film, though it may go for narrative realism, as Losey's *Don Giovanni* does, foregrounds the artificiality of the genre, not as something exceptional, but as basic to all representation. *Owen Wingrave* in that sense needed to have its artificiality stressed, not played down, and those critics who found the television production too 'operatic' studiously missed the point that was on offer: that through this work the signifying practices of Britten in his other works were also being held up for comment: the devices that inform, say, *Billy Budd* and *The turn of the screw* being reviewed. The work, of a complexity just sufficient to make it worth much further investigation, and questionable enough in its thesis and stages towards a conclusion, seems admirably suited for television.

NOTES

1. 'Mapreading', a conversation with Britten about television opera, in *The Britten Companion*, ed. Christopher Palmer (1984), p. 90.
2. Quoted in *The Times*, 2 June 1971. For accounts of the opera filming, see *The operas of Benjamin Britten*, ed. D. Hamilton (1979), pp. 8–21; Michael Kennedy, *Britten* (1981), p. 100; Christopher Headington, *Britten* (1981), pp. 136–7; and the essays of John Evans in Palmer, *op. cit.*, and Peter Evans in *The music of Benjamin Britten* (1979). I am also in debt to John Warrack's discussion in *Opera* (May 1971), pp. 371–9.
3. The *Collected short stories of Henry James*, vol. 9, ed. Leon Edel, p. 30. Subsequent page references are given in the text.
4. Leon Edel, *The life of Henry James* (Harmondsworth, 177), vol. 2, p. 171.
5. Peter Evans, *op. cit.*, p. 502.

CHAPTER 6

Opera as culinary art: Bergman's *Magic flute*

The meaning of a work of art is not inherent to it; there is no 'transcendent signifier', as Derrida would put it, to guarantee that the meaning stays in place, remains the same; rather, meaning is produced through the relationships that obtain within the way it is set up by its particular mode of production, and the way it is received: meaning is to be negotiated through different interests wishing to take a text in one manner or another, and the text becomes the site of a contest. Within that struggle, the institution that is being used to display the text is itself a constructor of meaning. Television opera in its short existence has moved towards a further conformity to dominant tastes: ones that will simply reflect the canons that prevail in the opera house. The radical elements within *Owen Wingrave* have not been much repeated. British television opera since then has been a relatively anodyne affair: the BBC2 screenings of the Patrice Chéreau *Ring* came at the end of that particular version's cycle, when it had received a status of its own, and was no longer merely to be sneered at. Zeffirelli's versions of *Cavalleria rusticana* and *I Pagliacci* shown on British television in 1984 neither troubled the accepted popular status of those works nor provided any reason for thinking that they ought to be made more widely available than they are in the opera house. And Bergman's version of Mozart's *Magic flute* provides another apt example of a text and its mode of production creating meaning, in this case a fairly conservative meaning.

The film was commissioned by Swedish Radio, to celebrate

The Magic Flute. Urban Malmberg, Ansgar Krook, Erland von Heijne (the three boys). Courtesy Swedish Television.

its golden jubilee and was shot through the first half of 1974. Eric Ericson conducted the Swedish Radio Symphony Orchestra, and the singing was pre-recorded and then replayed in the studio. It was first presented on television in Sweden on New Year's Day 1975. The following Boxing Day it was shown on British television, and opened the same night as a film in London. Its status thus has been dual: the film of Bergman, the disturbing existentialist director turning his attention to the most metaphysical of Mozart's works, and the family fare that it presents in its televisual form, suitable to endorse Christmas and New Year values with the universal genius of Mozart behind it. A further accentuation of meaning to the work might be seen further in Sweden, where Bergman's work as a stage producer is, of course, well known: this *Magic flute* (*Trollflöiten* in Swedish), presented as though it were the recording of a stage production, becomes also a definitive production of a great work, a tribute to the theatre direction of Bergman, who is on record as saying that the opera 'offers a producer more hurdles than any other opera'.[1] It suits with this that in the quest to offer the definitive version Bergman should have made a study of the original production details of *Die Zauberflöte*, guaranteeing authenticity in small details, even if, actually, altering the work quite structurally as far as its second act is concerned. And, of course, this *Magic flute* was shot as a stage production, to be a simultaneous tribute to Bergman as theatre and film director, and to Swedish tradition. For the theatre to be used was that of the Drottningholm Palace, in the royal park outside Stockholm; only it proved necessary to make a studio reconstruction of that stage. The uses of tradition may be important, and may be stabilising for a New Year family audience, but the tradition itself is synthetic. The boys, who pelt Papageno with snowballs as he is about to hang himself, in their actions not only participate in the plot but act out the standard seasonal images of boys playing in the cold weather that is associated with a northern Christmas: the mythology is complete: the impression of seamlessness is perpetuated; the world outside corresponds to the world of the theatre. It is of a piece with that that the camera not only plays upon the action, but also shows the actors in their dressing-rooms, or donning their costumes, or peering through the curtain, or, in the case of Sarastro, casting a look at the next part he is to play—in *Parsifal*. The impression to be conveyed is that actors and audience all belong to one unified experience, and that as much magic happens offstage as on: the world of the opera, of the theatre and of the audience in that sense being in a continuum.[2] That sense of a continuum is even perpetuated in the idea that one opera leads into another: that *The magic flute* leads on to *Parsifal*. Of course, so it does, in one way of looking at German opera, and the point is neat, but it also produces the myth that the world of opera is seamless and can be thought of as a whole. It denies difference and discontinuity; it plays up the escapist role of art—as, say, *Fanny and Alexander* also does. The camera-work was by Sven Nykvist, and the stress was on sharp colours: scarlet forces for Sarastro, for example, and the camera looking intently on the characters while they sang, impassively.

Meanings thus become imposed upon the Mozart text: or, rather, within the ascription of meanings that are being placed upon the work, even Mozart becomes a text: the source of childish delight, of wonder and magic—the last being a word that is invested in pretty heavily in popular discourse about the composer. The family fare sense is created by the ideology of a Mozart that the film text both buys into and creates: during the playing of the overture, the camera plays upon the audience's faces, and repeatedly cuts back to a child's face, lost in the magic of the (instantly accessible, because universal, because Mozart's) music. The BBC bought the film, and found it definitive: it was Channel 4 that was to buy Losey's *Don Giovanni*; the BBC was not interested. That says a lot about the differences between the two opera films in the range of meanings that each production allows, and suggests that two relatively equivalent texts—the two operas—do not yield up an inherent meaning; it has to be produced, and fought over. No doubt the buying of *Giovanni* for Channel 4, and the screening of it during the Christmas of 1985 (two days after BBC2 had shown the Zeffirelli *Traviata*) represented a simple competitive commercialism, as well as indicating what big business opera now was for peak viewing times, but there are still differences, and precisely the quality about the Losey film is that it is not receptive to being reduced simply to what Brecht described as 'culinary art'.

'Culinary art' is Brecht's sense of opera, where the music washes over the privileged spectator, increasing and heightening the sense of unreality and unclearness. Opera is in no position to criticise or even educate, in Brecht's terms, and even the best examples of the genre—in Mozart and Beethoven—which included 'elements that were philosophical, dynamic' were compromised. 'And yet the element of philosophy, almost of daring, in these operas, was so subordinated to the culinary principle that their sense was in effect tottering and was soon absorbed in sensual satisfaction. Once its original "sense" had died away the opera was by no means left bereft of sense, but had simply acquired another one—a sense *qua* opera. The content had been smothered in the opera.'[3] As opera, the text receives a new accentuation; it becomes something culinary, for consumption only, and emphasising by its form and by its place within the cultural practices of the smart audience it attracts that it has nothing else to say than to confirm the mode of social existence of those consumers.

In *Don Giovanni* there is enough complexity of attitude set up within the opera to allow for a univocal reading to be impossible: the status of the stone guest who is certainly not celestial at all but who confirms the good of the Christian *ancien régime* is a single example of an ambivalence that prevents a one-way understanding of the situation. But in the case of *The magic flute*, written though it was for a much less privileged audience than *Giovanni*, the possibilities of interpretation, though wide ranging from the view that here is superior pantomime to the sense that an elaborate allegory is being played out in Masonic terms[4]—conduce much more to one end: the terms of the narrative do not permit any doubts to be put on Tamino's eventual success, and the interest in the tests in Act II has nothing to do with a question as to their possible outcome. Nor is it possible, in narrative terms, to see the Queen of the

Night in terms other than those Sarastro presents her in: even her opening aria is decked with a florid coloratura, as if to suggest by the regression to *opera seria* that here is a figure of reaction, who will not fit into the Enlightenment mode of thought, where 'Mann und Weib, und Weib und Mann' fit together, and where Pamina's singing of 'Die Wahrheit' in the finale to Act I can receive such firm underpinning by the movement of the music, to ensure that here are affirmations that need no further comment upon them. It is quite possible to see the black Monostatos—the Caliban figure in a work that bears some relationship to *The tempest*, a work which, in any case Mozart wished to set but was unable to do—as a reflection of an Enlightenment ideology on all fours with growing imperialism. The allegorical name indicates with what freedom he may be chastised, as he is by Sarastro at the end of Act I. (Yet Sarastro's no. 15 aria explicitly eschews revenge: the point may be significant for the way that Monostatos has been marginalised.) This would emphasise that the opera, far from being the expression of eternal truths, is actually the expression of some fairly standard sentiments that belong to the Enlightenment: in this world it is impossible that the prince and princess should not be together, and that male supremacy—Sarastro's over the Queen of the Night—should not triumph; the narrative, far from being separate from the informing viewpoint, as though the product of high art in its natural rightness striving towards a perfect resolution, is the expression of the ideology that thinks through it.

In a sense there is no more dangerous opera of Mozart's to film, for all the 'magical' properties of the theatre can be turned to such good account in the cinema that the work affirms more and more fully its unity, its success in bringing to a resolution its own proposed valuations and conclusions: it can make look even more 'natural' and inevitable the textual selection of things to be called good or evil. Whereas a modernist text such as *Lulu* conveys its unease about its own status and its representational ability, the Mozart text presents itself far more seamlessly (even though there have not been wanting voices which have suggested drastic changes being made a third of the way through), as a work of an achieved vision. No better way for an artist like Mozart to go out than having had this vision of reconciliation, and of a world put right by the power of music to instil harmony. It is all too neat, sanctioning through the privileged place given to Mozart's music a view of art as untouchable and attaining a transcendental status. For the music is held to unity: as Joseph Kerman puts it, 'everything about [the opera] matches the temper of Mozart's genius. All the diversities—of musical style, action, tone and mood—are perfectly controlled to a single dramatic end'.[5]

Thus it may be argued customarily that whatever is absurd in the plotting—the work of Schikaneder and perhaps of Giesecke—is swaled away by the music which either ennobles or works wittily to underscore the comedy. No nearer access to the work is possible. Bergman's film, it must be said, fails to deconstruct those terms of reference: the semi-official conditions under which the film was made promote a rarefied Mozart, not the demotic composer who wrote for the Theater auf der Wieden in the suburbs of Vienna, far from the court. What is promoted is a slight vein of whimsicality: the 'dragon' that attacks Tamino is funny; Papageno (Håken Hagegärd), without the feathers of the bird-man, is very young and innocent: defined from the first as an ideal by Bergman's business where he has to race from his dressing-room to the stage as he hears the playing of the introductory music for 'Der Vogelfänger bin ich ja'; his carelessness (in an ideal sense) presented through this apparent equation being made between the carefree actor and the character. When comedy is so lightly worn, there can be little sense that its values are to receive a serious challenge. He and Papagena (Elisabeth Eriksonn) are like Jof and Mia in *The seventh seal*, save that their progeny is more vast at the end: they are seated under the greenwood tree surrounded by children, and their witty removal of winter clothes to reveal spring-suited ones beneath, recalls similar unmaskings in the *Hour of the wolf* where the nightmarish figures remove their masks to reveal only unreality beneath. Papageno becomes less Rousseau-like, as a child of eighteenth-century nature, and is rather an innocent in the theatre, where all actors are, finally, to be seen as innocent. To return to that child-like world, as Isak Borg (the initials are significant) is enabled to do in *Wild strawberries*, is Bergman's aim through the use of the theatre: an aim in which he constructs his sense of Mozart wishing to do the same.

For the citation of earlier Bergman motifs is the reminder that the film wishes to become part of his own dialectic. Cowie quotes Bergman on the despairing lines of Tamino (Josef Köstlinger), when he is at the nadir, 'O ew'ge Nacht! Wann wist du schwinden? Wann wird das Licht mein Auge finden?'— 'O everlasting night, when will you vanish? When will the light reach my eyes?'—and makes Tamino's question, Mozart's. The dying composer 'asks his question in darkness and from this darkness he answers himself—or does he get an answer? I have never felt so close to the deepest secret of spiritual intuition as just here, in this moment'. 'Bergman refracts Mozart's despair through the prism of his own experience', Cowie adds; but the Mozart who despairs is no more than a Romantic creation, probably Bergman's; and it can only reproduce the stereotypes of the suffering artist whose vision is nearly divine, to argue in this way. In the film the Speaker holds a lamp as he listens to Tamino, and blows out the flame as he goes, leaving Tamino in complete darkness: the gloom is lifted slowly till the point arrives where Tamino plays the flute to attract Pamina (Irma Urrila), and a backdrop of a landscape descends. It is an attractive moment which depends for its piquancy on the recollection of the *Hour of the wolf* discussion about art. There the tormented artist is shown, as a kind of torture, an extract from *The magic flute*, by Lindhorst, in the castle: the puppet sequence involves using real people as puppets; they are completely manipulated. Lindhorst, whom Borg, the artist (Max von Sydow), has already portrayed in one of his sketches as a bird-man, a Papageno constructed by a non-benevolent, non-enlightened nature, follows up this display of control by talking to Borg about Pamino and Tamina. Borg as Tamino should have his Pamina in Alma (Liv Ullmann); the wife's name has obvious symbolism. But this Tamino can make no connection with Pamina–Alma; the sources of his art are not the impersonal

F

wisdom that Mozart invests in, but have instead a selfish and pathological basis.

Passion in *The hour of the wolf* has a destructive character: whereas the answer given to Tamino about the restoration of light to him is implicitly connected with the search for Pamina, an eternal feminine figure, just as Alma is, so that enlightenment and love are brought together, love here can do nothing; the mistress, Veronica Vogler in the film—again, the bird-name is relevant—is in the company of demons, and all conspires towards Borg's disappearance, which Alma, the helpless wife, can only speak about.[6] None the less, Cowie speaks about the importance of Alma being pregnant; and the courtship of Papageno and Papagena ends with their thinking of the joys of having plenty of Papagenos and Papagenas, so that ideology is instilled here. Reconciliation, though deferred, is to be brought about. And Bergman's *Magic flute* only intensifies this production of harmony. Amongst the alterations that Bergman has made to the script is the presentation of Pamina as the daughter of Sarastro (Ulrik Cold) and the Queen of the Night (Birgit Nordin). Some of the last shots of the film bring these parental figures together as united in the triumph of the young lovers. W. J. Turner says about the Queen of the Night that 'such a being could not have existed in the plot of *Die Zauberflöte* as it stands';[7] she has to have a small part, despite the strong build-up she receives in the opening act. Turner thinks this is fitting, since the re-introduction of the Queen of the Night with Sarastro in opposition to her in overt form would have been an 'all-sufficient theme for another drama', but this begs the question: it assumes that the existing theme of *The magic flute* is sufficient in itself, and that it needs no disruption; the theme can be taken as it stands. It is part of the strong investment in the unity of the work of art, and the conviction that its disparate parts can be harmonised: that last word both recalling the metaphysical power ascribed to music, and the Romantic to American new critical sense that the work of art grows into its own definite, united form. But what ideology produces this, what does it serve? In the case of this Mozart opera it produces something culinary, and Bergman, far from laying hold of a genuine difficulty in the text—one which has provoked discussion about revisions in the course of the writing—has chosen to close the gap, to domesticate the Queen of the Night, as it were. That feminine fury, which produces 'Der Hölle Rache' as the expression of hysteria in a frustrated mother, is not countered by Sarastro's following solo; it rather exists in permanent opposition to male patriarchal assumptions of rationality.

It would be a more interesting work that opened up these fissures in the text rather than marginalising them. Mozart's own text makes something marginal out of the Queen of the Night; and this is intensified by Bergman: though she is associated at the start with the guiding properties of the flute and the three boys who will lead Tamino, by the end she is reduced to Monostatos (Ragnar Ulfung), who leads a crowd of women, Alberich-like, to destroy the new harmony set up with Tamino and Pamina. Female power is reduced to such low male aid. Bergman even reduces the attempted seduction of Pamina by Monostatos, and the Queen of the Night's intervention, with her aria (played with the use of a green filter and with sharp close-ups of the Queen) to the status of a nightmare: an hour of the wolf, indeed, from which Pamina will be awakened by Sarastro. In itself, the idea is simplifying the tests that the three or possibly four lovers are undergoing, but should the actual contest be so collapsed into the merely subjective? Is not the Queen's voice being occluded? Bergman is often credited with making males passive witnesses of a female agon, and it is true that the arrangement of events that he uses in Act II, as we shall see, does stress Pamina's role, but here both the reliance on Mozartian allegory, which means that character can be reduced to the status of cypher, and the master device of the theatrical imagery, which increases the sense of the culinary, serve as a method of preventing the female voice its full weight. This does not mean that the film conspires to reduce the woman's status: on the contrary, Bergman cuts the Priest's words to Tamino about the need not to believe women, and cuts, too, no. 11, the duet that the priests sing about men being snared by women. Though the allegorical sense of the Mozart may suggest that Maria Theresa is the subject of that (Masonic) anti-feminism, its place in such a humanist text is still indicative of the discourse of the Enlightenment; Bergman's omissions merely sweeten the culinary fare. Or they suggest that a more than heavy weight is being laid on Mozart to produce him as the spokesperson for a universal, and reconciling representative of art, whose innocent, naive (in Schiller's sense) vision may act as a corrective to the tortured mind of the twentieth century, both showing it how it has lost such an ability to be absorbed in its own creations, and also exalting, by contrast, twentieth-century angst.

This implies that the opera-film cannot afford to allow disturbance of Mozart's text, must, indeed, homogenise the material so that the elements in it which differ from its general direction should not be allowed to assert themselves. In the interests of this, Bergman made small but significant changes: dropping the emphasis on Masonic ritual and on the Egyptian setting, and emphasising art as enshrined in the temples. In the second act the separate trials are virtually presented as one, with some cutting back to the priests outside the room, solicitous for the welfare of those inside. Thus Papagena makes her appearance much earlier: after the singing of no. 20 'Ein Mädchen', which comes before the Quintet, no. 12. The torment of Pamina follows (nos. 13, 14, 15) and this leads in to Pamina's suicide scene, which follows her singing of no. 17, 'Ach, ich fühl's': the boys reappearing here, but their no. 16 trio having been omitted, as is no. 19, the trio for Pamina, Tamino and Sarastro. Papageno's suicide attempt is put adjacent to Pamina's, and the resolution of this with the re-entry of Papagena leads to the finale, with Tamino and Pamina going together through the fire and water. After the purgation the armed men remove their helmets to reveal their smiling faces, and the end follows fast with the rebellion of Monostatos and the Queen of the Night, and the final wedding dance, where the various characters hold up placards with the various aphoristic phrases of the libretto inscribed on them. The cuts, easy to make with *Singspiel*, of course, do not, perhaps, make the music hang together as well, (Max Loppert in the *Listener* of 8 January 1976 complained that they made the key shifts ungrammatical), but there is nothing inherently objectionable in them: only it increases the feeling of joyful celebration where the trials are not, ultimately, that testing. The prevalent atmosphere of youth, and of the comic, where the women ogle the audience in close-up, each one trying to get in front of the other, in their opening trio, and where no threat is posed—this sounds very culinary, and indulgent. It might be suggested that the use of the placards with such inscriptions as 'love soothes all pains' is Brechtian alienation, a commitment to the difference between Mozart's text and Bergman's world, and an insistence that this is mere representation and no reality, but then Bergman has already indicated his complicity with the vision the film offers by the cuts and the insertion of such a line as Sarastro's, after no. 15, 'in true love between two people you shall find the source of wisdom'. It is of a piece with this that when Tamino looks at Pamina's portrait in the first scene, that the picture should be mobile, and be Pamina herself looking at Tamino. An equality of relationship is set up.

Irving Singer argues that '*The magic flute* never accords the female an heroic mission comparable to the male's',[8] so that the emphasis is entirely on the ability of the male to go into death and return (the aspect of the opera that most links it to the *Requiem*). Like Bergman, who links the progress through fire and water to sexual intercourse, by surrounding Pamino and Tamina in the fires by naked couples caught in the fires (shades of Dante here), Singer sees the flute as the expression of male potency and the sign of victory in death as in *le petit mort.* The boys who help Pamina when she is near to death fit here, so do the concerned priests. It would not involve a difficult extension of this argument to suggest that the flight from the serpent embodies fears of sexuality before there is an object of desire, and that the quest to gain Pamina from Sarastro's temple is in displaced form, with its stress on rationality, a sexual possession, where the apparent injustices that Sarastro's temple embodies, belong to Tamino's imperceptions as he has to grow into awareness of male power. If that is the case, then the emphasis on Reason and Enlightenment disguises the nature of power in the male's possession of the female. The text may accord

Pamina a new kind of aria in Mozart opera, one that no woman before her in the da Ponte operas could have sung, her G minor (so possibly associated in Mozart with pathos), 'Ach ich fühl's', with its lingering postlude on the strings, and its sense of wishing for death, but it receives no other consolation, is followed, indeed, by comedy with Papageno and the priests and Sarastro complimenting Tamino on his ability to withstand the tests thus far. Since Pamina is not in on the secret of why Tamino is silent —whereas the male knows, because he is reasoning, with a rationality that is the condition on which his sexuality may be accepted, in this Enlightenment world—and indeed has been mortifying his instincts in not speaking to her, it seems that there is an injustice, one that involves the putting down of the female as inherently less able to control whims and instincts that may indeed be, as they were in Pamina's aria, desires for death. Was there not something of this attitude to the woman in *Così fan tutte*? Did not the men there learn something about themselves that the women—such is the structure of that plot— could not?

Those elements in Mozart that encourage ambivalent attitudes to be taken up towards passion, both celebrating it and yet moving away from its endorsement towards both a distortion in the representation of women and a pre-Schopenhauerian pessimism, are not merely personal but aspects of Enlightenment thought in its own contradictoriness. Bergman's film is clearly aware that the fissures are there, and it would have been a fine opera-film that accentuated those contradictions, and did not soften the harshnesses by foregrounding the female for pathos and interest: not to show her—as also her mother—as what gets left out, but to make her equal with the male. The film removes contradictions and builds up the image of the universal Mozart who is suitable for Christmas and for all families everywhere. In doing so, it promotes further the idea of art as the comforter and reflector of bourgeois truths, and does not allow for a contestation of those positions. Bergman's film reduces its subject and allows for an overall passivity towards the opera. If Mozart disturbs, he is less likely to do so as the result of Bergman. Perhaps he was too much nobbled by

Hesse's view of Mozart in *Steppenwolf.*

NOTES

1. Quoted from *Opera news* (5 May 1962) in a review of *The magic flute* by William Moriz, *Film quarterly* (fall 1976), pp. 45–9.
2. A full account of the shooting of the film is offered in Peter Cowie, *Ingmar Bergman* (1982), pp. 295–9. See also Cowie's review in *Sight and sound* (summer 1975), p. 159. Bergman in interview said 'it's not a film—it was made as a television play', by which he was affirming the collective (family) response to the film, rather than the solitary film-goer's. See Lise-Lone Marker and Frederick J. Marker, *Ingmar Bergman: four decades in the theatre* (Cambridge, 1982), p. 232.
3. See *Brecht on theatre*, ed. John Willett (1964), p. 39.
4. See Jacques Chailley, *The magic flute: Masonic opera* (1972). Useful on the opera in general is E. J. Dent, *Mozart's operas* (1947) and Dorothy Koenigsberger, 'A new metaphor for Mozart's *Magic flute*', in *European studies review* vol. 5, no. 3 (1975). The account of the Masonic thread should be supplemented by Wolfgang Hildesheimer, *Mozart*, trans. Marion Faber (1983).
5. Joseph Kerman, *Opera as drama* (New York, 1976), p. 124.
6. Paisley Livingstone, *Ingmar Bergman and the rituals of art* (Cornell, 1982) discusses in detail the relationship between *The hour of the wolf* and *The magic flute.*
7. W. J. Turner, *Mozart, the man and his work* (rev. ed. Christopher Raeburn, 1965), p. 323.
8. Irving Singer, *Mozart and Beethoven, the concept of love in their operas* (Baltimore, 1977), p. 102.

CHAPTER 7

The modernist and minimalist aesthetic: *Moses und Aron*

Jean-Marie Straub and Daniele Huillet's film of Schoenberg's *Moses und Aron* was made in 1975, and first shown in Britain in the Edinburgh Festival of 1977: since then this country at least has hardly seen it, just as Straub's work in general has been poorly received. *The chronicle of Anna Magdalena Bach* (1968) was recently shown on British television, and the *Observer* heralded it as a film tedious beyond belief: that reaction to Straub was typical. A film as severe as the *Chronicle*, juxtaposing brief episodes of Bach's second wife speaking about Bach's life, his accounting, his religion and his career against broad slabs of Bach's music, being played in long, single-shot sequences, was not appropriate to an audience that thought a film had to do with action. People who would boast of their ability to listen to Bach for long stretches would find the same thing dull when it was presented on the screen, as a demand to listen—and to do so in a slightly distanciated way, epitomised by the camera's diagonal position, de-centring both the music and the listener to it. Yet the *Chronicle* seems to me crucial in the consideration of Straub's work, and the connections between it and the Schoenberg film seem interesting.

The *Chronicle* is shaped like a Bach oratorio: the passages of Anna Magdalena Bach's reflections are positioned like recitatives against the fuller music that is both the substance of, say, the *Matthew Passion*, and, in the film, of the selected passages of Bach's music that are being used for five- or ten-minute stretches at a time. The film, in its refusal to be indulgent about the life

Moses und Aron. Günter Reich (Moses) and Louis Devos (Aron). Courtesy Janus Film.

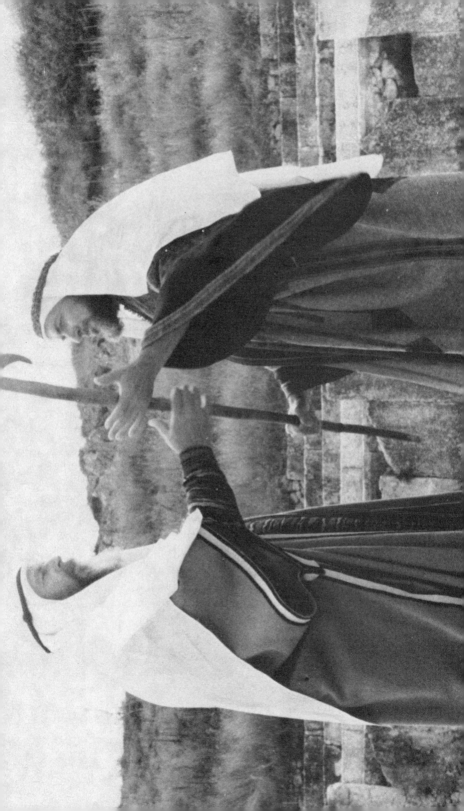

of Bach, and its lack of sentimentality, differentiates itself sharply from any attempt to gather Bach into the category of 'inspired artist'. Rather, it insists on the realism, or better, the *materiality* of the music, and the non-use of playback techniques, the use of direct sound, with the microphone placed next to the camera, so that there is no sense of the viewer of the film receiving a privileged, high fidelity recording of the work—the illusion in hi-fi being that a performance, or indeed a work, can be lifted out of its moment in history, and can be made ahistorical, something for all time—all this works in a way that is genuinely disturbing to the Romantic sensibility of the average late-twentieth-century listener. For such, Bach represents effortless genius, spontaneous creativity, in the way he has been mythologised. The film rejects that in its presentation of those hard edges around which the music moved—the demands of money, of family, of town politics, of church requirements, all of which are reduced to a few bare signifiers, not the less pressing for their minimal presentation. In these contexts, the music must assume an equal materiality, professionalism and objectivity; and the category of art as something separate, belonging to inspiration and to the voice of God, is thereby deconstructed.

Yet this oppositional thinking about the nature of art is anything but slick: the figure of Bach, the nature of oratorio, the political importance of the film for Straub, who identified it with his opposition to America's involvement in Vietnam—these are important motifs, and they compare interestingly with his later work on Schoenberg's musical text. For Schoenberg, like Bach, was intensely religious—he rejoined the Jewish faith in 1933, immediately after the writing of Acts I and II of *Moses und Aron*. The oratorio-like nature of the opera, and its political dimension, which is certainly accentuated in the film, these also recall *Anna Magdalena Bach*. Consideration of either film may well enlighten about both.

To speak of the opera first. *Moses und Aron* was written between 1930 and 1932, as to its first two acts, but left incomplete at the time of Schoenberg's death in 1951. The third act exists in libretto form only. When the opera was first performed in Zurich, in 1957, only the two completed acts were given: a revival in Berlin in 1959 tried to set Act III with music used from Act I, but it was held not to be a success. Charles Rosen, in his amazingly short—one page!—account of the opera, says that it is more effective in concert performance than in the theatre,[1] and if this is so it reflects strongly upon the oratorio-like objectivity of the work. The order of twelve-tone method, the original intention, in 1928, to compose it as a three-part oratorio, and the firm hand kept on its composition—where 'one starts with a very exact notion of the whole thing, and what takes some doing is not only keeping this vision vivid all the time but intensifying it, enriching it, enlarging it, in the working out of details . . .'[2] —all these things help to establish a work of great objectivity. Moses and Aaron have no psychological realism about them: they are the embodiments of two ideas. There is no concession to be made to naturalistic details: the only place where there seems some form of spontaneous, 'natural' behaviour is in the scene around the Golden Calf, which is written, musically, as a five-part symphony, almost Mahler-like, and where the descent into something more like conventional musical experience belongs to the moment which is at the antipodes from the idealism of Moses, or even of Aaron. In this opera, absorbed as it is with 'the thought of the inconceivable, of the chosen people and the leader of the people' as Schoenberg expressed it in a letter of 1933,[3] the musical dialectic is worked out against the background of ideas: those which have to do with Schopenhauer's sense of the opposition between the pure thing in itself, and its representation. Moses stands for the priority of a God who is outside the necessity of representation, of being presented in symbol or in image-form; Aaron represents the artistic spirit that desires *Vorstellung*—the creation of pattern, of music, of art to manifest, adequately, the unseen.

The issue may be one of particular Jewish relevance: that is, if Schoenberg's treatment of it may be compared with Kafka's, in *The trial*, and especially in that part of *The trial* that formed a short story before being gathered into the chapter 'In the cathedral'. The priest, who tells Joseph K. this parable about the man who comes seeking admittance to the Law, proceeds to interpret it in a bewildering variety of ways, which demonstrates that 'the scriptures are unalterable and the comments (i.e. the interpretations of the parable) often enough merely express the commentator's bewilderment'.[4] In other words, there may well be an original text, but the nature of that text is that it is itself representation; because it is a text, it functions as a sign, and therefore opens itself up to plurality of meaning. Thus, the priest continues, having baffled Joseph K. further with yet more possibilities of meaning: 'The right perception of any matter and a misunderstanding of the same matter do not wholly exclude each other' (pp. 238–9), which means that there can be no such thing as a right interpretation, and lying becomes, as Joseph K. decides, with melancholy, 'a universal principle' (p. 243). There is a split, viewed one way, between truth and meaning: there can be no final articulation of the meaning of a truth. Moses, of course, thinks that there can be, in this opera, and the letter already quoted from Schoenberg connects him to Michelangelo's Moses: the comparison illuminating Schoenberg's sense of the titanic power of patriarchalism that Moses, for him, represents. Though Kafka's novel does not deal with a specifically Jewish context, and the priest is no doubt a Christian, yet the interest in the 'law', in those final writings, is clear enough. And the philosopher who has done the most to deconstruct the terms of the opposition between original statement and interpretation is also Jewish— Jacques Derrida. His work in 'deconstruction' has to do with the overturning of any such thing as the idea of an original statement, an original writing: *any* kind of proposition is already inserted into language, into representation, for Derrida, and partakes of the sign-nature of all writing. Derrida's philosophy would eliminate Moses' propositions from the start by showing him that he is incoherent in wishing to think of a God who can be located outside language, or representation: even God can only be a representation, a being whose meaning does not reside inside of himself but points beyond himself in a further regress.

What is radical in Derrida is that he detects a violent and

repressive tendency behind the attempt, in Western thought, to situate thought in relation to a prior 'presence', a prior 'truth'. Derrida's argument that Western philosophy has privileged 'logocentric' attitudes, or 'phallogocentric' attitudes, assuming that there can be a final original presence, incarnated in speech, which is thus nearer to 'truth' than mere 'writing'—arbitrary marks, mere signifiers—is wholly relevant to the discussion of *Moses und Aron*.[5]

For to Moses, the puritanical spokesperson of the concept of the pure, original word, Schoenberg opposes Aaron, who appears first in Act I scene ii, turning the twelve-tone row into melody, singing as an operatic tenor, and accompanied by the sensuous tones of a flute solo with its accompaniment. It is a dance tune, and alluring. Moses speaks throughout: the tiny passage where he is allowed to sing (if he wishes: there is a choice) epitomises his puritanism of thought—'Reinige dein Denken, / lös es von Wertlosen / wehe es Wahrem: / kein andrer Gewinn dankt deinem Opfer'—'purify your thinking, free it from worthless things. Let it be righteous. No other reward is given your offerings'. There is no room for the creative word here. But at the end, when he inveighs against the Golden Calf, and Aaron's complicity in that, Aaron quite justifiably rounds on him with the very Derridean point that the tables of law he carries are themselves images, part of the manifestation that there must be of a God, whereupon Moses nihilistically breaks them. (The differences from Exodus XXXII.19, where Moses simply breaks the law out of anger at the people's perfidy in making the golden calf, are crucial.) Aaron has the victory over Moses in argument, but the opera closes with Moses' feeling of futility—so that *his* is the privileged voice in Schoenberg's work —as he speaks of 'O Wort, du Wort, das mir fehlt'—'O word, thou word, that I lack', where the violin accompanies him sensuously, and softens the puritanism. It is possible to think of Moses as himself winning some kind of redemption through this final orchestral pathos.

Schoenberg's second act thus finishes with a feeling of uncertainty: in Act III he gives the advantage to Moses, and Aaron dies at his feet, while Moses speaks of the preferable nature of the desert for any insight into the nature of God, since there can be no visual distraction there. But the opera remained incomplete for those last twenty years of Schoenberg's existence, and it is impossible not to feel that the failure to write is connected to a sense that the argument cannot work on the terms proposed. Moses, as I have said, is the privileged one of the two: he starts and finishes the work; in narrative terms he must take the lead, and Aaron must be a substitute, at best, for him. Yet the very form of writing—opera, music, spectacle— indeed, the very act of *writing* itself is the final criticism of Moses' purist attitude, and exposes his position as philosophically invalid, since he wishes to pull apart the concept of the pure truth of God from its manifestation in history, culture and language. As a leader of the people, Moses embodies finally a repression by an assertion—an assertion of a final authority, which is beyond plurality, doubleness, multiplicity of meaning, since it is not imbricated in language. The assumption of absolute rightness, of course, becomes a concomitant of Fascism, and Moses belongs to the 1930s in composition and manifestation alike. And in so far as the twelve-tone method becomes a device for the imposition of objective order, and is the refusal of subjectivity, there seems a kinship between the method and Moses. And whatever might be said about the justice or otherwise of Thomas Mann's use of Schoenberg's row system in *Doctor Faustus*, it does seem that the critique of a music there with its 'composing before composition', where 'the whole disposition and organisation of the material would have to be ready when the actual work should begin', thus cutting out subjectivity, lends itself more to the ideas of a Moses than an Aaron. Leverkühn says that the musician is 'bound to a self-imposed compulsion to order, therefore free',[6] but the point may well be the non-sequitur in his statement, and *Doctor Faustus* remains an important critique of the twelve-tone method as involving an overuse of the concept of order, where the musician seeks to derive an authority for the details of composition by referring back to an original tone row.

If the drift of these comments implies a linking of aspects of Schoenberg with Moses and with dodecaphony and with the impulse towards authoritarianism, then some reason for the non-completion of the work may well be found there: Aaron's voice is too important to let that of Moses triumph ultimately, and the people, who are to the foreground of Schoenberg's thinking, as the letter makes clear, cannot be allowed just to come under the sway of a voice that evokes authority merely. Schoenberg's return to Judaism in 1933 becomes, in that light, a gesture of solidarity with the people rather than a reversion to an established form of order, manifested in Judaic tradition. Or rather, the step itself is ambivalent, and *Moses und Aron* epitomises the sense of split.

What does seem clear is that Schoenberg's satisfaction in being able to derive the whole opera from one tone-row, at least as much of the opera as he was able to write, implied a strong objectivity, a disdaining of subjective truth and of the personal. The 'Supreme Commander' motivated him: so he called whatever historical process, or personal pressure, or God lay behind his work. (Rosen begins his account of Schoenberg by recalling the story of how he replied to a question as to whether he was Schoenberg—'No one else wanted the job, so I had to take it on'.) And a religious–political aim motivates the God of the opera—'God loves the folk, more than he loves Moses, as we gather from Act 1 scene 1, but cannot communicate with them directly, and they do not know or love him'.[7] It needs a Derrida to disentangle the hierarchical implications of all that as a formulation: to bring out the point that there cannot be this one original truth that is free from representation; that all truth is itself a representation, and that all 'truth' partakes of the character of a sign. That does not invalidate the possibility of 'communication', though it pluralises it, and brings about the installation of the possibility of difference being perceived in the most univocal statement: but it does deconstruct the character of the God, the truth, that cannot enter into communication. It questions its possibility of being.

Straub's opera-film performs a Derridean function. Like the films of *Giovanni* and *Parsifal*, it is intended initially as a critique of opera-house productions of *Moses* and *their* inherent hierarchies: Straub and Huillet were in opposition to the 1959 Berlin version, a review of which, by Desmond Shawe-Taylor, may be found in *Opera* magazine for December 1959. It was, apparently, both spectacular and advanced in audio-visual terms: there was, for example, the use of pre-recording for the voice of God in the first scene—which was, of course, the composer's intention. Specifically, the production refused naturalism—'it would call for the resources of a Cecil B. de Mille if it [the Golden Calf sequence] were to be put on stage literally, according to the composer's intentions' (Shawe-Taylor)—in favour of something more abstract. But the evasion of realism, which surely does *not* have to be de-Mille-like—that seems a reflex response merely to the problem of staging works that have a Biblical reference—runs the danger of de-historicising the piece, of giving it a mythic, exalted status, so that its issues are treated as though they involved permanent problems of the human condition. No such mystification is allowed in the Straub film, and if it is objected to that that the remorseless stripping away of anything mythic, anything that could have a mystificatory feel about it, only makes the film tedious, then it can at least be asked what it is that people expect more in a performance of a work which presumably they might be quite happy to listen to in the even more abstract conditions of hearing it on record. (The Peter Hall production at Covent Garden in 1965 had no doubts, and pitched the orgy, for then, fairly hot and strong.) As with the *Chronicle of Anna Magdalena Bach*, Straub and Huillet begin with the music, and with its *materiality*: Bach and Schoenberg are both *religious* composers whose music is remorselessly organised, mathematical, not subjective, not wrung from them at the price of their sanity or as part of the angst of their unconquerable minds. What is religious in the music is its non-spiritual quality. To return to that sense of the music is crucial, for Straub and Huillet: to put the point philosophically, they are trying to eliminate the influence of Schopenhauer in his ideas about music, where he sees it as abstract, not involved with representation, but existing as a reflection of the absolute will. To speak like that is, at the least, to be metaphysical, and it lends itself to the view that music has an eternal reality, that it is not part of a mode of production, part of the discourse of a particular society. Not to allow for the strongest form of realism is, then, to risk letting abstract, ahistorical ideas about music reflecting a timeless human state take over.

Hence the thinking behind the film of *Moses und Aron*. The Austrian Radio orchestra was pre-recorded in Vienna, conducted by Michael Gielen, and the singers sang on the set—which was an open-air location—a Roman amphitheatre near Arezzano in Italy. The singers were fed with the orchestral sounds with hearing aids and with singing voices playing gently to act as a guide. The elliptical arena drew attention to the non-naturalism of the work; emphasised its character as artefact. At the same time, it was an arena without an audience, which both left space, as it were, for the cinema audience the more fully to recall their double distanciation from the events—separated by not being part of the same experience as the singers on the set, separated by the medium of film, the materiality of which is also emphasised from time to time as the screen goes blank—especially at moments where a coup de théâtre would be expected, like the building of the calf. Syntagmatic links were erased: each scene finished with a blank screen: narrative continuity was broken: the relation between Moses at the bush in the first scene and the arrival of Aaron in the second was not perceived. In that way, the opera again approached the condition of oratorio.

Materiality is stressed, too, in the way the opening scene of the opera is played with the camera looking at Moses from behind his left shoulder, and downwards: he is not seen to speak, and the effect not only softens Günter Reich's performance—in contrast, say to the Solti recording with Franz Mazura as Moses, where the words sound far more strident in their addressing of God. Frontal close-ups are avoided: Moses' face is only seen facing outwards to the camera in the middle of the second scene with Aaron, and then the camera is above him, so that it looks down, and avoids a full confrontation with the figure.[8] The objectivity is maintained; no easy access to a private person is to be made. In this, there is a sharp contrast to be observed with the Aaron (Louis Davos), whose performance, though it involves the same kinds of camera positioning as for Moses, also uses much more eye contact, and involves the singer in half-smiling, which implies that access to the personal-emotional and to the subjective artist which is what Aaron embodies.

The film sharply distinguishes the two: Moses appears always to the left of Aaron, and both front the chorus who appear in the third and fourth scenes of the first act in a single block, one character. No attempt is made at distinguishing them as individuals; they form a unit. And what is political about the film emerges in this treatment. Whereas a traditional operatic production would wish to individualise the chorus members, and give each separate aspects of character, the film deliberately reverts to something much more like oratorio in seeing the chorus as a single, unified entity.

Martin Walsh, in a very sharp and interesting critique of the film, sees the people as the centre of Straub and Huillet's concern,[9] and argues that in the accentuation of Schoenberg that is being made Moses and Aaron's dialectic is a false one in that *both* figures are adopting an hierarchical position in regard to the people—they differ only in the method by which they would lead. And the absence of the people in the last scene of Act II, when Moses has returned from the mount, would bring that out: the leaders quarrel, but the people for whom they profess such concern are actually excluded from sight: they sing offstage, significantly coming round to Moses' point of view rather than to Aaron's, dominated by the power of his hierarchical position. That would not, of course, be Schoenberg's position: we have already seen that something of the pose of Moses works through the putting together of *Moses und Aron.* Yet Derrida's reversal of hierarchical structures (the central argument of his *Of Grammatology*, his sense that the inherent pluralism of any sign, any glyph, is reduced to the status of being a 'dangerous supplement' by a logocentric tradition that insists on the primacy of the Word, on the possibility that there can be truth outside signification and the play of signifiers) enables us to deconstruct Schoenberg's text in just such a way as Walsh suggests Straub and Huillet do. What is involved is not a 'playing against the text', for that assumes that there can be some pure meaning to the text itself.

It seems important to register the point that there is a political dimension to the film: not for nothing was it dedicated to Holger Meins, a cameraman friend of Straub and Huillet, who died on hunger strike in 1974, having spent two years in prison awaiting trial on 'terrorist' charges, associated with the Baader-Meinhoff group. None the less, Walsh's reading for me can only ironise Moses and Aaron, as leaders, and while it de-centres the Schoenberg text, usefully, it misses what opportunities the text itself has to prove itself plural, to resist being gathered up under the heading of one authoritative reading. Schoenberg's own text is richer than Walsh, for all his acuity, takes account of, and it seems to me that one of the achievements of the film is its respect for the music. It has been listened to, and however austere the film may be, and however much it seems that Schoenberg wrote an 'anti-Marxist' work,[10] it pays attention to the possibility of the music being considered in its own right: it makes that music lucid. The end of the first scene is a case in point: the words of God taking over from Moses' *Sprechstimme.* Schoenberg has introduced a plurality into the conception of God that in itself acts as a criticism of Moses' conception of monotheism wrapped up in a non-articulated truth. A speaking chorus says the lines while six voices sing along with the instruments they are paired with in the orchestra: the effect is tender and anything but authoritarian. As the words are heard, the camera shifts position from looking downwards at the floor of the arena to looking at the opposite side of it from where Moses is standing, and then slowly pans right round the wall of the arena, on its return missing out Moses, who is thus occluded as a privileged voice, and it comes to rest after 300 degrees on a view of distant peaks (Monte Velino), to the right of Moses as he has been standing in the arena. The effect is, I think, very tender. The point that it is a camera gaze which is at work is never forgotten, but the limitations of Moses' outlook are caught finely, both in musical terms and in the circling around the arena.

Another example of this is finely described by Walsh in his account of the second scene: he points out how the camera moves from Aaron singing in the direction of Moses, with gaze fixed from right to left; the response from Moses is frontal, and the next shot of Aaron is of him singing left to right, again in profile. 'Aaron metaphorically surrounds Moses' is Walsh's way of putting it: the effect, I think, is analogous to the earlier moving around the perimeter of the arena, and it again privileges music over speech: gives music a plural value (as also Aaron over Moses): it is not the people who are drawn attention to, but the possibility of signification in music seems to be brought out, and the subtlest, most minimal effect has been used to suggest that.

The ending of Act I works in this manner too. The people break into a nationalistic hymn of triumph and expectation there, and the words express their rejection of Egypt in favour of the land of milk and honey. Straub and Huillet make this chorus the voice-over to shots of the Nile from Aswan and Luxor. It is actually the only part of the opera (save for Act III) which is filmed from the arena and its surroundings. If the music sanctions a nationalism, the film interprets that as false consciousness by its presentation of these attractive landscapes, which focus especially on wide expanses of water: ochres and blues relieving the eye after the scene in the enclosing amphitheatre. The effect is to dissolve the urgency of the political movement; relativising the visions of both leaders and people. Something of plurality is inserted into the text, and the music, which clearly may be seen as parodying political action, as well as allowing for its possibility, receives that further accentuation from the visual slant.

The effect of these panning shots is to cause a forgetting in the audience of the more brutal aspects of Jewish nationalism: stresses that might have seemed highly necessary in the 1930s may require a softening in the 1970s, and there is clearly a softening going on in the Golden Calf sequence in Act II, for these scenes are presented tactfully and in no spirit to encourage a voyeur-like reaction from the film audience. Whereas in the Schoenberg text, the 'orgy' seems to validate the authority of the leaders, and implies what depths of degradation may lie within a nation, thus giving no space at all for the people's wisdom—the anti-Marxism of the work—the film responds differently by its use of hints only, by its strong metonymic displacements of the action—a hand pouring out wine with growing unsteadiness conveys drunkenness, for example. If the end of Act I worked both to countervail the nationalism while Schoenberg (though ambivalently) heightened it, then the dance around the calf in Act II softens the antithesis in Schoenberg's stress: the violence and the lapsing out, expressing the people's servitude to false consciousness, is not presented as brutally. The music, which might be regarded as approaching a more nineteenth-century mode in order to indicate the relapse in the people, as Schoenberg conceives it, need not be taken in that univocal way; it may be presented as the expression of a kind of warmth, however flawed this may be. The holocaust of the animals (never seen) may be barbaric, but the dance of the butchers has its own grace. Schoenberg's own attitude to the scene—that it displays the grossest descent into the unrelievedly sensual and unthinking—receives a relativising; while not forgotten, it is still qualified.

The decision to play Act III, set in the Lago del Matese, in the film is important in the light of this. It may well be that the film is doing something that could not be handled in the opera house, in giving that short scene in the simple form of voices speaking. What Schoenberg left unfinished, no doubt because it represented a crux for him that he could not solve, Straub and Huillet have used. Act III, as it exists, shows Aaron reduced, now having to speak as he has not had to do before, and Moses' is speech unbacked by any orchestral sound. The contrast from the richness that there has been could hardly be greater. Hearing voices merely speaking, as Aaron lies in the mud with Moses standing to his left, and soldiers guarding the body of Aaron to the right, so that there is a strong sense of the prevalence of the vertical, the upright, in uncompromising shape, is to emphasise the dangers of letting one voice only prevail, of letting the authoritarian personality gain the upper hand. All that Straub and Huillet do is to play the text as written, save that they do not show Aaron's death, the camera having cut away to Moses' face in profile, but the choice to play the scene without music provides a vital justification for the whole of their procedure throughout the film, in being as minimalist as possible and letting the music offer its own powerful images.

For the opera opens, it will be remembered, with what Tippett calls 'the representation, the symbolisation of pure spirit, of the single, eternal, omnipresent, invisible and inconceivable God. The sound that we hear is a six-voice choir. There are no words to this, true to the music of the angels, only a single vowel, 'O' . . . the whole of *Moses und Aron* can be shown to derive from these chords and this theme'.[11] In Straub and Huillet's completion of the opera, the musical absence implies several things. It means, firstly, that the opera affirms a God who sings rather than speaks initially—speaks only when speaking to people, sings to himself, so that the ultimate descent to pure speech with no musical background is the ultimate denial of that God: Moses at the end is the ultimate in atheism. At least the Golden Calf episode involved music: *this* apostasy is worse than the first, and the resolute minimalism of the last scene is not just an aspect of Straub and Huillet's technique: it is also a criticism of the barrenness that Moses' point of view leaves us with, even in comparison to the barrenness involved in the dance around the calf. Moses at the end represents male, logocentric, as Derrida would say, authoritarianism, and the soldiers are with him, so that the political register of this bleak assertion of power is made clear. (I said 'male' advisedly: the six-part choir is partly female: in both singing and speaking choruses, God sounds androgynous.) Secondly, the opera, by giving a God who both speaks and sings, affirms the people's point of view, rather than Aaron's, who just sings in the first two acts, or Moses', who just speaks, as I have already discussed. The people do both: they sing and speak. The people are absent in the last scene, and the absence of the people is also the absence of God. All that is left is a Moses who speaks, and who forces Aaron into his own mode of discourse.

Act III in Straub and Huillet's film may construct a different opera from the one presented in the theatre, but it seems to me that it engages with the debate that Schoenberg sets up in a way that advances it quite considerably. The scene becomes a supplement to the opera as written: it shows the results of its vision not being carried through. The reaccentuation of Schoenberg for Marxist thought seems to be exemplified in the playing of Act III as it exists: Schoenberg's inability to complete it shows, with good reason, his inability to side with the potentiality of a Moses.

Of all the films discussed in these chapters, *Moses und Aron* is the one that respects the music the most: that is not to say it is the best played, or sung. (There seems some serious underplaying in the case of the chorus singing: or so it appeared on the soundtrack.) But as with the *Chronicle of Anna Magdalena Bach*, the materiality of the music, its lack of complicity with the soul of the performer, its anti-romanticism, therefore, seems to be emphasised. Straub is often spoken of as highly influenced by Robert Bresson, and is quoted as having said that the 'only truly mystical film was *Les dames du bois de Boulogne*'.[12] The statement as it relates to Bresson might have to do with the Racine-like Jansenism that André Bazin found in his films: the original title for Bresson's *Un condamné à mort s'est échappé* was *Le vent souffle où il veut*; and Richard Roud has connected this suggested title with the frequent shots of trees, clouds and skies in the *Chronicle*,[13] as though the music was presented as material, yet at the same time, not reducible. Despite all the determinations of Bach's music provided by his home circumstances, presented with documentary detail as they are in the film, the signifying value of the music is in excess of whatever meaning might be ascribed to those particular historical situations. That the signifier can be so capable of further and further accentuation and re-emphasis is the mystical thing: and it requires a minimalist aesthetic to say anything like that, for the film that is 'filmic' in the sense of already being replete with meaning and interpretation is hardly likely to allow the audience to ponder on the possibility of the barest image being itself a rich signifier. It seems to me that this point is crucial to *Moses und Aron*, and shows the quality of the debate that is being conducted with Schoenberg's text in the film.

For *Moses und Aron* seems also a mystical work, and not in the sense that it has to do with the manifestation of God. Derrida's emphasis seems necessary to show the incoherence of the idea that there can be a God outside the sphere of the sign, and once that is so, God becomes a sign himself, not a final truth. And the opera makes this plain: God is not incomprehensible, but is heard at the opening of the opera, and the four three-part chords heard at the beginning initate the tone row from which everything is to be derived: they are the *langue*, in Saussure's terms, that will enable the *parole* to be heard. The representation is already there: anterior to the development of the distinctive and individual aspects of the parole, a system of differences, an initial set of choices, must have dictated the production of the langue. As far back as you go, you can only find representation, or the image: you may yearn for the original, as Moses does for the word that he lacks—but this desire for an ultimate authority itself will produce nothing more than the word: nothing more than a signifier; a mere word, empty in itself, marked out, as Derrida would say, by absence, by its deferring of meaning. The twelve-tone row may try to root the arbitrary nature of the signifier in some form of objectivity, but in itself that objectivity has been produced and stands for no natural principle.

None the less, it is the possibility of the tone-row generating numerous further significations that gives it its fascination, and makes it apt symbol for the idea of God, who similarly embodies all possibilities of signifying practices within himself, presumably. What is modernist about *Moses und Aron* is that the opera is about itself; about music, and its possibilities of signifying, or creating reverberations in the minds of those who hear it: the people in the opera being those who listen. If we reject the hierarchical stance implied in the idea that the composer has an idea to communicate, and that people have to become educated enough to pick up that message, difficult as it may be, with the aid of mediators such as Moses and Aaron, and if we start asking why the person should be listened to in the first place, it still seems that another emphasis may run through both Schoenberg and Straub and Huillet: that is that significance cannot be contained; it is the inherent quality of the signifier, and it has little to do with the intention of the musician, or author. That, perhaps, is the mystical sense.

Thus when Moses expresses his tragedy—'meine Kraft ist zu Ende: Meine Gedanke ist machtlos in Arons Wort'—'my art is at an end; my thought becomes powerless in Aaron's word' (Act I scene iv)—what is implied is the death of the author, as Barthes deals with that concept. Moses as authoritarian personality can work no more. But the power of the music can continue, and in no programmable way: what follows is the generating of images: in the film, the cobra on the ground, the leprous hand, the blood, then the water on the ground, the images of the Nile. As Schoenberg's score unfolds itself in plural forms, deriving from the one first image—the tone-row—so the space is opened for the generating of significance. What seems so admirable about the Straub and Huillet film is that the objectivity before the music that shapes the film, recalling it as more akin to oratorio than conventional romantic opera, respects the materiality of the music and its non-material quality: that in its absence of meaning, it continues to signify. The absence of distraction visually, the fidelity to the music as having its plural and suggestive significance—which makes its absence in the last scene so striking—further emphasises the point of Straub and Huillet have gone along with Schoenberg in their sense that this is a film about music: and if they have used Schoenberg against Schoenberg in the process of the film, subtly reaccentuating the emphasis of the film, that only brings out the way that the 'supplement'—as Act III is—will always prove 'dangerous' in effecting an unsaying of the deeply meant statement.

NOTES

1. Charles Rosen, *Schoenberg* (1975), p. 104.
2. Letter of 1931: quoted in Willi Reich, *Schoenberg: a critical biography*, trans. by Leo Black (1971), p. 178.
3. *Ibid.*, p. 179.

4. Franz Kafka, *The trial*, trans. Willa and Edwin Muir (Harmondsworth, 1953), p. 240.

5. The arguments from Derrida are all to be found in *Of Grammatology*, trans. Gayatri Chakravorty Spivak (Baltimore, 1976); the best introduction to Derrida in English (apart from Spivak's introduction) remains Jonathan Culler, *On deconstruction: theory and practice after structuralism* (1983).

6. Thomas Mann, *Doctor Faustus*, trans. H. T. Lowe-Porter (Harmondsworth, 1968), p. 188. The passage is part of the chapter 22 where twelve-tone method is discussed, and which Schoenberg objected to, as intrusive upon his ideas.

7. David Lewin, in *Perspectives on Schoenberg and Stravinsky*, ed. Benjamin Boretz and Edward T. Cone (New York, 1972), p. 62.

8. The film of *Moses und Aron* has been well written upon: see Martin Walsh, *The Brechtian aspect of radical cinema* (1981), pp. 91–107; Richard Roud, *Jean-Marie Straub* (1971), p. 123; Richard Roud, *Guardian*, 26 February 1975; John Sandford, *The new German cinema* (1980), pp. 27–35.

9. Walsh, *op. cit.*, pp. 94–5.

10. Roud, *Jean-Marie Straub, op. cit.*, p. 123.

11. Michael Tippett, *Music of the angels*, ed. Meirion Bowen (1980), p. 107. Useful musical analysis of *Moses und Aron* exists in Karl H. Worner, *Schoenberg's Moses und Aron* (1963); and Luigi Rognoni, *The second Vienna school*, trans. Robert W. Mann (1977), pp. 218–74.

12. Roud, *op. cit.*, p. 102.

13. *Ibid.*, p. 72. For discussion of the metaphysical element within Bresson's work, see Amedee Ayfré's essay in *The films of Robert Bresson* (Studio Vista, 1969)—a book which also reproduces the Bazin essay. The account of Daniele Huillet of the shooting of *Moses und Aron*, in *Enthusiasm*, no. 1 (December 1975) is fascinating in its own right.

CHAPTER 8

Losey's 'fenomeni morbosi': *Don Giovanni*

After the 'definitive' (thus the BBC) *Zauberflöte*, the contro-versial and 'non-definitive' Losey *Don Giovanni*.[1] It was inspired by Rolf Liebermann, the Swiss composer and former general-director of the Paris opera, whose intention it was to demo-cratise opera: to draw it out of the privilege of the opera house, and give it more accessibility. (And it is an interesting statistic that suggests that more people have seen Losey's film than have seen the opera in the theatre since the time of its first pro-duction.) Liebermann had filmed stage productions before, while working with Hamburg State Opera, but opera-film was a new venture. The location eventually chosen for the film was the Palladian Veneto, not Spain, and thus immediately the text was opened up to a free interpretation, one whose setting could not be ignored but was rather insistent, so that a whole history was implied within it: and not the history of da Ponte and Mozart's work. Also, this placing meant opting for a mode of presentation that would, by stressing specificity, put the events of the opera into a shared world: make the audience also figures of that landscape. Palladio here is not part of a museum-experience, but democratised, his patrician dwellings now lived in, as much by the servants in the kitchen below stairs in the Villa Rotonda as by the aristocracy above, so that there was a shared space for Palladio, Mozart and da Ponte, Losey and the twentieth-century personnel of the Paris Opera. Not only a different history, then, but a new one that breaks conventional ways of seeing the past, 'the continuum of history', as Benjamin puts it, and makes it 'time filled by the presence of the now'.[2]

Losey's liking of location-shooting allows, too, for the firm imposition of a narrative, and so another history, upon the operatic material: incidents are no longer loosely attached, and the social reality is not easily slipped out of into timelessness, or the situation of being mere metaphor. Giovanni's wealth is derived from the glass-blowing factory at Murano, and the overture is played against shots of Donna Anna and her father being shown the furnace by him: great play being made of the eye contact between the male and female. The stress on the fire, emblematic of sexuality, will return, particularly in fresco form when Donna Elvira sings 'In quali eccessi', looking at Tiepolo-covered walls, with a last judgment upon them, as she meditates on Giovanni's state, and seeing, in her recitative, the grave opening beneath his feet. It will come back at the end, when the flames engulf Giovanni: he is caught, it seems, in his own industrial world, licked up by the flames that manifest the extensions of his energy beyond the sexual. The flames at the start, dividing the man and woman, are soon to be contrasted with the rain falling in the Piazza dei Signori (in Vicenza, where the first scene is set), as the Commendatore dies: water mingling with blood, with the initial redness recalled in an extension of its initial significance. From there, the action moves outside to the country owned by Giovanni: he occupies the Villa Rotonda; Zerlina and Masetto belong to the *campagna* around the villa; while there is a separate villa (the Caldogno) for Donna Anna, to which Giovanni travels in a coach with Anna and Ottavio during the sequence of scenes (11–13) of Act 1. Ottavio is a melancholic romantic, whose 'Dalla sua pace' needs to be sung while he is being rowed in the waters of the lagoon around Torcello, while the rest of the act is set around the Villa Rotonda, to which the 'maschere galanti' arrive by water.

But the second act makes this sense of narration difficult to sustain, implying the plurality of the discourses that underlie this film, where in any case the libretto and the rewritings involved in the change between the original productions at Prague and Vienna prevent any sense of a narrational flow being sustained. Act 2 begins in the villa, but soon moves away to the

Don Giovanni. Ruggero Raimondi (Don Giovanni) and Eric Adjani (valet).
Courtesy Artificial Eye.

Palazzo Valmarana for the Donna Elvira sequence. It is followed by a scene with a Brechtian distancing of the action: an indoor sequence set in the Teatro Olympico, (scenes 7 and 8) for the sextet. It is played on the stage and in the wing space, in front of a cardinal and court sitting in the audience, appreciative of the drama played out before them. The theatre, Palladian baroque, apt emblem for the stilted emotions performed by the various outraged characters, had appeared before, at the start of the overture, when there was a movement out of it to journey to Murano: here it stresses the acted nature of the sentiments, just as Leporello is 'really' acting, as Giovanni. The naturalism is fissured, and not resumed with 'Il mio tesoro'; Ottavio appears out of a door into the grounds of the Villa Rotonda, and sings of the need to console his beloved, and that vengeance will soon come, to groups of sleeping peasants, who have drunk too much of Giovanni's good wine: the servant kicked by Ottavio reverts to slumber again. Elvira's last aria, 'Mi tradi' is sung into the lattice-work of a confessional, emphasising how her new love for God is a displacement of her sexual desire for Giovanni: then there is a long shot of her walking through the courtyards towards the camera, suggesting her future cloistered existence, but then the aria concludes with her going into the fields and so away from this claustral world: the fissured nature of her feelings, between liberty and self-opperssive fear is suggested. The cemetery scene and Donna Anna's aria, no. 23, follow: during this, servants remove the veils from the statues and pictures; she herself takes the veil from the image of the father, whose authority is stressed, creating the torsion in the woman's feelings. The last scene returns to the Villa Rotonda, with the final *buffa* sextet delivered with the characters going out of the door into an autumnal morning with dead leaves, and are then seen out in boats on the lagoon, in brilliant colour, while back at the villa, the valet in black shuts the door: the last vision.

There is an only partial narrative coherence: this suggests something radical: a switching of codes. Roman Jakobson's distinctions between metaphor and metonymy, which link with the Freud–Lacan argument about the two crucial ways in which thought is constantly condensed and displaced in speech terms, may be useful here: metonymy acts by replacing one item of thought by a contiguous one within the same area of investigation, the same syntagm, and so belongs to a mode of thinking that works in order, from one item to the next, displacing one term by another along the chain of signifiers that make up the range of possibilities held to exist for thinking about a subject. It fits the novel, and anything that relies on narration, itself the mode most given to working onwards in a metonymic chain. Metaphor, however, perceives a similarity of thought within two different sets of syntagms, and projects a comparison of one item within one symbolic order on to another. Metaphor is habitually allied to poetry in that it demands the perception of immediate, non-logical, non-sequential connections; and it may be that film is metonymic in character, displacing image by image, working strongly, traditionally, from the shot of one aspect of things that calls up all the other related aspects. Theatre, and opera, however, would be more metaphoric in their mode of presentation. On the stage a total image is offered, however much there may be an attempt to foreground one signifier only; the eye is not confined to one single signifier which is about to be replaced. The spectator's ability to see everything at once seems itself an apt figure for the theatre's lack of ability to handle narrative easily; for its tendency, rather, to present total images that contain the whole vision of the play within them.[3] *Don Giovanni* in the theatre resolves itself into a succession of musical sequences, which might even be cut at will, as indeed happens. In Losey, the sequentiality is stressed; less escapes; everything has to be seen as part of a history.

Opera may work on the metaphorical axis of thought; so the conception of the opera-film involves the clashing of two codes, metaphoric and metonymic. In Verdi all the action takes place between scenes: *opera seria*'s derivation from the classical theatre meant that action began near the end of a plot, certainly *in medias res*; opera usually relates on formulaic and traditional situations, so that narrative becomes inessential: these points stress that its usual form is a series of tableaux that function as metaphor.[4] Indeed, it may be argued that this gives opera-film a new possibility: if opera house performance is for most a sensuous spectacle, and complex analytic listening is not possible, it is different in the cinema, where the realm of the intelligible is foregrounded over the visible; as Gilles Deleuze proposed that in the cinema, the spectator's view is not free, has no natural anchorage, no independent point of reference.[5] Possibility of attention to the way narrative is constructed is intensified; analytic possibilities are opened up. Opera thus needs film, since it relies on a plurality of conventions, narrative, drama, music, both vocal and orchestral, spectacle. The spheres of the sensuous and the intelligible need separate examination, including a prising apart. It is not part of the democratising of opera, that it is made to give up its status as unquestionable, and that it is asked to relate itself to the real world? A strong social context is enforced upon the events and arias in the work: nothing can escape the necessity of being framed within a discourse.

No opera, probably, has invited more contextualising than *Don Giovanni*, from Hoffmann and Kierkegaard to Otto Rank— while Julian Rushton's monograph is a recent attempt to impose an adequate reading, based, in his case, on a conviction that what is meant to be said is what gets said. Thus, while repelling boarders when coming to the defence of Donna Anna, he writes about her aria, no. 21, 'she loves Ottavio; the recitative and the aria cannot be understood otherwise. Music cannot lie. If Mozart and da Ponte wanted us to understand . . . that Anna is a liar and a hypocrite, they could have found some way for music and text to contradict each other. They did not'.[6] Music means what it says, then: there can be no Hoffmann-like shifting with Donna Anna, with the sense that her real love is Giovanni. But 'music cannot lie' is straightforward metaphysics: in one way, music cannot lie because it cannot *say* anything: in another way, as Eco would suggest, it can do nothing else, seeing that music functions as a sign, and semiotics is 'the discipline studying everything that can be used in order to lie'.[7] Since it is a sign, it cannot possibly be taken in one way only, and Rushton's formalist analysis of Donna Anna's music, adorned with such qualifiers as 'heartrending' and 'poignant', and the reference to Berlioz's sense of the music's 'poetry of love' represent readings-in, self-confirming strategies for taking the music text in one way only. This is not to return Donna Anna to that in any case overstated category of 'hypocrite and liar', but it suggests that the text is being used to confirm assumptions—mildly Christian, liberal–humanist—that the critic started out with. It is no coincidence that two pages later Rushton decides that Giovanni has no depth, is marked out by 'vacuity', is the 'perfect counterpart to the empty, frigid atheist of Molière'. So much for seducers, then. For Bernard Williams, in an earlier section, 'it is notable that he has no self-reflective aria' (p. 82). The absence of introspection is the disqualifying feature. (Losey's self-reflective characters—Anna and Ottavio—are seen through mirrors, characteristically: Donna Elvira confesses into an empty black box: these are the introspective types: and the gap is marked by Giovanni in this film: he owns a glass factory: very suitable for those who wish to be self-reflective.)

Williams says this discussing Kierkegaard's thesis that music is the art-form uniquely qualified to express the sensuous-erotic, and that *Giovanni* is the work that incarnates this principle, evoking it in the figure of the seducer himself. Kierkegaard's thesis will not allow Giovanni the criticism that 'seducer' implies: since reflection and consciousness are necessary to the category, and they do not mark out Giovanni as characteristics.[8] In this opera, if anywhere, therefore, music and subject-matter come together, and the innocence of Giovanni figures the sensuous eroticism of music. Kierkegaard stresses Giovanni as the successful lover: points out (p. 92) that the number 1003 for seductions in Spain is 'odd and accidental, which is not at all unimportant, since it gives the impression that the list is by no means closed, but that, on the contrary, Don Juan is in a hurry'. No Rank-like sense of failure here: psychoanalysis belongs to a different discourse, one that is determined to bring Giovanni to consciousness, as it were, to textualise his sexuality.[9] In Michel Foucault's terms, in *The history of sexuality*, classical

psychoanalysis belongs to the systematic turning of sex into
discourse that belongs to the post-Renaissance episteme; the
subject is constituted as having something to confess to in
sexual terms; is the site of some hidden deviancy or inadequacy
that needs to surface.[10] That new form of knowledge, associated
with the classical period, of quasi-scientific knowledge (which
is also power) over those thus constituted as subjects inter-
pellates them as individuals subject to guilt, and with the
capacity, derived from the new vocabulary of sexuality, to
reflect upon their individualistic egos and drives. In Kierkegaard's
sense, Giovanni resists such classifications: is not to be brought
into such manipulations of power, acquired through this newer
discourse of sexuality: has not been pushed into the subjection
of having to define himself, with a character created for him. In
Foucault's terms, too, that might be positive: in Rushton, it is
negative, Giovanni is shallow. But perhaps that definition of
shallowness rests upon the sense that someone has resisted
classification: has not accepted a prevalent discourse: has,
indeed, walked out of it.

Yet da Ponte's Giovanni is complex: he may resist power
acquired through knowledge, and have to be taken at the end
by mere power which punishes the dissolute: yet at the same
time the irony of events works against him: he has no joy in
sexual terms on this his last day of existence. The text is
fissured: though the *buffa* terms of the music relativise the
moral outrage of those who sing in *opera seria* style,[11] yet it can
show nothing else, and the comedy works similarly against
Giovanni. Losey's film opens Act II with Giovanni and Leporello
sitting, a naked woman between them, which may favour
Giovanni's reading of events of himself as the successful seducer,
but elsewhere Losey emphasises the artificial nature of the
claims. For Leporello's 'catagolo' aria, the servants bring out
books that contain the list of Giovanni's amours and lay them
down before Elvira: concertina like, the leaves of the books
open up and cascade down the steps of the Villa Rotonda.
Wealth in the factory is capped by wealth in possession. While
Leporello sings 'Voi sapete quel che fa'—you know what he
does—in that leering, insulting manner that gets at Elvira's

status in class and sexual terms, and which makes her pull down her veil angrily and shamefacedly, the camera has moved elsewhere to Giovanni on his estate. He is looking at a woman bathing, Ingres-like, with lustral water, figuring her innocence, upon her: 'Sua passione predominante / E la giovin' principiante' —his main passion is for the beginner. There are shots of eyes looking into the camera: and they recall the audience's who are also constituted as subjects of Leporello's voyeur-like cataloguing of the names, and indicate our own complicity in the sensuality evoked: and they are eyes looking back at that artificial eye, the camera, seducing, erasing the power of censorship, and thus mocking the Elvira response. Here the film allows the amours of Giovanni: yet it does so at the same time not refusing the text's mocking question of their reality. 'Questo non picciol libro' ceases to be a mere litotes: instead, the books are prolific as Giovanni on this day is not: and his seductions are emphasised as artificial, texts, signifiers only, with an absence of the body, pointing to the endless desire, never fulfilled, always deferred, that is in any case inscribed in the number of loves the text describes him as having.

Losey's film has its strength in drawing attention to the dual nature of the signification; to the fissured nature of all discourse; and thus opens up the text as problematic, not asking for a single, unified, and thus closed reading. For the sense of fissure is in the Gramsci epigraph selected for the film, 'il vecchio muore, e il nuovo non puo nascere: e in questo interregno si verificano i fenomeni morbosi più svariati'—'the old is dying and the new cannot be born: in this interregnum, a great variety of morbid symptoms appears'.[12] For Gramsci, Fascism was one of those morbid symptoms, and Losey has made much of the political register of the opera, written two years before the overthrow of the *ancien régime*, seeing it as 'a piece of rebellion, a drama of social class'.[13] Commentary on the film took its hint from that: Leporello (José van Dam) was seen not as the product of the *commedia dell'arte* tradition, where Dent derived his name from, but as 'the archetypal bourgeois jackal living shamelessly off the aristocracy until he can retire into bourgeois respectability';[14] while class differentiations are made clear in the finale to the first act, as Losey himself tells Michel Ciment: 'when the servants move towards the house while "Viva la Libertà" is being sung, quietly a row of valets from the house prevent them from going any further'.[15] Traces of the feudal *ancien régime* remain within the film: the near-seduction of Zerlina is carried on in full view of the servants, and the openness of the villa is significant, and 'Là ci darem la mano' is sung in the house while a dog—medieval symbol of fidelity—lies stretched out before the fire.

Rushton's approach separates Giovanni from the rest, morally: my argument is that the opera collapses these distinctions, and that Losey's film draws attention to the contradictions they imply. Elvira's 'Ah! chi mi dice mai' contains within it the *buffo* style of 'Poverina' sung by Giovanni as he plans another seduction: both comedy and dramatic seriousness depend on the imbrication of one emotional voice within another and the refusal to privilege one: the *buffo* note acts as a revolutionary voice, qualifying sharp distinctions of character and attitude. Elvira's music in no. 15—'Ah taci, inguisto core', fully analysed in Kerman's *Opera as drama*, is significant in that it is a register that accommodates itself to Giovanni's sensuousness itself: the *seria* tone is gone, replaced by a sense of the indissolubility of Elvira and what she represents, and Giovanni, and what he embodies. Nor is that indissolubility denied in her last solo, no. 21b. If Giovanni were the evil principle 'out there', which could be destroyed, it would be at the cost of Elvira herself: something of this, indeed, is involved in the position she takes up at the end. So too Donna Anna, after her highly ambiguous *recitativo* (no. 10) about what happened that night, will not yet marry her Ottavio: she receives no new life from the restoration of socially approved order: the loss of the anarchic figure does nothing for 'goodness': this is no world of binary oppositions. As Christopher Ballantine points out, 'these differing relationships (to Giovanni) are articulated musically: the closer the character is to Giovanni, the more deeply touched by him, the more will his or her music approximate to that of the hero'.[16]

Though the opera's title may privilege Giovanni and his aria, 'Fin'ch'han dal vino', significantly accompanied by full orchestra, set out his energy in anarchy (he wishes to mix up the dances), as something positive, the work does not function as the privileging of the spontaneous individual against society, where the hero disrupts social and patriarchal order: indeed, both Giovanni's feasts, at the end of either act, are disrupted by the unexpected putting in its appearance: the maskers and the stone guest, undermining figures as Giovanni is himself. The self is not an absolute, but is the effect of the difference that exists between it as an element in a signifying system and other elements. Giovanni's absence of theme or aria, save for 'Fin'ch'han del vin', emphasises that he exists not as something discrete, but in those other to him, mirrors indeed, and the urge for possession is the desire for possession of the imaginary wholeness displaced down the chain of signifiers, and this motivates his sexuality.

There is more here than the articulation of the conscious subject. He is a displaced, decentred figure, not adequately named, dispersed, though with traces of him in the whole order set up within the opera: binary distinctions do not work; for within each term is the repressed other; everything that functions as a signifier is riddled with doubleness. Losey, indeed, creates an additional character: a valet in black (Eric Adjani)—the suggestion, it seems, of Franz Salieri, the pseudonym of Francis Savel, who took Losey through the score. (Savel, by his self-ironising name, and proposal to give Giovanni an extra cover—since the valet is on hand to perform any necessary acts of unpleasantness, so acting as a front for Giovanni, to make him seem more gracious—seems to be satirising the musical establishment's need to see Mozart and everything associated with him as divine. A Mozart performance, and a radical Mozart film, requires a scapegoat, and Salieri will act as that, as will the valet in black.) Losey's valet belongs to the unconscious of Mozart/da Ponte's own text: suggests what is excluded in the da Ponte. For Leporello may function as a double to Giovanni, as Rank suggests, and the opening music for Act II may proclaim, by its lack of character-differentiation, the identicality of interests between the two; but the valet in black makes all that a problem, opens up ways that Losey feels

Giovanni needs supplementing beyond the conscious of the text, with its Leporello. The idea of a 'right reading' of this opera, or of any work of art, involves ignoring the text's unconscious: assumes that a line can be drawn around the signifiers, that they do not involve the play of 'supplementarity', that elusive property discussed while looking at *Moses und Aron.* Supplementarity as an 'idea' removes unitary concepts with their truth value, so definition of it as a unitary concept is impossible; but a quotation from Derrida will help: 'Man *calls himself* man only by drawing limits excluding his other from the play of supplementarity: the purity of nature, of animality, primitivism, childhood, madness, divinity. The approach to these limits is at once feared as a threat of death, and desired as access to a life without difference'.[17] These 'others' are set outside 'man' in binary oppositions to 'him', whereas Derrida's 'supplementarity' and 'différence' show that philosophical thought customarily rests on the assumption that there can be a purging of all these elements of dualness, doubleness, and the 'other', in the name of creating a unitary concept. On such, hierarchies of meaning are built up. The use of the valet in black—an illegitimate son of Giovanni's? just a valet? a suggestion of homosexuality? death?—is an example of Losey's refusing to let *Giovanni* have that kind of univocal truth: the text is seen as problematic, neither affirming a civilisation nor the individual, and neither 'morality' nor sexual freedom, nor nature or art. What are the effeminate young men doing lying around in the background to Giovanni's feast in the last scene? Do they point up a homosexuality, or do they imply that his success with women necessitates seeing other men as emasculated?—just as Ballantine finds Ottavio suspiciously passionless in his relationship with Anna, and his protestation that he will be a father to her admonitory. There is a doubleness here, no either/or. The film resists an imposition of meaning.

Against the mathematical, classical, Palladian architecture there is the swelling of hysteria, of morbid phenomena, that goes with Losey's American interest in the decadence of the aristocracy, the decay of the house, of Venice, of Europe: inspirations crucial to *The servant* and *The go-between* for instance, and to the unmade *Proust*. These interests suggest one way of taking Gramsci: in his notes to the cast, Losey reflects that the key words in Act I, 'Viva la libertà' (sexual as well as political liberty) are not sung by the peasants: 'the underlings stand at feeble attention like a lot of whipped middle-class English standing to attention for the National Anthem at the Haymarket theatre'. If the revolution, hailed in C major, with trumpets and drums and martial rhythm, is to appear, it will not be so much from Masetto, but from Giovanni, whose anarchism can both subvert the peasantry—as those erotic flutes seduce Zerlina in 'Là ci darem', and the aristocracy. Losey traces dual aspects of the socially radical and destructive in the Giovanni that Ruggero Raimondi creates: Gramsci's morbid symptoms are evoked in the black costume and diabolic look. Mozart's evocation of the *diabolus in musica* as the Overture repeatedly brings back a phrase that descends from the tonic D major to the tritone (Rushton quotes an anecdote about the recurrence of this phrase to Mozart during the course of writing, and falling asleep over it) receives a reaccentuation here. It was a common reviewing complaint to say Losey had missed the humour, and there is cause for puzzlement why he should have accepted Patrick White's description of Giovanni as 'dangerous and cold as steel'; but certainly the characterisation involves a sense of the morbid: black for most of the film, and tightly buttoned up, he is seen bathing and dressing in the recitative sequence after aria 10a, and then is in white, with open-neck shirt, in a way that makes him not only innocent and feminine, with the hair hanging down in a tail, but also, as Felicity Baker suggests in *Paragraph*, vulnerable. These opposites again are doubles, contradictions. The character is not 'natural'; the white costume and the pastoral wide-brimmed hat are artifices, there is nothing of Rousseau here, as the previous romanticism of Ottavio, singing 'Dalla sua pace' is also death-like: studied isolation, with the figure (Kenneth Riegel) standing upright in the boat being rowed along in silence along the misty lagoon, while he reflects that what displeases Anna gives him death. And that retreatism relates back to Anna (Edda Moser), with her black dress, which aligns her to Giovanni, and her mourning, her living surrounded by statues, equally chill.[18]

None of these three is out of the atmosphere of artifice, and the connection between that and hysteria is made by Elvira (Kiri Te Kanawa), first seen framed in nature, between the trees, (as later, between the doors of the courtyard, in no. 21a), and with a headdress of architectural qualities. When the veil is pushed back—and no film could make more use of veils and masks, as the latter are a prominent feature of all Mozart's operas, her hair is grey, a morbid symptom itself. What is natural in her is breathed into the confessional: sexuality is forced into that secret mode of discourse. The hysteria that makes her describable as mad—'pazza'—with that strong coloratura that seems to sanction Giovanni's description, is the morbid symptom that has to do with the frustration of the female.

The maskers at the end of Act I try to assume control as they commend their enterprise to heaven, walking through the villa in the deepening gloom, while the camera cranes down on them from above, emphasising their smallness within the moment. Each of these three represents a frustrated sexuality: their definition in these terms is the motive behind their desire for revenge on Giovanni, the figure not so caught. These promptings of the sexual both express a decadence and a revolutionary fervour. The *ancien régime* subverts itself: plays out its etiolated feelings in the Teatro Olympico, before an audience, which confirms the validity of these feelings. Yet the weakness of response of the non-Giovanni figures (though affected by him, and not separated) is stressed. After the sextet comes 'Il mio tesoro', florid, *opera-seria*-like, self-repeating in its use of the ritornello, and though sung very theatrically—Riegel walks away periodically and then turns back to face the camera—played to no audience, for the peasants are either asleep or indifferent, disengaged from these self-regarding emotions. The singer's movement enacts the ritornello pattern: as the emotion is for ever self-repeating, too, caught in its own fixity. The contrast between the two worlds, two classes, is evident.

A morbidity that affects all, that renders the sexual energy both creative and sterile, caught within the very discourse it would wish to subvert: that is basic to Losey's film. There may be an anti-feminism in the attitude to women here that structures them as depressive, near hysterical—if so, it belongs with the ironic statement in *The go-between* that the woman is never to blame, and it suggests, too, the presence of feelings that hardly know themselves, in Ottavio, and crucially in Elvira and Anna, while they do not speak in Giovanni, save in the 'Champagne' aria. And there his energy may be seen as deliberately evoked, and the absence of discourse about the sexual may not represent merely a freedom or a mere spontaneity. It is interesting that Losey's Zerlina (Teresa Berganza) by being too old, probably, for the part should have looked so motherly; the idea of a positive pastoral and innocent sexuality is given little stress; just as the boorish aspects of Masetto (Malcolm King) are played up strongly: the revolutionary fervour there is seen as all too much like the rancour that Nietzsche sees as central to European political and emotional thought in *The genealogy of morals.* Where is the sexuality here that is untroubled by thought and consciousness?

For Mozart and da Ponte, the opposition between Enlightenment and Romantic thought may well have provided the basis for some of the unresolved parts of the text, those seized on by Losey, but the morbid symptoms here belong to the twentieth century, and Losey is writing the history of the present, drawing on Marx and Freud. Hysteria is seen as the effect of power, working in all ways: endlessly repeating itself: in father to daughter, in master to servant, in man to woman and woman to man, from class to class and from the institutional forms of religion, and civilisation which produces its own discontents in its way of concealing feeling behind control. The sexual is the agent of power, as the key to knowledge about a person. The product of this bottled-up feeling is nineteenth-century opera, which in *Don Giovanni* is in process of separating itself from *opera buffa* and which speaks the language of suppressed and displaced emotion, allowed the codification of aria. Fissures are inherent within the opera to imply the presence of just that repression, of that inability to create a whole vision, and they point to a whole subconscious behind the text, that needs bringing out, not in a univocal way but in a manner that stresses the gaps in the work, as Losey does.

Far more than Syberberg's use of Brecht, this film seems to be Brechtian opera in its drawing attention to inconsistency and contradiction.[19] The *buffa* ending is ironised. It is bright with light, comic-opera music, as Giovanni has in his last scene been dressed in bright and light clothes, and it finishes the opera with the figures far out on the water, that glittering and insubstantial element. Losey finishes with the valet in black shutting the door; inserts a different emphasis. Of this film, more than any other discussed here, it can be said that there has been the creation of a separate work: not passive, merely dependent on Mozart, but a film that deliberately contrasts that older text with a present-day sense of history, montage-like. It works in tandem with the opera, and the two texts are seen to need each other. Mozart's text enables a new articulation of the present, in the way it flashes up the past.

NOTES

1. See John Higgins, *Times*, 18 September 1980.
2. Walter Benjamin, 'Theses on the philosophy of history', *Illuminations*, trans. Harry Zohn (1970), p. 263.
3. On Jakobson, see David Lodge, *The modes of modern writing* (1977), pp. 73–124; Keir Elam, *The semiotics of theatre and drama* (1980), p. 20. See also Christian Metz, *The imaginary signifier*, trans. Celia Britton and others (Bloomington, 1977), part iv.
4. I am disagreeing here with the views of Peter Conrad, *Romantic opera and literary form* (1977) where he links the rise of nineteenth-century opera to the novel.
5. Deleuze (*Cinema 1: L'image-mouvement* (Paris, 1983), pp. 84–5) is quoted by Felicity Baker, 'Operatic character: cinematic form', *Paragraph* 4 (October 1984), pp. 20–61: see also her article 'Don Giovanni and the trapped spectator', *Quarto* (May 1982).
6. Julian Rushton, *W. A. Mozart: Don Giovanni* (Cambridge, 1981), p. 102.
7. Umberto Eco, *A theory of semiotics* (Bloomington, 1977), p. 7.
8. See Kierkegaard, *Either/Or*, trans. David F. Swenson and Lilian Marvin Swenson (New Jersey, 1971), i, p. 97.
9. Otto Rank, *The Don Juan legend*, trans. David G. Winter (New Jersey, 1975). This stresses the fear in Giovanni of women, presented as the avenging mother; and the homosexual component in Giovanni, with the commendatore as the father figure.

10. Michel Foucault, *The history of sexuality*, trans. Richard Hurley (Harmondsworth, 1981), p. 60.

11. For the distinctions between the *buffa* and the *seria*, see Edward J. Dent, *Mozart's operas* (Oxford, 1947), pp. 155–74, 185–7.

12. A. Gramsci, 'Passato e presente', *Quaderni del carcere* (Turin, 1951), vol. 6, p. 38. On the statement, see Thomas A. Bates, 'Gramsci and the theory of hegemony', *Journal of the history of ideas* 36 (1975), p. 358.

13. Quoted by Martyn Autry, *Monthly film bulletin* (September 1980), p. 175. Losey's detailed comments on his film are available in the Losey archives, donated to the British Film Institute. I have drawn on them fully.

14. Rodney Milnes, *What's on*, 26 September 1980.

15. Quoted by Michel Ciment, *Conversations with Losey* (1985), p. 370. The whole interview on *Giovanni* is relevant, though I have not felt bound by all of Losey's authorial interventions.

16. Christopher Ballantine, *Music and its social meanings* (New York, 1984); chapter 3, on Mozart, is worth reading.

17. Jacques Derrida, *Of grammatology*, trans. Gayatri Chakravorty Spivak (Baltimore, 1976), p. 244.

18. Ciment, *op. cit.*, p. 235, quotes Losey on the importance of statue-like positions for the characters in *The servant*, and on the importance of the statues. The master–servant relationship, the interest in the house, with the shots wandering through it, the architectural styles (Regency and Palladian)—these are important connectors between the films.

19. See James Leahy, *The cinema of Joseph Losey* (1967), p. 22, for Losey's use of Brechtian contradiction, and p. 133: 'The truth which *The servant* conveys is the truth which results from the dialectic between the movie and the individual members of the audience . . . *The servant* is an essentially Brechtian work.'

CHAPTER 9

Between the spectacle and the specular: *La traviata*

Zeffirelli's *La traviata* (1983) is more akin to *The magic flute* than *Don Giovanni* in its inspiration: cutting freely, ministering strongly to a market, and unprovocative in insight. At Cannes in 1982 Zeffirelli was recorded as saying that the consumer interest in opera-films was because of the lack of other spectacular musical films. 'One notices an increasing demand in the world for music and a desire to see the great singers in close-up.' The most beautiful film-opera remained *Jesus Christ superstar*, 'a great pastiche of the music and style of our society' (which music, which style?). This aspiration after Hollywoodian opulence goes with a moralism that is a reminder of *Jesus of Nazareth*: 'It's more difficult, of course, to adapt Verdi, Wagner, Rossini or Bizet to suit our consumer society'. Such a canon demands a worthy audience, it seems. With such confidence in the idea that opera makes the best musical, Zeffirelli, already unaffordable by Covent Garden in terms of fees, seems to be on his way up: at the time of writing, his *Otello* is virtually complete, and there is talk of an *Aida* as well. *Otello* comes with the same cameraman (Ennio Guarnieri) and Lorin Maazel conducting his third opera-film (James Levine conducts *La traviata*). Again, Zeffirelli presses the musical comparison: 'When was the last real musical? *Hello Dolly* perhaps? For the kids, there are, of course, the rock operas, but for an adult audience, films like my *Traviata* and Rosi's *Carmen* have won big new audiences everywhere.' And conveniently, the market's interests are art's interests too: 'Great performances such as

La Traviata. Teresa Stratas (Violetta). Courtesy Producer Sales Organisation (UK) Ltd; thanks to Franco Zeffirelli.

these offer an exercise in culture which is accessible to those
who want to feel they are looking at something of artistic
quality.'[1] What registers from this is a slightly disingenuous
simplicity: Zeffirelli does not seem to know enough to do more
than subjugate all other questions to the mere criterion of
whether it will look fine. His *Otello* looks as if it will suggest
that syphilis—for everyone had it then—and demonic possession
will do everything necessary to account for Otello, especially
in the scene of his delirium, at the end of Act III, and for Iago's
behaviour, his 'motiveless malignity', which is not at all
explained by Boito's insertion—perhaps under the inspiration
of *Mefistofele*—of his 'Credo in un Dio crudel'. What could it
possibly explain, to say that Iago happened to think that way?
It is not enough to leave everything to the power of the music,
and to the effect of the location-shooting, and to assume that
good and evil are wonderful absolutes: together, they can
explain everything. If Shakespeare needs the kind of strong
historicist criticism that will suggest that behind the confrontation between Othello and Iago there is the abuse of the
Caribbean's trust by the European mind,[2] then that kind of
insight cannot be left with Shakespeare: it ought to affect the
way that Verdi is seen: if nothing else. To film an opera is not
to be passive before it: to be passive is to collude at the
perpetuation of an older attitude, and to reduce the possibility
that the work might speak again, differently.

Otello plays on such strong myths, of ideal woman and
husband turned monster, an exhibit from Dr Caligari's cabinet,
that it remains a licence for an unthoughtful production that
stresses blasphemous and pagan rites—Iago's 'Credo' is sung in a
chapel—in contrast to the heroine's 'Ave Maria', that product
of late-nineteenth-century overstress on *pietà* in the face of
gathering secularism. It is a pity that Baldini did not live long
enough to complete his argument about *Otello* suffering from
Boito's preciosity: the challenge to the work's status needs
making.

Zeffirelli's enthusiasm for opera on film belongs to the cinema-
maker's interest in spectacle: what are the 1950s and 1960s
Biblical epics if not twentieth-century versions of grand opera?

And *Aida* clearly fits the requirements of film: its 'theatricality' (Verdi's term)[3] associates it with grand opera, and the desire for spectacle. In this sense, it is more interesting to look at *La traviata*: more domestic, intimate, less open to spectacle— though Zeffirelli has emphasised the latter, with the dancing getting faster and faster in Flora's party, with beautiful land- scapes, including a pastoral spot for Violetta to die in, with a stress on glitter generally. Mosco Carner refers to Verdi's 'elemental masculinity',[4] which ensures that of all the operas, only *Luisa Miller* (1849) and this one, based on the Dumas play, are named after women. The context for the name of Traviata (sung to the mirror in the Zeffirelli) defines the woman's necessary role as sufferer—'Ah della traviata sorridi al desio; A lei, deh, perdona; tu accoglia, o Dio'—this is striking contrast to, for example, the Duke in *Rigoletto*, whose wanderings sexually receive no ultimate criticism: where maleness is its own reward. Verdi's liaison with Giuseppina Strepponi is beside the point: the opera assumes a punitive attitude to the woman which Violetta's prayer at the end, where she asks pardon for the wanderer by the way, shows that she too has internalised and made her own.

It would have needed a director less bourgeois in his view of romantic love than Zeffirelli to have constructed a text out of the Verdi material that would do something with such anti- feminist sentiments, and that would have shown up the contra- dictions in the opera's conception, those based on the need to entertain a dual thought about the woman (both seeing her as eternal, trans-historical, essentially: in contrast to the male)— as the brilliant *demi-mondaine*, with sexual attractiveness that is deep opposition to the middle-class tradition that Germont represents, and as the Magdalen figure, who can be spoken to favourably on her deathbed, and who can be reunited safely with her lover once she's there. No opera more than this one needs its nineteenth-century costuming more: the 1700 costuming, discarded by Zeffirelli for the film, is a dangerous irrelevance: *pace* Budden, it *does* matter in the least in what epoch *La traviata* is set . . . its feelings are not those of 'individual humanity down the ages'.[5]

Zeffirelli's production captures the bourgeois notes of the work well, in creating a series of pastoral vignettes of Alfredo and Violetta together to go against his singing of 'De miei bollenti spiriti' at the beginning of Act II (just after the text has colluded in presenting an entirely fallacious view of Violetta as the emblem of female honour, by referring to the 'pompose feste' where she received homage from everyone on account of her beauty. If it's Alfredo who believes this, then his degree of self-deception about the function of those parties, and their brittle reality is horrifying: if it's Piave, the librettist, the text confirms its dishonesty at this point). Again, Germont *père*'s singing of 'Pura siccome un angelo' is accompanied by a sight of the daughter in Provence, about to enter into the state of marriage: it's a touch which yields itself to irony, thus adding another voice to the total number of texts within the film. It is possible to take both glimpses of the discreet charms of the bourgeoisie as being commented on for parodic effect, and it goes with that other strong element in the film—casting its whole action into the focus provided by preparations for an auction. Top-hatted bailiffs, right out of Daumier (so the *Observer*, 23 October 1983), are weighing up all Violetta's personal property and effects. The historical Marie Dupleissis's goods were auctioned off after her death in 1847, and the idea is incarnated in the Dumas novel: Zeffirelli's use of the idea here shows tact, and goes along with the reminders that the opera provides that the parties Violetta gives are financed by the Baron: that she needs, in Act II, to sell her possessions, and that she can be treated as a prostitute in the second party scene when Alfredo casts his winnings at her feet. These are the moments in the operatic text where it differs from itself: where it articulates the sense of the woman as a creation of a bourgeois taste, and finance. The text conceals something of that internal contradiction by making Violetta give her money to the poor via Annina in Act III: again, this is a moment that the film omits, perhaps because of its contradictory nature. (In the Dumas play Marguerite is obliged to sell a bracelet which she has received as a present, at this moment, and has to help finance a superannuated member of the *demi-monde*,

Prudence, who has come to her for help: thus sharpening the sense of the number of ways in which the woman pays.) Another way in which the film emphasises the nature of the care of the middle class is displayed where the father, after his first visit to Violetta, continues to lurk about in the gardens, to make sure that she is doing what he has told her to do.

These elements within the film are strong, yet they function as incidental criticisms only, and the sense of an unhappily interrupted idyll still lies firmly within the film's vision. More, to return to the opening point, its gaze is definitely male: the phrase belongs to E. Ann Kaplan's discussion of the objectifying of women in the cinema, just as her discussion there of Cukor's *Camille* is entirely relevant for any view of *La traviata*.[6] What there is of male looking inherent in the act of cinema-going itself (the darkened room, the individuated spectator, in no significant relationship to the person next to them, but gazing straight ahead, the element of sexual pleasure in looking which is played on) is intensified by the male gaze of the camera (usually controlled by a man) and the sense that in the film women are created as objects of male gaze, which the spectator—even if female—must identify with, because of the absence of a countervailing look. This is intensified in the film of *La traviata*. The film opera opens with a view of Paris and Notre Dame (another accentuation being given to the virgin–whore split that underpins the vision of women held by the opera), and then moves into the apartments of Violetta, very bleak and smokey-blue; this being while the orchestra is playing the first act prelude— that haunting theme which in Act II will become the 'orgiastic outpouring' of emotion[7] at 'Amami Alfredo': love me, Alfredo. The prelude may be read as a musical portrait of Violetta, intimating her death, as it will be re-heard at the opening of Act III when she is on her deathbed; and it conveys a sense of her yearning. Zeffirelli's use of this thematic material is intelligent, as the opening shots of Violetta's apartments, with bailiffs in attendance, lead to the sight of Violetta herself, consumptive and dying, gazing into the mirror, and evoking all the incidents of Acts I and II as a flashback, so that the return of the Act III preludes unifies the time and place, and continues with the present after these visions of the past. But what needs accentuating, however, is not the deftness of the unifying, but the way that Violetta is shown to be under the male gaze of the bailiffs, so that she turns from these where she is objectified as the famous Parisian courtesan, to objectify herself in the glass. That implies many interesting concomitants: the elements of fantasy, of dream fulfilment in watching a film which psychoanalytic critics have drawn attention to are acted out here as the fantasy is generated by the gazing into the mirror: a film within a film is set up, and the male fantasies that play about the notion of the infinitely desirable woman (who will die, however: the consumption that she carries around with her being the adequate superego for *this* society) are continued into the fantasies Violetta continues to create *as* object—while the orchestral theme of passionate yearning lasts. (The theme, it will be recalled, is heard just at the point when Violetta is leaving Alfredo, and is thus one doomed to be left merely as the expression of desire, as having nothing more tangible than that: 'Amami Alfredo' can only be sung precisely because there is no chance of his being able to do that except in nostalgia and hopeless regret.) The film enacts the sense of being held in a state of mere desire which the opera fails to lift itself from.

Further, the inward, specular gaze, looking in the mirror, as the father does at the end when he wonders what he has done, is structural to the whole film, as to the technique of flashback, and recalls Lacan's 'mirror stage', discussed earlier in Chapter 2. It will be recalled that it has to do with the moment that the child recognises its own image and thus begins to see itself in ideal form. Laura Mulvey comments on it that it occurs when 'the child's physical ambitions outstrip his motor capacity, with the result that his recognition of himself is joyous in that he imagines his mirror image to be more complete, more perfect than he experiences his own body. Recognition is thus overlaid with misrecognition: the image recognised is conceived as the reflected body of the self, but its misrecognition as superior projects this body outside itself as an ideal ego, the alienated subject, which reintrojected as an ego ideal, gives rise to the future identification with others. This mirror moment predates language for the child.'[8] What is important here is the sense that the mirror stage begins the phase of thinking of the self as separate, alienated, not the same as the body that feels and suffers. From there it is a short step, in Lacanian thinking, to the entry into the symbolic state—that which is imposed through the agency of the Father. For the woman (and Ann Kaplan refers to the psychoanalytic work of Nancy Chodorow here), the presence of the Father imposes a double loss on the female—firstly, and in a way common to the male, because here is the entering in of the Law (because the Father is not part of a dyadic relationship of mother–child, but a third term),[9] with the reduction to language of what the already split self is, so that the self is not articulated through discourse, but remains always poised in a state of desire, and secondly, in a way unique to the female, because the presence of the father and the existence of the phallus confirms her plight to be one of loss. She is in the position of need as far as the male goes, and her link with the mother is broken, for the mother has also the phallic lack, and the separation is accentuated by the way the mother has had a child, which is to replace that lack. Only through motherhood can there be a return to the mother, then.

The device of the mirror in Zeffirelli's film, however intentional or not, opens the work away from the merely cinematic, in Barthes's terms, to the filmic,[10] and makes it possible to construct a reading that also exposes several aporias in Verdi's conception. Perhaps cinema-going itself is a regressive activity, harking back to the mirror stage and to those early fantasies; as Rosemary Jackson puts it, 'to get back, on the far side of the mirror, becomes a powerful metaphor for returning to an original unity, a "paradise" lost by the "fall" into division with the construction of a subject'.[11] Exactly so, and Violetta's gazing not only comments as a metalanguage upon the activity of cinema-going but also images her split-off stage, her position as the woman whose subjectivity has been constituted as a *traviata*, a sinner, someone who can have no authentic emotions of her own. Just as the cinematic selves we greet on the screen from our darkened places in the stalls are the *Je-idéal*, the perfect bodies that invite identification and a marking out of the sense of difference, so the self that Violetta, worn down by the tuberculosis, that symbol of the self as divided against itself, looks at in the swirling dance music of Act I, represents her in a different order, a state of desire which leads to a return to the imaginary order—that state of non-individuation, of union. The moments of rest and games with Alfredo come in here: though I have previously suggested that they might be seen as lightly ironised (and certainly Domingo suggests the bourgeois more than he does the lover), it might also help to see them as an attempted capture of the imaginary order before the law of the Father—Germont *père*—supervenes. Framing, then, the film by means of the mirror and the flashback, following a hint in Verdi, with his use of preludes, gives to all the events the quality of something dream-like, of a fantasy; what we are seeing is the expression of Violetta's subjectivity not a wholly objective account. Stressing this idea would intensify further the notion that Violetta's self, constituted not only psychoanalytically but sociologically by her place in Parisian society, as a creature of desire, of someone who is working out of a sense of loss, makes the incidents the way they are, reads Alfredo, for instance, as both lover and father at the same time, splits the desired male into those two aspects that the female cannot reconcile in the male—that he must epitomise both desire and the law. To see these qualities in two men, father and son, only emphasises the way that both attributes are contained within the same person. Actually, both opera and film show themselves aware of this split, in that solo for Violetta that closes Act I, 'E strano!'. After the recitative, she moves into her aria in the mirror key reflecting 'fors'e lui', as she thinks that Alfredo managed to turn her fever into the fire of love. At that point the change to the major is effected, as she moves into the expression of 'quell'amor ch'e palpito / dell' universo intero / misterioso altero / croce e delizia al cor' (that love that throbs, belonging to the whole world, mysterious, exalted, curse and delight to the heart). It is a powerful emotion this, related to her own theme heard in the prelude (not yet sung, of course), and, interestingly, Alfredo's music: when she begins to describe love it is important to note that she has no language of her own, she must borrow from the male. It is a point that should be taken in feminist reading of *La traviata*: it is not just that thus far Violetta has no experience of love, and therefore cannot articulate a sense of it (that point would, equally, apply to Alfredo), it is that love for her is part of the ordering of language that comes from the male: she has no language which is authentically hers. After that highly emotive note, she rejects the passion as folly, and turns to her cabaletta, which is sung by Teresa Stratas in the film with vivid coloratura that conveys a giddiness and strain in the character—'sempre libera degg'io / Folleggiare di gioia in gioia' (always free, I ought to go from pleasure to pleasure). The antithesis between andante and cabaletta makes more than a musical point; it has to do with the split in the perception of the male she has. 'Sempre libera' is the rejection of the male as father, of the idea of law. Though she articulates to herself the sense that she ought to please herself only, since she is a lonely woman in this 'popoloso deserto / che appellano Parigi', it is important to see there is a displacement here: she is not being asked to make a choice between loneliness and pleasure, but love and pleasure, and the split is rendered musically: the cabaletta flurrying perhaps implying the criticism of this female desire for liberty rather than for the male.

The 'croce' (the cross), that is one side of love is felt more by the female than the male: it is what is involved in being linked with the male as representative of bourgeois order. Hence the excitement as she breaks into the cabaletta: an overwrought passion, complete with traditional breaking of the champagne glass against the mirror, to break any ideal sense of herself, and the running from room to room, going like a caught bird. All this time, Alfredo is singing offstage, with harp accompaniment (recalling Act III of *Trovatore*, and the offstage singing of 'La donna è mobile' from *Rigoletto*)—that singing which in that work establishes the supremacy of male desire, and its indomitable nature. It is a similarly privileged voice, here, too: accentuated in this version by Zeffirelli showing him singing in the courtyard, outside, in the rain: the director's enthusiasm for musicals will be recalled, and the Gene Kelly echo may be intentional. The point is that the male singing that hypnotic melody increases the sense of a trap: makes the necessity to run from room to room more pressing. The harping may make Alfredo a troubadour just temporarily, or even like 'a visitation from, or a vision of, a better world', as Kimbell suggests,[12] and they fit with the film's lushness of treatment, which is aimed, as surely as the Verdi is, and as the musical may be thought to be, in catching the spectator in an emotional complicity, so that a sob in the throat is the appropriate response to the work. None the less, both these responses to Alfredo, while partly true, are partial: for both seem very male points: what seems more interesting is the dramatising, in Violetta, of the split she intuits, of her sense that in the way her subjectivity has been constituted, there can be no satisfactory male relationship. In Violetta's fevered mind at this point, Alfredo actually appears to her in her apartment, ready to take her in his arms, and for this 'vision' section, the acoustic of the recording was subtly altered.[13] The frequent visions of Alfredo make him inescapable, a *huis clos*. Male dominance is projected further in the film, then, through Violetta's own internalisation of the nature of a love relationship.

The cabaletta after Alfredo's initial Act II aria is omitted in the film: there is no 'O mio rimorse! O infamia'. There has been a fashion in Verdi criticism to wish the cabalettas away as relics of older styles of operatic writing, but there seems an important logic to this one: it is the sequel to his sense of having been tamed by her love, that he should suddenly break into this passion. The libretto makes the excuse the sense that he has not given heed to his financial affairs as he should—has not been the complete bourgeois, while honeymooning with Violetta; but it seems important that there is a displacement here: that the remorse *is* that of the bourgeois, who, having idealised the relationship in ways suggested above, now realises its improper basis, its questionable shape. The film's softening of this note of anguish seems to exemplify its weakness in accepting some of the clichés about Verdi as composer, in allowing this cabaletta to be wished away. It would have been a more interesting reading that could have played up the opposition between the bourgeois in his words and his meaning: that could have exposed the complex basis that underlies Alfredo's attitude to Violetta, and that associates him with the father. For the father's association with Violetta is similarly ambiguous and Freudian: Cornell McNeil in the film looks the perfect member of the bourgeoisie, but is it possible to suspect Zeffirelli of having nothing more in his mind than trying to involve static direction and a monotonous placing of two characters, by giving the vision of the pure daughter in Provence, when much sharper points could have been made. These would have centred on the way the father can only free himself and his son from the impermissible force of Violetta by idealising his daughter: the way that he replaces, in the course of the opera, this pure daughter by the 'other' daughter, Violetta, and the way that his attitudes to her seems to display a sublimation of a sexuality. Father and son seem to come together in more ways than one during the course of the opera: it is more than just the triumph of the bourgeoisie that it witnessed at the end when Alfredo and Violetta are together under the permission of the father, as though middle-class marriage was being evoked: it is also a proxy relationship whereby the father possesses the girl. The film does see some of those ironies, though it is hard to be sure, especially when it is such 'safe' material as Verdi, and so uncritical a director as Zeffirelli, one who sees 'society past and present with rather optimistic eyes . . .', who deals with 'great values, great feelings with competence and extreme professionalism'.[14] But the film is clearly thinking of something when at the end there's a glimpse of that ideal daughter again, this time with a five-year-old child! (The time sequence, of course, has been distorted.) A feminist reading of the film-as-text might suggest that what is important here is the suppression of the idea of motherhood for Violetta: the role of mothering having, in Julia Kristeva's terms, a potentially subversive role (though motherhood is more usually seen as the instrument whereby women are fully stereotyped, brought into the male symbolic (and economic) order). Ann Kaplan traces in Sternberg's treatment of Dietrich the suppression of the idea of motherhood, and the intention to eliminate fears of female sexuality, and she discusses how, in Kristeva's terms, in motherhood the woman is 'closer to her instinctual memory, more open to her own psychosis, and consequently, more negatory of the social symbolic bond'.[15] Violetta's state of non-motherhood acts out further the way she is created by male desire. In giving the sister a child, the film may wish to emphasise sentiment, but the signification is open, anyway, and the other reading may be constructed.

Germont *père* upholds the bourgeois patriarchal order, and the opera allows itself some moments of irony in reflecting upon him: especially in his aria 'Di Provenza il mar'—sometimes thought of as a bit of fustian to meet the requirements of the baritone. It seems subtler than that by its placing, immediately after the return of the old man to the house to discover Alfredo distraught over the news just received that Violetta has gone. It involves an idealisation of the bourgeois way of life, but this is set against the lacuna left by her going. The choice is stark, the appeal fake, and what there is of triteness in the aria's strophic form makes its criticism. But for whom is the aria sung? Merely for Alfredo? Or also for the old man himself, whose second need to idealise that afternoon this is? Kimbell's comment on the lyric is apt—'The objective statement is followed by the catch in the throat, the intimation that Germont is emotionally involved himself, and from that stage he works himself up into a kind of spiritual exultation.'[16] The film is not able to bring out this level of irony: it follows the text lamely, cannot construct a reading. It would have been a finer and more discriminating work had it brought more to awareness the contradictions apparent in the father—in the symbolic code itself, that is, in the way meaning and order are arranged in bourgeois society, that had been able to suggest that the internal contradictions that Germont and his music knows, but which the libretto knows perhaps less (since its purpose is wholly served by its only needing to be functional) have produced the decidedly ambivalent relationships that underpin Germont's attitudes to Violetta. The father–daughter theme is Verdian anyway: it belongs to his abortive wish to set *King Lear*.[17] But Violetta is not supposed to be anyone's daughter: that she finds

herself so unaccountably under this old man's domination—
and more, that she puts *herself* there, giving herself more of a
'croce' than she had before—says a great deal, probably, about
the element of the 'law' in Verdi himself, and certainly suggests
that there is a lot to be said for a reading of the text that sees
it as the fundamental way in which woman is driven under the
subjection of the symbolic order, from which she cannot
extricate herself, though she may have fantasies about doing
so; may have wishes about returning to a state of primary self-
absorption, where she is complete unto herself. Usefully,
Baldini emphasises that *La traviata* is about sacrifice:[18] but it
needs a more precise documentation to see that sacrifice is
ideologically suspect; that it belongs to the male order that
ensures that it is something Violetta does all the time, and
which means to destroy. Zeffirelli shows little of this kind of
awareness. Gilbert Adair points out the presence of that haunting 'Zeffirellian ephebe in the guise of a furniture remover'[19]
whose sympathetic gaze in the Act I and III preludes follows
Violetta and seems to display the readiness of male youth to
fall for the older woman in her sickness. She is made thus a
creature of positive sexuality: it is an important countervailing
note, perhaps, but elsewhere there is little sense of the positive.

What would help would be more sense of the '*croce* e delizia',
but this is provided by Radin Gabrea's film *Ein Mann wie Eva
(A man like Eva)* made just after the Zeffirelli, probably with
some knowledge of it, and commenting alike on *La traviata* and
La dame aux camélias, as well upon Fassbinder, who is portrayed
directing a film of the Dumas play with Verdian backgrounds,
and in love with both his Marguerite (Lisa Kreuzer) and his
Armand (Werner Stocker). The film is a highly melodramatic
expansion of some facets of Fassbinder's own life, with his
lover (Charly Muhamed Huber) committing suicide, and the
Marguerite finally killing the Armand to keep Eva (Eva Mattes)
who has married her during the course of the film. Fassbinder
actually had married Ingrid Caven, a member of his own stock
company, and after their divorce had made *In einem Jahr mit
13 Monden* (1978) with her and Eva Mattes. All the cast, crew
and director are gathered in one derelict old country house to

film: the camera moves from room to room as it does in the Zeffirelli. The ironies that play about this film are directed at Fassbinder here, not least in the way the role is taken by a woman, though the ironies play round her, too, and the suggestions of what her life off-screen must be or have been (hence the title): they equally work against Verdi and Dumas. The words 'quell' amo ch' e palpito . . . croce e delizia al cor' run throughout and strikingly during the film: so does Callas's voice singing 'Amami Alfredo', defining that position of desire and hopeless yearning. What is at work in the film is how the 'croce' can really work where the audience is not merely the censoring bourgeoisie. Thus Eva forces Lisa Kreuzer to crawl along the floor while on set, thus re-writing the moment of humiliation Alfredo subjects Violetta to when she faints in Flora's arms, making the point about subjection the more painful when it is not to the background of sensuous Verdian passion that inevitably dignifies the sufferer and gives her a pleasure in pain. Similarly, the male lover of Eva hangs himself after his rejection; and thus brings out fully that element of masochism that hangs over the opera, and explains why 'croce e delizia' goes into the minor key; and in key with this, Eva fancies himself as the dying heroine of Act III of *Traviata*, planning a James Dean-type car crash. But his security is maintained: he is, as it were, turned from being a Violetta to being an Alfredo (he had wanted the former part because he had witnessed his Marguerite and Armand making love: it is *his* masochism). What keeps him safe is that Lisa Kreuzer murders Werner Stocker (who has, after all, been made love to by Eva) as a rival and substitute for her husband's love. It must be the woman who remains the *traviata*: so the last few moments of the screenplay imply, as Lisa Kreuzer dances with blood-stained hands—this film's version of the camellias—while, in true melodramatic style, in the next room, the Armand lies dead with a knife in his chest.

It may not be the *ne plus ultra* of those various shifts of the Dumas play: but it must have the effect of relativising Zeffirelli's vision. His film, in turn, belongs with the twenty-three films that have been made of the Dumas text up to 1981, as well as the infinite number of stage *Traviatas*; it cannot be considered in isolation; for its meaning and significance is a matter of the way it changes ways of seeing these, as well as those other films and presentations modifying it. Itself, it is a homage to the absent Callas, with whom Zeffirelli had wanted to make the film. 'The long straggling hair, blue-blackened sleepless eyes, flimsy nightgown and pale, ghostly presence—all are hallmarks of that earlier definitive performance.'[20] The mirror image gains further suggestions. Myth is built on myth. Just as the idea of the irresistible woman outside normal society is a highly literary conception—Dumas's heroine owes something to *Manon Lescaut*, a text Verdi had some thought of setting before going for *La dame aux camélias*, it also owes something to *Scènes de la vie de Bohème*, which appeared between 1847 in serial form. Mérimée's *Carmen* and the myth of the gypsy even lies somewhere near the opera (the appearance of the gypsies at Flora's party has some point, after all). At any rate, *La traviata* belongs *now* with *Carmen*, *Manon* and *La Bohème* in its evocation of the beautiful woman who lies dead at the end, utterly marginalised (the price for still living, if a female, in *La Bohème*, is to be the prostitute, Musetta, whom no one takes seriously). The creation of life by literature, and particularly operatic literature, is the point. Callas, whose life on and offstage becomes as much of a myth as the nineteenth-century heroines she plays, demonstrates the way the myth continues: the woman must be invested with continuing evanescent, somehow mysterious powers. *La traviata* is a text based on further texts: the endowing of Marie Duplessis with the mythical qualities she was given ensures that behind the woman is a further series of texts. What is important about these is what they want to affirm about the position of women in relationship to the dominant male order. Callas fits too well within that sense of the need to mystify the woman, to cast over her the quality of myth, so that the singer, as in this film, becomes textualised—and the film thus guarantees that in spite of—or rather because of—its beauty, its visual appeal, its daringness in movement and dance—it can say little that is new about the Traviata theme: can only perpetuate the old myths.

In the opera house, that is something usual: in any case, the same revival may stand for years and thus foster its own myths as audiences see it again and again. In the art of the cinema, where the equipment of the opera house was available, with international stars, the Bolshoi dancers, and evocative and attractive location-shots of Paris, it seems disappointing that no rethinking of the myth should have gone on, but that rather the same form of traditionalism should have been pursued. Yet film, like dream-work, opens itself up to signification, and the film is open-ended, a text to be read by the spectator so that he/she is not necessarily to be impelled by the myth and thus to be, in part, created by it. It loves that myth of a fun-bent Paris, and it colludes in it, but it also opens up aporias within the text. Only something with the hardness of *A Man like Eva*, with its trust in the open nature of the text, could go further, and show some of the further implications of romantic love as idealised by Alfredo, and as absorbed into herself by Violetta. The last shots, when she says 'rinasce', and we see her and Alfredo in the pastoral world together again before she dies on the carpet in the room she is really in—are no return to that possible imaginary order, but seem more like Zeffirelli's sentiment at work, endorsing the idea too fully of sacrifice.

NOTES

1. I have quoted Zeffirelli out of the files of the British Film Institute, and from John Francis Lane, in *Screen International* no. 526 (7–14 December 1985). Among the many reports on *Otello* in progress, see Norman Lebrecht in the *Sunday Times* colour supplement, 9 March 1986.
2. See on this Stephen Greenblatt, *Renaissance self-fashioning* (Chicago, 1980), pp. 232–54.
3. Letter of Verdi quoted in Julian Budden, *Verdi* (1985), p. 272.
4. Mosco Carner, *Puccini: a critical biography* (1958), p. 232.
5. Julian Budden, *The operas of Verdi*, vol. 2 (1978), p. 165.
6. E. Ann Kaplan, *Women and film: both sides of the camera* (1983), p. 41 especially.
7. David R.B. Kimbell, *Verdi in the age of Italian romanticism* (Cambridge, 1981), p. 656.
8. Quoted in *Women and the cinema: a critical anthology*, ed. Karyn Kay and Gerald Peary (New York, 1977), pp. 416–17.
9. See Juliet Mitchell, *Psychoanalysis and feminism* (Harmondsworth, 1975), p. 392.
10. Roland Barthes, *Image, music, text*, trans. Stephen Heath (1977), pp. 64–8.

11. Rosemary Jackson, *Fantasy: the literature of subversion* (1981), p. 89.
12. Kimbell, *op. cit.*, p. 657.
13. See review in *Classical music* (11 June 1983).
14. Comment on Zeffirelli, *Screen International* (12 November 1983).
15. Kaplan, *op. cit.*, p. 203, quoting from Julia Kristeva, *Desire in Language* (Oxford, 1980).
16. Kimbell, *op. cit.*, p. 663.
17. G. Baldini, *The story of Giuseppe Verdi*, trans. Roger Parker (Cambridge, 1981), p. 97.
18. *Ibid.*, p. 190.
19. Review in *Monthly Film Bulletin* (November 1983).
20. Review by Stephen Pickles, *TLS* (11 November 1983). Zeffirelli wished to film *La traviata* in the 1950s, but his first opera-film was a version of *La Bohème* (1965), using the La Scala, Milan, production of 1963. His *Otello*, for Cannon, has Domingo as Otello, Justino Diaz as Iago, Katia Ricciarelli as Desdemona, uses the chorus and orchestra of La Scala, and was pre-recorded, with locations in southern Italy (Barletta—near Bari); in Umbria and Venice, and in Crete, at Iraklion.

Too late for this book, *Otello* opened in London on 22 September 1986. Its cutting (reducing the text to two hours, with startling omissions, e.g. 'Fuoco di gioia', the concertato at the end of Act 2, and the 'Willow Song'); its poorish sound-track (the initial storm almost unheard above the sound effects); and its abrupt scenic switches to increase the stress on the spectacular ensured that the film received largely tepid reviews. Domingo's singing, while resonant, had no sense of a man moving into excess of *gelosia*, or passionate convulsion. In line with that, he did not kill Desdemona on the bed, nor die on it himself. The internalised distorted sexuality of Otello was strikingly missed, as though it could not be handled. The nearest the film approached to a treatment of the sexual was a set of shots of Cassio in onanistic mood, to accompany Iago's fantasising 'Era la notte': presumably to indicate sexual tensions in Iago himself. Yet one visual motif that recurred was the sense of looking out—through windows, through bars, through distorting mirrors, via flashbacks; this idea backed up the sense of voyeurism incarnated in the action, that is, a feature of the text itself, Shakespeare's and Boito's, in its invitation to an audience to look on the corruption of its central character, and which is further generated by the actual conditions of cinema viewing. The film could have embodied the sexual if it had wished.

I think it did not because it was being traditionally 'operatic': reactionary and sentimental (even to reprising the *bacio* music over the last credits). Its near racism was apparent in its creation of Oriental motifs in both the people of Cyprus and Otello in a manner that finely illustrates Said's thesis. It was encrusted with Catholicism: a Grünewald-like Christ crucified was shown during the Credo, again at the end of Act 2 (the moment, which, according to Budden, 'the unsophisticated [sic] find . . . the most enjoyable in the opera'), and again during 'Tu alfin clemenza' in Act 3. Passive suffering was endorsed; the film allowed no feminist critique of the male maligning of Desdemona. Despite Zeffirelli's liberties with the text, no new reading emerged.

CHAPTER 10

The fusion of Brecht and Wagner: Syberberg's *Parsifal*

Parsifal, 'ein Bühenweihfestspiel'—'a stage dedication festival play'—opened at Bayreuth in the summer of 1882, a year before Wagner's death: the intention being that it should be performed there always, as a prelude to the Bayreuth festival, and nowhere else. A hundred years later, Syberberg booked the cinema at Bayreuth to run his film in opposition to the festival, thus combining three motifs that are central to the film's vision: the sense that the film is a report on the first hundred years of *Parsifal*; that film, not opera in the theatre provides the *Gesamtkunstwerk*, and that the terms of reference for 1882, that make it a play, and that sacralise it as an opera even more than conventional opera house productions do with the works in their repertoire, must not be allowed to stand.

The film cannot be seen in isolation from the *Hitler* trilogy: from *Ludwig, requiem for a German king* (1972) (co-eval with Visconti's *Ludwig II*, a more conventional bio-pic treatment, with its own operatic opulence), *Karl May* (1974) and *Hitler: a film from Germany* (1977). There were, too, films that were by-products of this: *Ludwig's cook* (1972) and the *Confessions of Winifred Wagner* (1975).[1] Behind each of these is the fascination with the imbrication of high art, of German romanticism, in Nazism, high culture and Fascism. It is the subject of *Doctor Faustus*, and it prompts Adorno's statement that Auschwitz has made poetry impossible,[2] liberal cultural values having been appropriated so easily by the right. Winifred Wagner on film refuses to see any connection between the Hitler she admired,

Parsifal. Edith Clever (Kundry) and Karin Krick (Parsifal).
Courtesy Artificial Eye.

intelligent and courteous and perceptive about Wagner's music and the way that *Parsifal* should be revived, and the misery of the third Reich: that is, culture is not political. It will be remembered how the right always sees politics as something engaged in by the left: what the right does is far more natural. The films suggest that cultural value is not inherent to a text: Ludwig built kitsch castles, products of a middle-class taste, and also admired Wagner; Hitler founded himself on *Lohengrin* and *Rienzi*, and would have made a religion out of *Parsifal*, but his other enthusiasm was Karl May (1842–1912), writer of Westerns. 'Anyone who knows what Karl May was for generations of Germans, how every schoolboy grew up with his books, knows how close we are here to a history of German feeling, the adventures of the soul and myths of the good, the German who fights for noble things and triumphs'.[3] Karl May's fusing of America and Germany (a theme in Edgar Reitz's *Heimat*), explains why the Statue of Liberty is seen going down at the beginning of *Parsifal*, destroyed along with Berlin and other German towns in the Allied bombings, seen in photographs floating in a slimy pool. Wagner becomes as escapist as the castles and as Karl May's work: thus Syberberg concentrates on what is cheap and flashy in the opera: when Gurnemanz (Robert Lloyd, looking much younger than the traditional singers of this role) leads Parsifal into the Grail temple in Act III, they walk up steps into what turns out to be a blow-up of Wagner's silk dressing gown, the indispensable insignia of the bourgeois mind behind the music: it will be remembered that Patrice Chéreau in the centenary *Ring* at Bayreuth made Wotan wear the same dressing gown.

In Syberberg's opera-film, as is not the case with the other opera-films discussed here, the composer is on trial. The thesis of *From Caligari to Hitler* was crucial to *Hitler: a film from Germany*, in that Syberberg was there fascinated with the cinematic aspects of the Reich: not only did German Expressionist films of the 1920s make Hitler possible, but the Reich mobilised film itself, and perished leaving only celluloid behind. To say that mass movements favour the art that uses mechanical reproduction,[4] to think of totalitarianism being enabled by technology, so that sound added to film is an important aspect of the growing power of the Nazis, is to begin to make the point. *Heimat*, too, is a commentary on the connections between developing communication technology and the rise of Fascism and the later possibilities of thinking in global terms about destruction. But the point could be furthered in saying that the Reich functioned in an analogous way to the film studio. Leni Riefenstahl suggests this in saying that the Nuremberg Rally of 1934, which was given documentary treatment, 'was planned not only as a spectacular mass meeting—but as a spectacular propaganda film . . . the ceremonies and precise plans of the parades, marches, processions, the architecture of the halls and stadium were designed for the convenience of the cameras'.[5] This fusion between art and life, going further than Benjamin's sense of the 'aestheticisation of politics' involved in Fascism, indicates that the Reich offers itself as the complete living out of a fantasy fuelled by a new technology: the realm of personal subjectivity and of image-making has become real. The silent viewer in the darkened cinema plays out fantasies in looking at the cinema screen, is pushed towards regressive behaviour in sitting still, like a child, passively taking in the cinematic image. The spectator is drawn into complete identification with the image, as the child was in Lacan's mirror-stage: thus is created as subject of that cinematic discourse by identification, both with the camera's gaze which has constituted the image (and which the spectator fits into without a gap between) and with the image, which, child-like, he/she cannot refuse. Hitler, on the basis of this psychoanalytic reading, derived from Christian Metz's sense of the 'imaginary signifier', becomes the representative of the imaginary of the German mentality in the 1930s: the imaginary being that state of lost plenitude the child identifies with. The American screenings of *Hitler* changed the title to *Our Hitler . . .*, thus implying the spectator's complicity in what is projected on the screen. Timothy Corrigan, who discusses the film in such psychoanalytic terms, makes a further point when he adds that Hitler is 'the repressed presence permeating the vast majority of commercial films since 1945'.[6] The image, suppressed, needs exorcism.

But that connection of art and life, with its sense that the Reich was a film coming soon to a cinema near us, lies behind *Parsifal* and Bayreuth, which might be seen as the original Odeon with the darkened auditorium. An opera where applause at the end of the first act is suppressed, where the composer meditates on secret brotherhoods and Bayreuth freemasonries around the time of writing, so that the pursuit of the Grail is in some ways akin to the experience gained from listening to a performance of the work[7] —these things suggest a mystification which Syberberg responds to by allowing Kundry to cradle the Grail in her arms at the end—as a model of Bayreuth under glass, an image of the lost innocence striven towards, the full presence of the imaginary where full subjectivity is experienced with nothing objective to intrude. A Wagnerian music-drama itself refuses to accept limits on its own fantasy, but strains itself towards extremes, of tonality and of feeling, to the limits of instruments, as with the trumpets pushed to the top of their register on the third repeat of the initial Love-Feast–suffering–spear phrase at the beginning of the Prelude. In Verdi, the curtain comes down every twenty minutes or so: the listener never forgets the theatrical nature of the experience: has, indeed, to applaud the leading singers every so often. That ironises what has gone before: prevents the fantasy from being dominant on its own terms: in that space—certainly not brief—singers negotiate a new role with the audience, neither quite acting in role nor yet not quite just themselves either. The lack of applause for the end of Act I of *Parsifal* is already cinematic. Wagner's seamlessness, leitmotifs, use of a continuous onward drive, desire for an invisible orchestra, and (half-jokingly) for an invisible stage—all these suggest a world-without-end fantasy, that will entirely interpellate the audience as subjects of its discourse. 'Du siehst, mein Sohn, zum Raum wird hier die Zeit' Gurnemanz tells Parsifal as they enter the Grail castle: 'you see, my son, here time becomes space'. It is an apt comment on the Bayreuth ideology, which involves the collapsing of historical detail and reality into an attempted timelessness, a mythological space, that, by being fantasy, eludes definition. (One of the hazards of reading Wagner criticism is the swathes of source material about mythologies that are found necessary to be gone through. Mythology, rather than history holds its fascination for nearly every Wagnerian.) Gurnemanz's line is sung as the Transformation music accompanies a scene change that is conceived of in almost cinematic terms; Gurnemanz could be singing about the power of the screen.

Already, then, there are ambiguities: Wagner opera is already the cinema of the future, and not Losey's cinema which involves narrative, and Syberberg is pre-empted. Yet, of course, he has projected *Parsifal* forwards, and is examining its importance as a twentieth-century text. The studio set is the death-mask of Wagner, upon which the characters climb, and which divides to allow people to emerge from its depths, as Kundry appears from under water, and as the flower maidens are seen in a valley formed by the parting of the mask under the nose. Wagner is the site upon which a number of readings of the text have been mounted in the last hundred years. The film begins with models of the first Bayreuth production, and moves from there. The inspiration is Brechtian: Brecht's dislike of the *Gesamtkunstwerk* which belongs to Wagnerian conceptions of the theatre speaks again. He uses Brecht wilfully: his own desire to see the cinema as 'the total work of art of our age' notwithstanding. Whereas Wagnerian ideas seek to gather up and unify, in Romantic fashion, the better to assail the spectator and secure complicity in the experience, Brechtian techniques insist on maintaining distinctions: 'words, music and setting must become most independent of one another'.[8] Thus the theatricality of the experience is stressed: not even the Good Friday flowers are real. The dubbing is done so that there is no synchrony between music and camera on actors/singers: we look at one while hearing another. The music was pre-recorded, and only two singers, Robert Lloyd and Aage Haugland, a young looking Klingsor (indeed, there is a strong stress on youth in the production), also act: other performances were taken by actors, only some of them professional. Amfortas (sung by Wolfgang Schone) was presented by the conductor,

Armin Jordan, whose facial gestures while trying to wrest a performance out of the Monte Carlo Philharmonic so impressed Syberberg that he gave him the part of the king with the wound; thus offering a sly comment on the extremities implied in Wagner's music and on the posturing that so often is encouraged when the camera is allowed to record concert performances, where expressions of angst on musicians' faces are taken to imply profundity of emotion. Armin Jordan defended pre-recording in an interview, saying 'a singer, obliged to sing with only half his voice (in order to hear the soundtrack) will never have the same gestures that he has singing normally. He can't wear headphones either (which permit him to sing in full voice), because the cameras are rolling'. But the inaccuracies in the dubbing were deliberate as was everything else that was alienating and found offensive by the reviewers: the use of puppets—to suggest the manipulations of life effected through Wagner, and the child-like quality of the imagination. Indeed, the set often looked like a child's ruined nursery—and the use of backdrops (Bosch, Titian, Caspar Friedrich), and the asynchronic stress in the production ideas.

Syberberg has picked up on negative critiques of *Parsifal*, from Nietzsche to Robert Gutman, who have reacted negatively to the overlay of Victorian Christianity, with its pre-Raphaelite, Sacré-Coeur-like overstatement and delight in masochism. Neither the attempts of Lucy Beckett, who tries to read *Parsifal* as though it were as (pseudo-) English as *Four Quartets*, nor the spirited defence of Mike Ashman, who tries to read the text for religiously syncretic and socialist views, seem to me to negate some of these criticisms, which seem ably embodied in Nietzsche's comment that Wagner's music never danced,[9] so that in that sense it negates contact with the human body: the contrast being, of course, for Nietzsche, with Verdi and Bizet. Negative critiques have picked up on the knot of ideas associated with the ultimate rejection of the woman, the refusal of sexuality, and the desire to lapse out—Kundry's 'O ewiger Schlaf / einziges Heil / wei . . . wie dich gewinnen'—'oh endless sleep, only release, how can I win you?' (Act II). Only suffering until

that time of consummation can be reached, is possible.
'Dienen . . . dienen'—'let me serve'—are Kundry's only words
in Act III; until she dies at the end, she is carrying out a ritual-
istic service at the feet of Parsifal, her passivity musically
enacting her desire for negation. That passivity is crucial. The
only act Parsifal performs, the killing of a swan, is blameable;
his central deed is a refusal—a denial of Kundry's kiss. In this
shortest libretto of Wagner, with least action, most feeling
and most tableau-like, with Acts I and II in strict symmetry,
there seems something missing: Gutman may overstate in
seeing Parsifal as the young Aryan leader, but still he is to be
a positive force. None the less there is little spontaneity, and
the rejection of the flower maidens, themselves reduced to a
near banality of melody, lacks delight. Adorno's point about
Tannhäuser in Act III is relevant: 'sickness and desire become
confounded in a point of view that imagines that the forces of
life can only be maintained by the suppression of life. In the
Wagnerian theatre, desire sinks to the level of caricature . . . In
a regression familiar from the process of bourgeois education
and known to psychoanalysis as "syphilophobia", sex and
sexual disease become identical'. Adorno sees Wagner's art as
involved in 'the conversion of pleasure into sickness'.[10] Though
Dahlhaus points out that 'in spite of the philosophy of renun-
ciation, Parsifal does not become an anchorite but the Grail
King',[11] this second stress seems hardly less healthy than the
former, for the male brotherhood which peoples the Grail
temple (no women here: though there are youths and boys—
'les voix d'enfants chantant dans la coupole'), seems confined,
merely macho, confirming a male brotherhood. Charles Osborne
may be right when he compares two final works, *Parsifal* and
Falstaff, and finds 'the temperamental contrast . . . immense:
[with here] *fin de siècle* sickliness and piety and sentimental
homoerotic religious yearning',[12] in which case the stress
should fall on the sublimation, the displacement, of feelings
throughout. The sublimation belongs to the language of sacrifice
employed throughout the opera.

J. P. Stern discusses the 'sacrifice syndrome' as crucial to the
ideology of the third Reich, an aspect of cultural pessimism.[13]

Parsifal, like Schopenhauer, the prophet of cultural pessimism for the Right, may be said to nourish this, as even Nietzsche felt the fascination of the decadence within *Parsifal*. Syberberg's film similarly admits pessimism, for it begins as the director says, with 'the end of the world, and all that follows is memory'.[14] Hence the photographs of bombings, and the ending with a crowned skull on a beach: such, perhaps, is the end of that Holy Roman Empire, alluded to in the conclusion to *Die Meistersinger*, in Hans Sachs's statement that welcomes the coming of the religion of art: 'und gebt Ihr ihrem Wirken Gunst / zerging in Dunst / das heil'ge röm'sche Reich / und bliebe gleich / die heil'ge deutsche Kunst!'—'and if you favour their endeavours, even should the Holy Roman Empire dissolve in mist, for us there would yet remain holy German art'. *Parsifal*, in Syberberg's version, negates that, as indeed it must, for art cannot exist in a vacuum, away from a society; like the creation of Bayreuth with its sanctifying of *l'art pour l'art* inscribed in its very construction, there is the evidence of a distance being kept from society and its problems, which coolness can only allow for a pervasive pessimism. It is no coincidence that Benjamin saw art for art's sake as a position that Fascism endorsed; and of course, these words, at the end of *Meistersinger*, provided a Nazi rallying-point. 'Mankind's self-alienation has reached such a degree that art can experience its own destruction as an aesthetic pleasure of the first order. This is the situation of politics which Fascism is rendering aesthetic. Communism responds by politicising art'—so Benjamin at the end of 'The work of art in the age of mechanical reproduction'.

Syberberg's tolerance of that pessimism can be turned against him, as will be seen, but in the meantime the antagonism to power should be noted: Gurnemanz leads Parsifal to the Grail temple via corridors of banners and flags—familiar shots in Nazi propaganda films. Titurel (sung by Hans Tschammer, played by Martin Sperr) calls out to Amfortas from the tombs of Saint-Denis, resting place of another site of power, and specifically male power is not far away. He works from a reading that sees interest in that as central, that in Wagner no contempt is too strong for Klingsor whose wound means he has feminised himself. The rejection of the woman and the mother—Kundry (Yvonne Minton, with Edith Clever acting), who offers Parsifal the breast in Act II, recollecting both the sexual nature of the temptation and the memory of *Herzeleide*—is of a piece with this. The music drama ends with the incorruptible male with the spear. His guilt-feeling, his recollection of 'Klage', is not endorsed by others, who see him as pure. The film offers no alternative utopia to Wagner's, cannot suggest a politics where power is not stressed, but what it does do is to change Parsifal's sex. At the moment of the kiss, the man Parsifal (Michael Kutter) is joined by a young woman (Karin Krick) who appears in the background, draws near, 'sings' with the man (while the voice remains that of Reiner Goldberg), and lets the man steal away. The two are united at the end when they embrace, but the effect of having a woman in the role for most of the time— so that it is to a woman that Kundry kneels in Act III—is radically disturbing. Power is denied, even while the music affirms it. That is not to make an essentialist point about the 'nature' of men and women, but only to speak of them as they are constituted by the opera: man as active, woman as obediently passive. The change occurs at the point where Parsifal turns from the recollection of the mother to self-possession. Syberberg restores the woman at just that assumption of single, narcissistic in effect, power.

And the film examines further the contents of this power base in its offering a reading of *Parsifal* as concerned with sexual purity, and then criticising it. Klingsor's loss of potency is, of course, connected to his fear of sexuality: Amfortas's wound, surely a castrating one, originally, represents loss of power through illicit desire: sexual relations, too, with one of impure blood, for Kundry's other name of Herodias, and her laughing at Christ would surely make her Jewish. Parsifal's return with the spear enables a new phallocentric universe to be brought about: no Oedipal fears mark him out. In any case his father died in battle before he was born. Resisting Gurnemanz's questions in Act I, the pure fool who is never caught up into the sphere of definition, he stands outside the sphere of the Symbolic, Lacan's term for the state of loss brought about through the child's entry into language and the law of the Father. He stands as an absolute, untouchable by the spear, which implies his inviolability before castration, the subjection to the law of the Father. Meanwhile, in the film, Amfortas carries his wound round with him on a cushion, as if to make the Nazi-type point that a decadent Europe has made a fetish out of its being feminised, and that its religion is a displacement of its' sexual fear. (The Nazi hatred of psychoanalysis will be recalled, for its sense of loss, and also of the vulnerability of the male's position: it will be recalled that Freud, in the *Three essays on sexuality* did not believe that types of sexual behaviour were 'naturally' given, but were produced through the entry into culture, into the symbolic realm, as it may now be called.) The wound is like a bleeding vagina: it thus belongs, in Oedipal terms, to the male's fear of that as the memory of castration. Here it seems that Syberberg is only working on motifs that are in the subconscious of the operatic text. 'Die Wunde' and the whole motif of Amfortas's suffering, which runs through the second half of the Prelude, is aligned quite easily to the wound in the side of the 'Saviour' (which also becomes a castrating one, as though the religious sense and the possibility of salvation also depended upon a prior castration, upon the annihilation of the male), and it fastens the anguish that actualises the opera as being deeply sexual in tone. Parsifal recalls the wound as Kundry kisses him, and the change of sex is important, for Parsifal is now, in the film, defined as already in the position of loss, as the female, the one who has never been able to glimpse the male fantasy of the possession of the phallus, putting him beyond danger of loss.

Yet all this area teems with problems. I have not seen an account of *Parsifal* which makes necessary sense of the transition in the hero at the moment of the kiss, so that he identifies with Amfortas and sees himself as a guilty sinner in a trance-like state. The difficulty seems to reside in the issue of why either he or Amfortas should feel so profane. If it is explained, as outlined already, that the sense of a taint comes from the fear of women, from the threat posed by the feminine, then, of course, Syberberg's reading makes good corrective sense in making Parsifal female anyway. And it is true that the one woman in this opera, reduced to total bankruptcy of emotion in a way that goes quite beyond the treatment of women in other nineteenth-century operas discussed before, and only allowed a subsidiary singing role in this scene in relation to Parsifal, is punished as an Eve figure. Edith Clever plays the part with intensity as an outcast woman who has internalised the accusations of the knights and of Klingsor, and accepted her deep guilt. Yet the mention of Eve recalls Jeanne Moreau's performance in Losey's 1962 film of that name, set in Venice, and—in milieu and theme (Stanley Baker as a reverse Giovanni: 'Bloody Welshman' is how Moreau—perhaps with affection—describes him at the end)—anticipatory of *Don Giovanni.* In *Eve* shame is the keynote: it starts with a shot of a statue of Adam and Eve on the Doge's Palace, and the voice-over says, 'And they were both naked, the man and his wife, and were not ashamed'. The sexual is posed as a problem there, as it is in *Don Giovanni*; for it is associated with shame. In *Parsifal*, by contrast, the sexual cannot be faced, but must be fled from: if the opera asks for a male who can stand away from the female, in a rejection of 'sündingen Verlangen'—sinful desires—it is not to instate male desire as pure, or to return to a myth of pure masculinity. Rather, it is more deeply investing in a desire for castration, as an answer to the issue of shame, and Parsifal's reaction to the wound is fascination. Which implies that Klingsor, the marginalised figure—object of fascination to the knights and squires in the first act—is the supplement, in Derrida's terms, who needs to be foregrounded as central, which he is, oddly, in his placing in the middle act, for the distinction between him and Parsifal is much less than between Parsifal and Amfortas: both, after all, refuse, out of shame.

The reading that assumed the opera's investment in power to be central is crucial: but in the hollows of that text is the contradictory desire for an unmanning: and Syberberg's version not only reconciles the sexes: the historical positioning of women, which sees them as defined in a position of loss in relation to both father and mother, is countervailed and male power is set aside; it also suggests the lability of sexual difference by implying that Parsifal's movement into independence of the woman is also very feminine. As such, it is a highly suggestive and beautiful surreal image. What is tender in the music, such as the lovely and sensuous flowing melody of oboe and strings for the Karfreitagzauber theme, can well up in a way that gains in spontaneity from the re-siting of male power. Those fantasies of the restoration of an etiolated power through the pure blood—of the perfect Aryan, never stained by miscegenation, however much part of the discourse of opera, or part of that of the 1890s and 1900s Wagnerians who appropriated the *Parsifal* vision—now look very different and healing. But that is not to imply that the opera should have its vision of the perfect fool made wise through compassion endorsed. That is not what is going on when Parsifal is kissed, and Syberberg's film points out the aporia in a way that should make it impossible to take the work unambiguously.

Having discussed how the film works formalistically, it remains to ask how appropriate as a procedure Syberberg's is. And two points need discussion: Syberberg's privileging of the cinema, and the place given to myth. In *Hitler* the Holy Grail is a miniature of the Black Maria, Edison's studio; this not only emphasises Hitler as film-maker but implies Syberberg's acceptance of Bloch's thesis that even with a negative, reactionary and regressive movement a positive drive forward may be discerned: as an argument, it implies the necessary demonism of *Doctor Faustus.*[15] For Hitler to be constructed as the cinema-maker contrasts with Benjamin's argument, and raises the question how it is possible to reaccentuate a text even by changing the conditions of its being reproduced: film, rather than challenging an order, may perpetuate it. Adorno drew attention to Wagner's desire to produce the mythic and the sacral in his conception of the *Gesamtkunstwerk*: the resources of sensuous art are supposed to provoke a feeling of the metaphysical: in that light, it was right that Syberberg should make the Good Friday flowers artificial. And not tragedy, Adorno argues, but film is born from the spirit of music: indeed he quotes H. S. Chamberlain writing to Cosima in 1890 about

Liszt's *Dante* symphony: 'perform this symphony in a darkened room with a sunken orchestra and show pictures moving past in the background—and you will see how all the Levis and all the cold neighbours of today, whose unfeeling natures give such pains to a poor heart, will all fall into ecstasy'.[16] It is the obverse of those practically useful ends that were discussed in Chapter 3, about the use of film in music: an emotional effect is connived at, and the technology of Bayreuth is a precedent for that creation of the aura through mechanical reproduction. If film is the *Gesamtkunstwerk*, what Syberberg perpetuates is the nineteenth-century ideology of art itself as the privileged bearer of meanings in the absence of religion: art as the new metaphysics. The work is not free from the accusation of being mystificatory. Indeed, inscribed within it is the conviction that the artist makes history, creates ideology. Whereas Adorno's argument as it affects Wagner insists on the bourgeois nature of the inspiration: just as Ludwig's castles, far from being Romantic escapes, attributes of a mind out of tune with materialistic reality, are themselves an expression of bourgeois kitsch; middle-class taste revealed and affecting the artist *manqué*. If Syberberg had not worked within that context, he could never have been so concerned with the artist's influence.

This relates to the second issue. Michael Tanner in a film review in the *TLS* (8 April 1983) makes an excellent point when he compares Syberberg's work with Chéreau's, televised by Brian Large, and says that the latter uses no myth. The *Ring* cycle set the four operas in the nineteenth century, from 1840 to the 1920s: the Rhine scenes are set around a hydro-electric power dam, and the maidens are clearly prostitutes. At the end, the Gibichung palace looks Art Deco in style, and the climax of the work takes place by the waterside in, say, Manhattan Lower West Side, with a backdrop of warehouses. In this environment, capitalists, industrialists and factory foremen push against each other and the end of the power struggle is the fire that brings out, in the last moments of *Götterdämmerung*, a casual crowd who watch the inferno amazed and then turn round to look at the Bayreuth audience, as if to ask what assurance there can be that this holocaust could not occur again.

Siegfried appears thuggish, Wotan is a smooth capitalist complete with tuxedo, Loge a Dickensian Heep-like creature, manipulating by his sham humility. It was a production that recalled Wagner as the contemporary of Ibsen.

Chéreau's intention was to strip the work of its 'universal significance' and to show that the cycle's values belonged to a precise moment of history which created them and allowed them to be meaningful: it is amusing to see Bryan Magee in the festival number of *Opera* (1977) attacking Chéreau precisely for not permitting universal significance. The moment of the *Ring* is that of the invention of tradition, when the Rhine and mountains and mountaineering are entering the German nation's mythology, when old narratives are being unearthed to prop up nationalist day-dreams, to give them the illusion of disinterested heroic action as embodied in their history, and ask what they are heirs to. Chéreau strips that away: there is no escape from a constricting urban environment here: the dragon's hoard in *Siegfried* is found within a city park enclosed by walls. Syberberg, however, works happily within myth: in the introduction to his *Hitler: a film from Germany* he speaks of Germany's loss of 'creative irrationalism', which he defines as 'the ultimate principle of infinity in our art, the indissoluble, the homesickness, the yearning for meaning in madness, in the cinematic artwork, and as a nation's desire for representation, a desire for myth'.[17] Postwar West Germany has so far pulled itself away from the Romanticism that made the Reich it has now lost its tolerance for fantasy. *Heimat* belongs to that desire to make reparation, to renew myth and story-telling; compare its title with Syberberg's 'homesickness'. Watching that film over four evenings, admittedly an artificial way to see it, only emphasised its use of myth: even of the mythic structure of the *Ring*: with the founding of the Nazi regime as the new Valhalla, with the blasting away of hopes in the catastrophe of 1945 as the equivalent to the deferring of hopes at the end of *Walküre*, Hermann as the new Siegfried, to dominate the third evening, and the deaths of Maria and Glasich, and the breakdown of Anton as the new twilight of the gods, the end of an old order.

Syberberg says of *Hitler* that he sought 'an aesthetic scandal:

combining Brecht's doctrine of epic theatre with Richard Wagner's musical aesthetics, cinematically conjoining the epic system as anti-Aristotelian cinema with the laws of a new myth'. His *Parsifal* acts out myth: one central one being that there was something specifically German about the Reich, and that it was the product of certain strains of Romanticism. That underpins Thomas Mann's sense in *Doctor Faustus* but it is, of course, un-Brechtian: 'Fascism is an historical phase which capitalism has entered, and thus it constitutes something new and at the same time something old. Capitalism exists in Fascist countries only in the form of Fascism, and Fascism can only be fought as capitalism, in its most naked, brazen and treacherous form'.[18] Thus Brecht's rise of the Nazi party is recorded in his *Arturo Ui*, where there is no room for any myth, where Hitler appears as the tool of monopoly capitalism; where the mythic, indeed, would appear as an evasion of an historical consideration of the causes of the resistible rise of the Reich.[19] Syberberg's film thus exposes the putative myth behind Nazism only by reinstating myth. To go into the reasons for the rise of Hitler would exceed the competence of this chapter, but it would have to be held that to see Wagner as central to it (whatever use might have been made of the music-dramas) would be elitism: if any cultural manifestations helped produce the Reich it would be more likely to be Fritz Lang's *Die Nibelungen*, as Kracauer discusses it (though *Caligari to Hitler* suggests within its very title that there can be a movement from fantasy to reality easily enough, and that assumption needs questioning), as it was an attempt to mediate German culture to popular tastes, and was quoted in Leni Riefenstahl's *Triumph of the will*. Wagnerian motifs sport there, at second and third hand. 'In shaping their mass ornaments, the Nazi decorators drew inspiration from *Nibelungen*. *Siegfried*'s theatrical trumpeters, showy steps and authoritarian patterns reappear, extremely magnified, in the modern Nuremberg pageant'.[20]

This is not said to exculpate Wagner, whose daughter-in-law's confessions reveal what the implications of Bayreuth idealism so often were: none the less, it cuts at the mystification within Syberberg's film, which uses a complete set of cultural references—Aeschylus to Marx—as puppets in the initial moments of the film, and thus extends myth way beyond itself, not ending it or the sacralised appeal of Wagner's music. When he concludes the *Confessions* by saying that it is easy not to be a Fascist when there is no Hitler around, one response might well be to agree, but then to wonder whether, beyond the *ad hominem* statement, Hitler himself has not been mythologised, taken out of history. The 1967 Mitscherlich thesis of the German 'inability to mourn' might seem to necessitate the need to exorcise the image of Hitler: but that cannot be done by using Wagner: there is no separation from what needs to be deconstructed. The Chéreau *Ring*, blamed as it was for leaving things out (not from the music) and for wanton re-setting of the action, makes the more striking statement by its ability to defamiliarise the audience from Wagner. At least the Chéreau production brought things down to a point where they could be argued with at the level of human motivation. Wagner suffers from people's displaced interest in mythology, Deryck Cooke's admittedly incomplete *I saw the world end* being a fine example of kind of study of Wagner that could never approach the drama because of its preoccupation with Germanic legends. Something of the buoyancy of the musical is needed to counter-act the tone of criticism: *The pirate* acts as a fine comment on *Der fliegende Holländer* in its parody of Senta's obsession with the portrait of the Dutchman, with Micaela's misplaced longings after Macoco.

The difficulties are immense: there is that hypnotic music, which Adorno sees as incorporating in its use of the leitmotif, the commodity function: 'the music is designed to be remembered: it is intended for the forgetful':[21] so again Wagner is seen as writing for popular middle-class tastes; and the leitmotifs are likely to catch the listener second or third time round and insert him/her into that onward dynamism, that long statement of grief and of a psychic wound. Syberberg is too thoroughly moulded by that discourse, and the psychic wound joins with a Romantic melancholia, an inability to mourn, itself a questionable sentiment: was Germany bereaved of Hitler that it should be thinking about mourning? From these motifs, what is constructed is a nostalgic requiem—the motif behind each of his films; inscribed in the very idea of playing *Parsifal* over the death mask of the composer. The film records a lament that things cannot be otherwise, and that art moulds—and is—the political: it cannot go beyond and be more critical of this privileging of art; of opera, and film.

NOTES

1. On these see John Sandford, *The new German cinema* (1980), chapter 8.
2. See Martin Jay, *Adorno*, pp. 19–20.
3. Hans-Jürgen Syberberg, introduction to his *Hitler: a film from Germany*, trans. Joachim Neugroschel (Manchester, 1982), p. 16. See also Susan Sontag's preface to this, a longer version of which is in *A Susan Sontag reader* (Harmondsworth, 1982), pp. 403–21.
4. Walter Benjamin, *Illuminations* (1973), p. 253.
5. Quoted by Susan Sontag, 'Fascinating fascism' in *Movies and methods*, ed. Bill Nichols (Berkeley, 1976), p. 36.
6. Timothy Corrigan, *New German film: the displaced image* (Austin, 1983), p. 159.
7. Barry Millington, *Wagner* (1984), discusses some of the ideology underlying the opera, and refers to the work of Hartmut Zelinsky for Wagner's anti-semitism and for the use made of that in the Reich. See pp. 47–8, 118–23, 135–6. Further work on Bayreuth in the Reich may be found in Geoffrey Skelton, *Wagner at Bayreuth* (1965), chapter 11, and in Martin van Amerongen's odd if entertaining *Wagner: a case history* (1983), chapter 16.
8. See *Brecht on theatre*, ed. John Willett (2nd ed., 1974), p. 38.
9. See Elliott Zuckermann, *The first hundred years of Wagner's Tristan* (New York, 1964), p. 19. See also Raymond Furness, *Wagner and literature* (Manchester, 1984). For Lucy Beckett, see her monograph on *Parsifal* (Cambridge, 1981); and for Mike Ashman, see his article in *Parsifal*, ed. Nicholas John (1986).
10. T. W. Adorno, *In search of Wagner*, trans. Rodney Livingstone (1981), pp. 93–4.
11. John Deathridge and Carl Dahlhaus, *The new Grove Wagner* (1984), p. 162. See also Dahlhaus's *Richard Wagner's music dramas* (Cambridge, 1979), on the opera, and on the works in the theatre. Dahlhaus reconciles himself to production changes (which no doubt would include film changes) by reflecting that the drama is in the music structure, and that production therefore matters little: it can be abstract (Wieland Wagner) or committed (Chéreau). This is certainly true as regards the composer as dramatist, but it involves an evasion, since Dahlhaus believes that 'one of the features rendering a work of art great is that it is above history' (p. 158), and new productions upset this belief.
12. Charles Osborne, *The complete operas of Verdi* (1969), p. 449.
13. J. P. Stern, *Hitler: the Führer and the people* (1975), chapter 3.
14. Quoted by J. Hoberman, *Voice* (22 February 1983), pp. 60, 64. See the interview with Syberberg in *Literature Quarterly*, vol. 10, no. 4 (1982), pp. 206–18. He has written at book length about his work: *Syberbergs Filmbuch* (Frankfurt, 1979).

15. See on this Fredric Jameson, ' "In the destructive element immerse": Hans-Jürgen Syberberg and cultural revolution', *October* (1981), no. 17, pp. 99–118; pp. 106–7 especially.
16. T.W. Adorno, *op. cit.*, p. 107. Cp. Ernst Bloch, *Essays on the philosophy of music*, trans. Peter Palmer (Cambridge, 1985), p. 165 suggesting that *Parsifal* is 'the most worldly of Wagner's major works'—a comment which fits with Adorno's criticisms.
17. Syberberg, *op. cit.*, pp. 10, 18.
18. Quoted by Keith A. Dickson, *Towards Utopia: a study of Brecht* (Oxford, 1978), p. 165.
19. John Hiden and John Farquharson, *Explaining Hitler's Germany* (1983) discuss orthodox and non-orthodox Marxist explanations for the Reich, especially those of T. W. Mason; see chapter 7.
20. Siegfried Kracauer, *From Caligari to Hitler* (Princeton, 1947), p. 95.
21. Adorno, *op. cit.*, p. 31. Jameson gives a more positive sense of the leitmotifs being designed not to be fetishised: *op. cit.*, p. 115.

AFTERWORD
and suggestions for further reading

Film theory has been well developed, and numerous summarising accounts of it have appeared: Dudley Andrew's *Major film theories* (1976) and *Concepts in film theory* (1984, both Oxford) being two good examples of places to start. Much of the interest in feminist readings, and psychoanalytic approaches to cinema, derived from Freud and Lacan, originates from the politicising of readings that stressed the heavily ideological structuring of an individual text that was associated with 1960s and 1970s French literary critical theory. No single useful term describes all this: it is familiar to literature and media students, English and American, through numbers of popularising works, from Terence Hawkes, Tony Bennett, Terry Eagleton and Jonathan Culler. I have used Derrida's work, and have found very interesting on it Vincent Leitch's book *Deconstructive criticism: an advanced introduction* (1983). Music criticism knows much less of this criticism, though an initial approach to it is provided by F. Noske, *The signifier and the signified: studies in the operas of Mozart and Verdi* (The Hague, 1977). For the semiotics of music, see *Musique en jeu* especially no. 5 (1971). I have referred in the course of this study to critical studies that take account of the political implications of music, from Adorno onwards: a fine salvo is fired by Cornelius Cardew: *Stockhausen serves imperialism* (1974), which I have not mentioned before.

In Chapter 1 I have dealt with representations of the gypsy, and of the female 'other', particularly in Hollywood: it might be worth comparing this with the stress on exotic and Russian features in popularisations from opera in Hollywood as discussed in Chapter 2. Susan Kane's debut in *Citizen Kane* will come to mind: it will be remembered that she should have sung in *Thais*, which like *Aida* is set in Egypt, though an early Christian Egypt. As it was, she appeared in *Salammbô*, thus evoking Flaubert and his interest in the East. Much of the book by Edward Said, *Orientalism* (New York, 1977), is relevant here:

for Said's interest in showing how the East has been constituted a subject for knowledge—which is also control—through nineteenth- and twentieth-century projections of it, of its women and its sexual incontinence, of its irrationality—means that it becomes a mythologised subject to be projected in a number of cultural ways, of which grand opera, and opera-spectaculars, are fine representatives. Said's book says nothing about opera, but provides indirect comment on the unconscious motivations behind the productions of meaning associated with Carmen and the popularity of, say, *Butterfly* and *Lakmé*.

There are plenty of cosy biographies of the stars of the 'Met' who appeared on the screen, such as *This was Richard Tauber*, by Charles Castle and Diana Napier Tauber (1971)—to take one singer I have only mentioned. The topic of the diva's singing needs more exploration: the Hoffmann tale *Rath Krespel* (cp. Offenbach's *Contes d'Hoffmann*—Act III, 'Antonia') deals with the singer who dies trying to evoke her dead mother: this has interesting bearing on the psychoanalytic ground covered in Chapter 2. The topic of the castrato can be followed by Angus Heriot's *The castrati in opera* (1956), and in Roland Barthes's brilliant reading of Balzac's *Sarrasine* in *S/Z* (New York, 1974), about a sculptor falling in love with a diva who turns out to be a castrato. Barthes reads the text, in a manner that derives from Lacan, to suggest that the horror of castration is the abolition of meaning produced: the loss of difference, wherein meaning resides. Sarrasine thought that in listening to the singer, Zambinella, he was in touch with the Imaginary, with pure presence, with plenitude; all distance abolished, but in reality it turns out to be an empty signifier, a voice that points to pure absence. The coloratura voice in the nineteenth century is ambiguous in status, similarly, hinting at loss, at absence, behind the voice of the diva.

For Gramsci, in the last section of Chapter 2, some helpful comments on his attitude to Italian culture are provided in Alastair Davidson's 'The literary criticism of Antonio Gramsci', in *The radical reader* edited by Stephen Knight and Michael Wilding (Sydney, 1977). For a more precise sense of nineteenth-century Italian melodrama, a good start may be made with John

Black's biography of Cammarano, the librettist for *Trovatore, The Italian romantic libretto* (Edinburgh, 1984).

The work on Schoenberg in Chapter 3 and later in discussion of *Moses und Aron* may be supplemented by Daniel Albright's literary treatment in *Representation and the imagination* (Chicago, 1981). Schoenberg, Mann and Adorno are brought together in Peter Franklin, *The idea of music: Schoenberg and others* (1985).

In writing about the various operas, I have said nothing about stage productions, many of which have been very radical or have rethought issues very carefully: Peter Stein's current *Otello* for Welsh National Opera is a case in point, so was Mike Ashman's new *Dutchman* for Covent Garden (opened 17 March 1986), which excited rage and hostility in the *Telegraph* letters column, for instance. There is a general sense, often registered in *Opera*, that producers have gone far enough, and too far (just as *Opera* clearly finds opera-film to be an impure genre—though how pure is opera?). In wishing for utter fidelity, it might be wondered if the opera purists wish to return to gas lighting, and an undarkened auditorium. I am not, of course, suggesting that the director should do just what he/she pleases; though I am suggesting that in practice that is precisely what happens: even what is intended to be faithful to the 'original'—that which can only exist as a result of interpretation—is actually heavily ideological, inscribed within a set of values that assume the authority of the work, and its ability to speak directly, or ahistorically. (A so-called 'faithful' production of an opera will look wrong when it is seen again twenty years later—as it frequently happens. A new faithful version will be required. Faithfulness is labile.) An empirical approach to the work (such as Peter Hall's *Ring* at Bayreuth) is not self-effacing and merely responsive to the text: the director's presuppositions are not the less evident because they are not recognised as being ways in which the text has been chosen to be read in one light rather than another. Even empiricism is ideological.

In any case, I am not writing from within an *auteur* tradition that assumes the primacy of the director's personality: though it is true that Bergman, Straub and Huillet, Losey, Zeffirelli and Syberberg have each made their mark in distinctive modes as strong personalities. I would rather emphasise that each of the opera-films discussed belongs to a discourse—to a mode of thought that is representative of moves within cultural thinking since the beginning of the 1970s. The director is him/herself a function of that discourse, not autonomous, but caught up in something more complex, and larger than the self and its vision. To read a film and decide that it has the stamp of X upon it is a rationalisation, a reading in from certain cues that have been read or mis-read. Textual practices create 'authors', who are then defined as such, and the marks that are taken by readers to construct them are then applied to other texts that bear their name. My own analysis of the films works with the directors, indeed, but there is always a metonymy here: the name of the director displaces many other names and aspects of a discourse.

INDEX
of names, operas and films